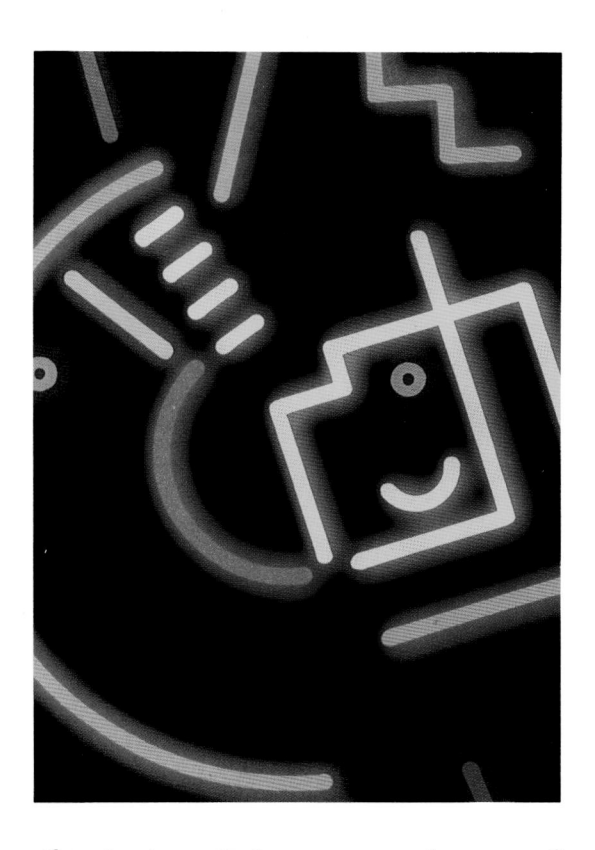

69th Art Directors Annual
and
4th International Exhibition

ADC Publications Inc.

Board of Directors
Dorothy Wachtenheim, President
Pearl Lau, Vice President
Jim Craig, Marketing & Promotion
Hugh O'Neill
Phil Thurman

ADC Executive Director
Diane Moore

Editors
Jeri Zulli
Jonathan Gregory

Hall of Fame Copy
Daniel M. Forté

Database Consultant
Marie Gangemi

Interior Design
Ryuichi Minakawa

Cover and Section Dividers Design
McRay Magleby
Lily McCullough
Linda Sullivan

Published in 1990 by
RotoVision SA
Route de Suisse 9
CH-1295 MIES/VD
Switzerland
for
The Art Directors Club Inc.
250 Park Avenue South
New York, NY 10003

While ADC Publications Inc. has made every effort to publish full and correct credits for each piece included in this volume, errors of omission or commission sometimes occur. For this ADC Publications Inc. and Rotovision SA are most regretful, but hereby disclaim any liability.

Since this book is printed in four-color process, a few of the images reproduced here may appear slightly different from their original reproduction.

ISSN: 0735-2026
ISBN: 2-8230-6041-1
Printed in Hong Kong

Media Conversion and
Digital Composition by:
I, CLAVDIA, Inc., New York, New York

Distributed to the trade in the
United States & Canada by
Watson-Guptill Publications
1515 Broadway
New York, NY 10036

International Distribution
RotoVision SA
Route de Suisse 9
CH-1295 MIES/VD
Switzerland

RYUICHI MINAKAWA

Ryuichi Minakawa, the *Annual's* interior designer, is art director of the Toppan Printing Company of America. He has also been involved in a similar manner with the 64th, 65th and 68th editions of the Art Directors Club *Annuals,* Volumes 7 through 11 of the *One Show* annuals, and *Illustrators 32,* the annual of The Society of Illustrators. At Toppan, Minakawa is responsible for the overall graphic production of *Graphis* magazine and the Graphis annuals.

Minakawa was born in Kumamoto, Japan. He is a graduate of the Art Center College of Design in Pasadena, California, and, prior to his current position with Toppan, worked for several major graphic design firms, specializing in corporate identity, logos, and package design.

Minakawa lives in New York City and is a member of the Art Directors Club.

SAUL BASS

Art Directors Club Hall of Famer and this year's designer of the 4th Annual International Call for Entries, Saul Bass has had a profound effect on visual communication. A designer and developer of numerous trademarks and corporate identity strategies, Bass's work for *Fortune 500* companies reads like a *Who's Who.* Alcoa, AT&T, Celanese Corp., Quaker Oats, United Airlines and Warner Communications are just a few of the clients who have benefited from his graphic design expertise.

In addition to his extensive and highly successful work as a designer, Bass, based in Los Angeles with his partner Herb Yager of Bass/Yager & Associates, has had an accomplished career as a filmmaker, motion picture graphic designer and title creator. Who can forget the shower sequence from ''Psycho'' or the final battle scene from ''Spartacus''? Bass directed special feature sequences for these classic films as well as many others.

His penchant for creating opening title graphics—as he did for over forty of Hollywood's most memorable motion pictures—is a credit to Bass's unique visual style and innovative technique. For example, ''The Man With the Golden Arm,'' ''Seven Year Itch,'' ''Vertigo,'' ''North By Northwest,'' ''Psycho'' and ''It's A Mad, Mad, Mad, Mad World'' contain some of the more unforgettable opening credits in film history.

Who's Who in America lists over 12 honors and doctorates under Bass' name from various organizations around the world. His work appears in the permanent collections of museums from New York to the Far East. It's only fitting for Bass to contribute his design to the club's 4th Annual International Competition.

MCRAY MAGLEBY

A 1966 graduate of the University of Utah, McRay Magleby, this year's national Call for Entries designer, has won numerous national awards in graphic design. His work has often appeared in *Graphis, CA Annuals, Art Direction, Print* Case Books, Japan's *IDEA* Magazine, AIGA and the *Art Directors Annuals.*

He is currently art director of the Brigham Young University Graphics Department, a position he has held since 1969. Mr. Magleby supervises a staff of ten designers and produces publications, books and posters for the university.

Many of his posters, originally designed for BYU, are currently being sold in galleries and reproduced on greeting cards. Magleby is also a professor of art at the University of Utah, where he teaches graphic design and illustration. In 1985 he was selected to receive the Distinguished Teaching Award.

CONTENTS

HALL OF FAME MEMBERS

1972
M. F. Agha
Lester Beall
Alexey Brodovitch
Rene Clark
A. M. Cassandre
Robert Gage
William Golden
Paul Rand

1973
Charles Coiner
Paul Smith
Jack Tinker

1974
Will Burtin
Leo Lionni

1975
Gordon Aymar
Herbert Bayer
Cipe Pineles Burtin
Heyworth Campbell
Alexander Liberman
L. Moholy-Nagy

1976
E. McKnight Kauffer
Herbert Matter

1977
Saul Bass
Herb Lubalin
Bradbury Thompson

1978
Thomas M. Cleland
Lou Dorfsman
Allen Hurlburt
George Lois

1979
W. A. Dwiggins
George Giusti
Milton Glaser
Helmut Krone
Willem Sandberg
Ladislav Sutnar
Jan Tschichold

1980
Gene Federico
Otto Storch
Henry Wolf

1981
Lucian Bernhard
Ivan Chermayeff
Gyorgy Kepes
George Krikorian
William Taubin

1982
Richard Avedon
Amil Gargano
Jerome Snyder
Massimo Vignelli

1983
Aaron Burns
Seymour Chwast
Steve Frankfurt

1984
Charles Eames
Wallace Elton
Sam Scali
Louis Silverstein

1985
Art Kane
Len Sirowitz
Charles Tudor

1986
Walt Disney
Roy Grace
Alvin Lustig
Arthur Paul

1987
Willy Fleckhaus
Shigeo Fukuda
Steve Horn
Tony Palladino

1988
Ben Shahn
Bert Steinhauser
Mike Tesch

1989
Rudolph de Harak
Raymond Loewy

1990
Lee Clow
Reba Sochis
Frank Zachary

It is no simple task to identify figures in our profession as illustrious as those who have already been elected to the Hall of Fame; but the Selection Committee has identified three people whose qualifications well match those already chosen.

They represent different aspects of our profession:

Lee Clow—for his ground breaking work in advertising.

Reba Sochis—for her influence and inspiration to a whole generation of designers.

Frank Zachary—for his extraordinary career as an editorial art director and editor.

There is also a Special Award being presented to **Robert Weaver**—for his equally impressive accomplishments as a teacher and illustrator.

For an organization to survive, it must have a history to believe in and standards to aspire to. Clow, Sochis, Zachary and Weaver provided these standards and history for us, in accordance.

Through these awards, we celebrate and thank them for their contributions.

Milton Glaser
Hall of Fame Selection Committee Chairman

HALL OF FAME

Lee Clow

This is the city, Los Angeles, California. It's a magical place known for burritos, celebrities, Disneyland, Dodgers, earthquakes, EST, freeways, palm trees, smog, tofu, valley girls and—advertising? There are ten million stories of people who work and play here. Lee Clow is one of them and this, is his story...

Born in Los Angeles in 1943, Lee Clow literally grew up at the beach. He credits his first grade teacher, Mrs. Rice, with recognizing his artistic potential. It all occurred very serendipitously with a little drawing of a boat Clow had made in class. It seems little Lee loved boats and realistically portrayed it right down to the curling eddies of smoke rising from its stack. Mrs. Rice immediately noticed his uncanny knack for detail and told Lee's mom of his impending future as an artist. As a result, Mrs. Clow encouraged her son to continue drawing and painting.

As Clow got older, he began to hone his artistic skills. He attended Santa Monica City College and received a two-year degree. His parents simply could not afford to send him to the more prestigious Art Center College of Design. Years later, as irony would have it, Clow was asked to teach there! It was also during this period that Clow's distinct California personality crystallized.

According to Clow, ''I spent a lot of time at the beach surfing. If the temperature soared above 80 degrees and the waves were four feet high, I didn't bother going to class!'' He was eventually drafted into the Army at the height of the Vietnam War. Clow's illustrative abilities got him assigned to the White Sands Missile Range in New Mexico. After his tour of duty was up, he went back to school, taking design courses at Long Beach State.

After the Army, he was hired as a paste-up artist at a local design studio. His first agency art directing position was with NW Ayer's west coast office. Frustrated by ''only okay work getting produced,'' Clow remained there a couple of years.

Inspired by the creative revolution of the just-completed decade of the sixties, Lee Clow was deeply influenced by the DDB team approach to advertising. At the time, it certainly caused a frisson of excitement, sending much needed shock waves of creativity throughout the industry. Wanting to have his cake and eat it too, Lee Clow set out to search for the perfect west coast agency that aspired to DDB's principles. He simply refused to trade in his bathing trunks for a Brooks Brothers suit.

Clow stumbled upon a young California agency called simply Chiat/Day whose creative credo was, ''Let's do good ads.'' Back in 1971, it was two years young, had a staff of 30 and billings just shy of $15 million. Lee Clow was determined to work there. He got his book together and launched a campaign of persistence. Phone calls, letter writing and kind pestering eventually led to a scheduled interview with Jay Chiat's associate, Hy Yablonka.

Clow, pumped for his big chance, waited patiently for Yablonka, who forgot about the meeting, instead opting for a long lunch. Resolved to seeing Yablonka at any cost, Clow staked out the building's lobby poised for his return. They met. Although Chiat/Day was not hiring, Yablonka did give him a great deal of time and constructive criticism.

In January of 1973, Lee Clow's tenacity finally paid off. He was hired by Chiat/Day as an art director. Clow recalls meeting Jay Chiat a day before he was to begin work. Chiat simply told him in his inimitable style, "Work hard and maybe you'll do some good ads."

Clow, under Jay Chiat's unorthodox working environment, was given great opportunities to grow. The agency was and still is, according to Clow, "a great forum of free association fostering creativity."

For someone whose formal training was in art and design, Lee Clow literally taught himself advertising. The on-the-job training provided by his boss, Jay Chiat, coupled with his well-thumbed prized possessions: a collection of New York Art Directors Club and Communication Arts *Annuals* from the 1960s, Lee Clow began his career in the world of advertising. So in tune with the swell of creativity spawned in the sixties, Clow even today goes back in time for help in creating new concepts when he needs inspiration.

In 1977, Lee Clow began his trip up the ladder at Chiat/Day. Notorious for shunning titles and the limelight, Clow was nonetheless promoted to associate creative director. In 1982, he became creative director of the Los Angeles office and two years later, he was named president, chief creative officer (and senior art director) of Chiat/Day/Mojo.

Clow attributes his success to Jay Chiat's anti-establishment concepts of horizontal management. "You must have a combination of talent and a good environment to work in, in order to excel," Clow says. Witness the open air atmosphere of Chiat/Day's offices. All are equal in size with no closed doors. Management is always accessible to both staff and clients. They really do consider themselves family.

The list of risk-taking entrepreneurial clients the agency has served over the years proved to be perfect foils for Clow's unique and quirky creativity. His work for Apple Computer, California Cooler, KCBS, KNBC, Nike, Nissan, Olympia Beer, Pacific Northwest Bell, Pioneer Electronics, Pizza Hut, Porsche and Yamaha helped create a counterculture and state of mind in advertising that quickly spread across the country like a forest fire. It was advertising California style; it simply could not be ignored or duplicated in the buttondown corridors of Madison Avenue. Through his clients, Lee Clow taught us that "California Dreamin" was no longer just a song reminiscent of pop culture, but a very serious and viable force advertising could not resist recognizing.

All one has to do is flip through the new coffee table book, *Chiat/Day, The First Twenty Years* to see Clow and his agency's incredible metamorphosis unfold. His Apple Computer "1984" spot. A concept so fresh, yet disturbing, it's been heralded as a classic from both a cinematic and advertising standpoint. Clow's irreverent "lifestyle" spots for California Cooler seem very autobiographical. Who better can portray a bunch of well-tanned surfers partying, dude?

Clow's most upbeat slice of California life shines through in his "I Love LA" spot for Nike. Randy Newman in an old red Buick, cruising down the boulevards singing, "From the South Bay to the Valley, from the west side to the east side, everybody's very happy 'cause the sun shines all the time." It's intercut with a wonderful montage of celebrities and ordinary people shot against a beautiful and glitzy LA background.

Lee Clow openly admits, "I haven't yet done an ad I'm totally happy with. When I reach that stage of the game, I guess I'll retire and go into the aluminum siding business." For Clow, as long as the forces of passion and insecurity tug at his creative psyche, he'll continue to search for that "all elusive, perfect ad."

Interestingly enough, Lee Clow has two heroes he's quick to mention: Walt Disney and Hobie Alter. Hobie Alter, you ask? Who's he? Alter's name graces many a surfboard and catamaran—the Hobie Cat, for one. Clow idolizes Disney because of his natural artistic abilities and uncompromising determination to succeed regardless of life's roadblocks. Alter because he reached a point in his life that permitted him to attend board meetings in shorts and sandals!

In order to maintain harmony and stasis between his career and private life, Lee Clow still enjoys surfing, cruising to Catalina Island with his wife of 21 years and yes—attending meetings in his ever present shorts and sandals! He also finds great solace commiserating with his two dogs on the finer points of advertising, especially after interminable client meetings. "It's very therapeutic," Clow says.

Lee Clow's stark individualism makes him a prime candidate for the "guru" of the west coast school of laid-back advertising. When asked to comment on his induction into the New York Art Directors Club Hall of Fame, Clow paused for a moment and said, "It's quite an honor, yet—ironic, too. Since my goal was to do good ads *without* having to move to New York."

From $15 million in billings to $1 billion; from 30 employees to 1500, Lee Clow is still Lee Clow and Chiat/Day is now Chiat/Day/Mojo.

Should you happen to see a large, bearded man decked out in shorts and sandals engaged in an animated conversation with two dogs on a sandy beach in Venice, California, chances are it's Lee Clow. He's probably in the midst of explaining to them his philosophy of life. With apologies to Carl Lewis's Nike spot, "Never give up. There's no telling how far you can go…"

Chiat/Day wants to join a motorcycle gang.

Yamaha ad, 1973

SPARE TIRES.

THE CHAPPY FROM YAMAHA

Yamaha ad, 1973

Our grown-up guide to football:

NEWS FOR GROWN-UPS CBS❷2

KCBS-TV ad, 1976

Apple Computer, "1984" TV spot, 1983

Take Macintosh out for a test drive.

Apple Computer ad, 1984

Apple Computer ad, 1984

Chiat/Day is working on your car.

Porsche ad, 1984

And Professor Porsche expects still more.

The windows in Professor Porsche's office in Zuffenhausen overlook a courtyard.

A courtyard lined with Porsches parked in a patchwork of colors and model designs.

Not shiny new cars, but the ones that have already met foul weather and potholes. Survived the winding kilometers between summer picnics and winter ski trips.

To Professor Porsche, these are very important Porsches.

Because when he stands at this window, hands crossed behind his back, rocking from toe to heel, and looks down at the cars in the courtyard, he imagines.

He is reminded of how much is yet to be accomplished.

It is the reason Professor Porsche drives his company much the same way one drives his cars.

With passion. Respect. Conviction.

The result, cars that set new expectations of what a car ought to be.

Cars like this one.

Porsche's latest project, the 959. Or, more affectionately known as the "Gruppe B" car.

A car powered by the same 6-cylinder, horizontally opposed, twin overhead cam engine used in Porsche's 956 race car. Producing 400 hp.

A car with such a sophisticated drive train you can actually dial in the power to each of the four wheels.

A car with a self-adjusting suspension system that automatically lowers it as speed increases.

Top speed: no one really knows. Yet.

And as far as Professor Porsche is concerned, it really doesn't matter.

Because no matter how close to perfection the Gruppe B car comes, there will be another day when he stands at his window.

And imagines.

959 (Gruppe B) 6-cylinder, horizontally opposed, four overhead camshafts, four valves per cylinder, water/air-cooled rear engine with twin intercooled turbochargers. 2850cc's, 400+ hp. Estimated top speed: 188+ mph.

Porsche ad, 1984

Pizza Hut, "Doug & Bob" TV spot, 1985

California Cooler TV spot, 1985

Nissan "Z" intro TV spot, 1989

Nike ad, 1984

Reba Sochis

Paccione

Oscar Wilde once wrote, "It is through art and through art only, that we can realize our perfection." Reba Sochis is the personification of Wilde's statement.

Born in Philadelphia, Pennsylvania, Reba Sochis grew up expecting to follow in her sister's footsteps: go to the university and study to become a teacher. Certainly, the proper profession for a proper young lady and most acceptable to our country's social attitudes at that time. Always interested in art, Sochis, however, saw her future develop differently. Not wanting to be confined to a classroom, she convinced her parents to allow her to enroll in the Philadelphia Museum School of Art.

The year was 1929. The country was about to be thrown into the depths of a great depression. Fortunately, Alexey Brodovitch had just joined the school's faculty. He was to be a great influence in her approach to graphic design. His teaching methods were as unique as he was. Brodovitch did not dwell on technique, focusing instead on the philosophy of design. According to Sochis, "The more he tried to provoke his students, the harder we worked," a character trait many an assistant would also lovingly attribute to Reba Sochis.

By 1934, she moved with her husband to New York City. In the midst of the Depression, to supplement their income, Sochis freelanced as a designer, creating various book jackets for small publishing houses. She eventually landed her first job in editorial layout design at *Esquire* Magazine, where she recalls being given the opportunity to experiment and take risks. After *Esquire*, Sochis headed for *Charm* Magazine.

By the end of World War II, she was hired as an art director for a large design firm in New York called Beacon Studio. Sochis resumed her career in what was, with the exception of her only female counterpart Cipe Pineles Burtin, then art director at *Seventeen* Magazine, the unchartered world of women in design. Interestingly enough, the same tandem remain the lone female members in the ADC Hall of Fame.

She was the only woman responsible for a staff of over 20 men. Sochis looks back on her pioneering days at Beacon as being a "jewel of a job." She attributes this to the fact that she never looked upon herself as a threat to the men and their jobs. Sensing this, they quickly accepted Sochis for her talent. She immediately became one of the boys without ever having to sacrifice her femininity. As long as her high standards of work were not compromised, there were no wrinkles at Beacon Studio.

One of Beacon's biggest accounts was Talon Zippers. Quite pleased with Sochis's elegant work for their promotional pieces, the client encouraged her to open her own studio. Late in 1949, Reba Sochis ventured out on her own with Talon as her first and only account. Because of the plethora of promotional materials Talon required, Sochis was swamped with work. She needed to hire a talented assistant and fast! Her first full time employee was a 19-year-old Pratt junior named George Lois. Lasting over 40 years, the mutual love and admiration both still have for each other is steadfast.

Mention Lois to her and you hear only superlatives. Lois also reminisces about his first boss: "In just one day working for Reba, you could learn more than in four years at Pratt or Cooper Union. She was the toughest boss in the world, but she was also the sweetest woman you could hope to know."

As Sochis's reputation for quality design grew, so did her studio, necessitating the hiring of more assistants. She turned it into a wonderful greenhouse of talent, recruiting Pratt and Cooper students as full and part time assistants. Among those who benefited from Sochis's tutelage, eventually moving on to outstanding careers in their own right, were: Seymour Chwast, Bob Gill, Kit Hinrichs, Steve Horn, Andrew Langer, Gilbert Lesser, Rick Levine, Tony Palladino, Tony Russell and Bob Tucker.

Reba Sochis instilled in her young assistants a motivational work ethic seldom seen today. She was able to mold them because, "They were young and talented and had no negative work habits to begin with." Known for being a perfectionist, Reba Sochis nurtured a generation of designers that certainly owe her an immense debt of gratitude:

Seymour Chwast: "For the short time I worked for Reba Sochis her dedication to design and craft amazed me. She would endlessly fuss over the letter spacing of type for a letterhead....Reba accepted only perfection."

Bob Gill: "Reba designs like an angel and swears like a cab driver. What more can anyone want in a role model? I love her."

Steve Horn: "Reba Sochis is the best thing since chopped liver! She began by putting the fear of God in me. In the short time I worked there, she gave me a well-rounded education that's proved invaluable. I learned more from Reba Sochis in nine months than most people learn in a lifetime."

Andrew Langer: "Reba Sochis was not an easy person to work for. When she liked your work, you received quiet praise. When she didn't, she really let you have it! Reba's a very stubborn person. But then the best usually are."

Rick Levine: "Reba Sochis influenced me greatly as a graphic designer. Her work was new, exciting and fresh. She taught me how to layout a page with great elan."

Tony Palladino: "Reba was a peer of mine, a work friend. A determined woman devoted to the quality of communication—which was a difficult role for a woman. She made us 'tough' guys think differently about women in design. Reba would rivet you against the wall about clear, intelligent communicative messages—and hold you to it. You couldn't walk away from Reba with a half-assed truth. You had to love her for that."

Tony Russell: "Met Reba the day after arriving in New York from England in November, 1963. Working with her and knowing her design standards cushioned the culture shock and persuaded me to stay. I value her friendship still."

The work Reba Sochis turned out from her atelier was flawless and the envy of conceptual designers. Her list of satisfied clients was a tribute to her professionalism. Sochis's work for Talon, Borghese, Bulkley Dunton, Lincoln Center, New York Telephone, Pappagallo, Revlon, JP Stevens and Shell Oil are marvels of detail and fine design.

A case in point was a shopping bag she produced for the newly launched Pappagallo shoe stores. In order to achieve the visual look of an intricate mosaic pattern, Sochis and her assistant, Andrew Langer, literally cut thousands of small tile-like pieces from sheets of gold paper. Each had to be positioned onto a mechanical with a tweezer! It took them weeks to complete the project, but the end result was a striking work of art.

For a Lincoln Center corporate fund raising brochure, Sochis decided to use safety paper, more commonly referred to as checkbook paper. Indeed, a very subtle, yet effective method of getting people in the mood to donate money.

More often than not, her incredible work was also the result of time being on her side. The majority of her jobs did not require deadline-insertions; thus, if Sochis was not pleased with a particular design, it was completely scrapped and redone from scratch.

At one point, she was asked to teach at Pratt. Sochis never realized how much she disliked teaching until actually setting foot in a classroom. After one semester, Sochis left Pratt, preferring instead to instruct eager young assistants from the comforts of her own studio.

Today, Reba Sochis is active in design, advertising and promotion. She selectively works on a wide variety of challenging projects.

According to Sochis, enlisting students from design schools presents a problem. "The George Loises and the Bob Gills simply don't exist anymore. The high caliber of young talent is not as prevalent as it once was."

Reba Sochis readily admits to being a demanding taskmaster. But it's done out of a deep-rooted love and respect for her craft. In an era of computer-generated design amidst a get-it-done-yesterday world, it's comforting to know that there are people like Reba Sochis. As long as she still cares, that twinkle in her eyes will continue to light up the design world.

Lincoln Center brochure cover

Lincoln Center brochure, inside spread

Pappagallo Shoe Shops, placemat

Pfizer trade ad

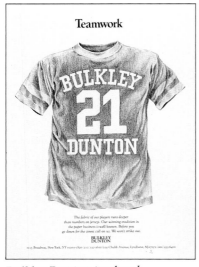

Bulkley Dunton trade ad

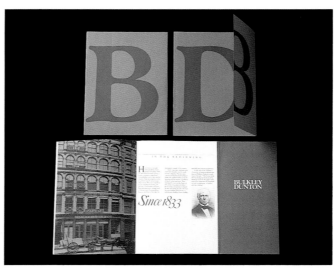

Bulkley Dunton corporate brochure

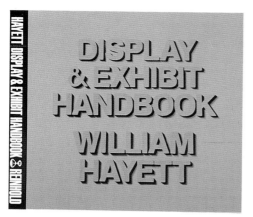

Hayett book jacket

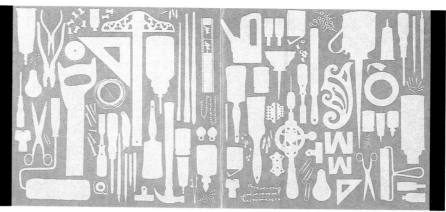

Hayett book endpapers

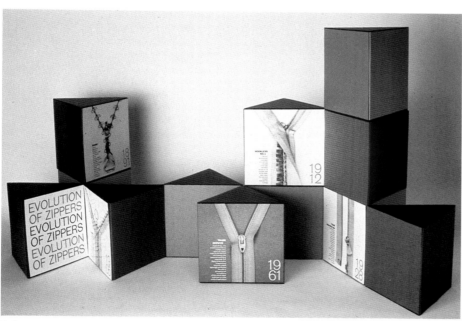

Talon traveling exhibit

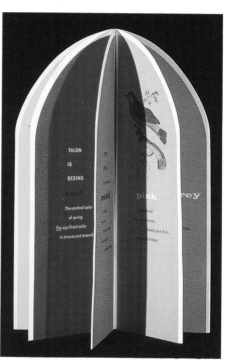

Talon spring color promotion

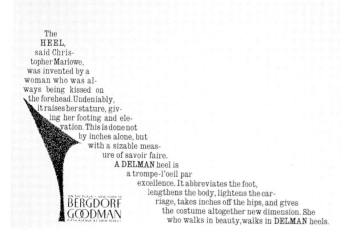

Delman Shoes newspaper ad

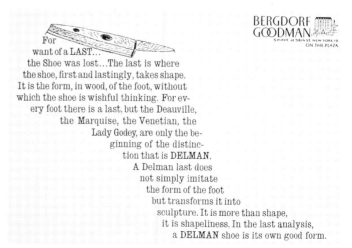

Delman Shoes newspaper ad

Frank Zachary

Countless people are probably asking themselves the following question: "Who the heck is Frank Zachary?" If ever there was an unsung hero who totally epitomizes the specialized craft of magazine editing and art direction, or as he puts it, "graphic journalism," Frank Zachary is that hero. He is living proof of the old geometry theorem, "The whole is equal to the sum of its parts." Indeed.

Born in 1914, the son of Croatian immigrants, Frank Zachary grew up near Pittsburgh, Pennsylvania wanting to become a writer. His mind loved to wander beyond the confines of the local steel mills to poetry and tales of science fiction. At the age of 18, Zachary gathered together a portfolio of short stories he'd written and took them to Henry Scheetz, who owned a weekly magazine called the *Pittsburgh Bulletin Index*. Scheetz was genuinely impressed with Zachary's indefatigable drive and enthusiasm, character traits still very much in evidence today. Zachary was hired on the spot! Not as a printer's apprentice, but as an all-purpose news hound. His growing list of responsibilities included: copy boy, beat reporter, layout artist and photographer. Zachary covered everything from society balls and golf tournaments to hard news stories.

While Frank Zachary was busy reporting the news for the *Bulletin Index,* the soon-to-be famous novelist John O'Hara became the magazine's editor. Nine months later, O'Hara left to pursue his career and Zachary replaced him as editor. To supplement both his experience and income, Frank Zachary also became the Pittsburgh correspondent for *Time, Life* and *Fortune* Magazines. This didn't sit too well with his boss at the *Bulletin Index.* They soon parted company.

In 1938, at the age of 24, Frank Zachary headed for New York City with $50 in his pocket. Through the aid of young Cyrus Sulzberger of the *New York Times* family, he was hired at Carl Byoir's public relations agency. Zachary found himself doing bland press releases for a variety of clients.

Feeling cramped and mired in a slump, he left the firm and went to work for Grover Whalen, the master publicist and showman. Client: The 1939 New York World's Fair. Zachary gained on-the-job experience unmatched anywhere—a far cry from those trite news releases he was accustomed to writing. As assistant director in charge of World's Fair magazine publicity, Frank Zachary fed countless feature stories and ideas to magazines on every "hook" imaginable. It was at the fair that he met and befriended a fellow PR writer responsible for radio publicity. His name was Bill Bernbach, the man who ten years later went on to open the legendary advertising agency Doyle Dane Bernbach.

After the World's Fair began to lose its luster and public attention shifted to crumbling world events outside the Fair's Utopian facade, Zachary moved on to organize a number of events for the United China Relief Fund. By 1942, the United States, already enmeshed in the global conflict, needed talented people to help bolster its patriotism. Frank Zachary was hired by the Office of War Information (OWI), where he helped create various propaganda publications to raise morale. He worked with a gifted group of people, from novelist Howard Fast and artist Ludwig Bemelmans to art directors Tobias Moss and Bradbury Thompson. Their combined efforts produced *USA* and *Victory* Magazines. It was Frank Zachary's job as editor and picture coordinator that was to distill his creativity into even greater accomplishments.

After the war, Zachary, already supporting a wife and two daughters, needed to earn more money—hopefully via editing a magazine. He became east coast editor for a monthly publication geared to tyro photography called *Minicam*. Zachary lobbied to change the target audience and format of the magazine. He won. *Minicam* became a wonderful vehicle for professional and artistic photography. He concentrated on stories detailing the stylistic and technical wizardry of Ansel Adams, Harry Callahan, Arnold Newman and others. It was then that Zachary purchased the name of "Modern Photography" for $200, soon replacing *Minicam* as the magazine's title.

While Zachary was preparing an article on *Harper's Bazaar's* master art director Alexey Brodovitch, he became totally amazed and immersed in Brod's style and the "art" in art direction. They became close friends and eventual colleagues.

In the late 1940s, Zachary decided to leave *Modern Photography* and wound up working at a Curtis Publishing Company test publication simply called Magazine "X". It was to be a tabloid similar to *Life,* heavy on features packed with photography. Its title became *People* and Zachary was to become senior editor. Curtis executives, fearing it would lose money to *Life* and compete against its own *Saturday Evening Post,* abruptly cancelled *People*. Instead, Curtis Publishing concentrated its efforts on a faltering travel magazine called *Holiday,* whose editor was Ted Patrick, Zachary's old OWI crony.

By 1948, Frank Zachary, disillusioned with the seemingly impossible task of putting together a successful magazine, took a job once again with Grover Whalen, this time to publicize the golden jubilee of New York's consolidation of five boroughs into one city. The 50th anniversary celebration was rivaled only by the 1939 World's Fair. Whalen, Zachary and crew pulled out all the stops on this project. Everything from the biggest parade in New York history to a monstrous fireworks display in midtown Manhattan helped make this celebration a tremendous success.

In 1949, Frank Zachary left Whalen for the last time. Zachary, along with friend and former *Modern Photography* colleague George Rosenthal, Jr., decided to collaborate on a glossy, *Graphis*-type magazine showcasing the best in graphic design, illustration and photography. Rosenthal got his father to put up $25,000, and the large 9 by 12 inch publication was christened *Portfolio*. No expense was spared to make it one of the most beauti-fully produced magazines of its day. From paper stock to specially tipped-in inserts, *Portfolio* was a visual feast not to be missed! Stories and artwork featured painters, photographers and graphic designers who specialized in contemporary visual communications. Zachary and Rosenthal lured Alexey Brodovitch to become the magazine's art director. They paid him a whopping $3000 an issue. Paul Rand also got into the act, designing an "absolutely exquisite" letterhead. *Portfolio* was indeed a labor of love.

Reality set in, however, when it came time to pay the bills. Zachary and Rosenthal decided to help defray costs by selling advertising space in the magazine. The ads turned out to be crude and detracted from the overall impact of the publication. So as not to destroy its cachet, advertising was dropped from its pages. This, and Rosenthal Sr.'s decision against further funding, led to the demise of *Portfolio*. From 1949-1951, three glorious issues were produced. Prized as collectors items today, *Portfolio* remains one of the greatest achievements in modern day magazine content and design.

Always seeming to be at the right place at the right time, Frank Zachary was offered the position of picture editor of *Holiday* Magazine. In 1951, *Holiday* was in trouble and needed a fresh injection of creativity. Realizing the challenge involved in turning *Holiday* around, Zachary accepted the job. To him, "The picture *is* the layout." If you have a great image it need not be overshadowed by the type. With that in mind, Zachary began experimenting with layouts of photographs and illustrations a la Brodovitch. Using almost cinematic principles of motion, scale and visual imagery, he transformed a stale and floundering format into a graceful one. Frank Zachary was *Holiday's* tonic!

According to Zachary, "You're only as good as the people you surround yourself with." He's quick to mention that the success of *Holiday*, as well as the success of other endeavors, may not have been attained if the caliber of illustrators and photographers were not top-notch. Among those whom he is especially indebted to are: Slim Aarons, Henri Cartier-Bresson, Robert Capa, Jean-Michel Folon, George Giusti, Burt Glinn, Edward Gorey, Tom Hollyman, Arnold Newman, Robert Phillips Ronald Searle and John Lewis Stage.

For *Holiday*, Zachary developed what he termed environmental portraiture. Common by today's standards, it rocked editorial photography in the fifties. Case in point: an article on New York's master builder, Robert Moses. A studio shot simply could not capture the essence of the man. For dramatic effect, Zachary thought it would be apropos if Moses could be photographed against the backdrop of New York City. He commissioned Arnold Newman to shoot Moses standing tall on a girder, rigged precariously out over Welfare Island! Needless to say, it was environmental portraiture at its best.

After being passed over as editor of *Holiday* in 1964, Frank Zachary left the magazine for: the world of advertising? Yes! At Mary Wells' request, he was made president of Pritchard-Wood, a McCann-Erickson subsidiary with nine branch offices throughout the world.

Based in New York, Zachary, sensing his lack of ability to succeed in advertising, stayed only eight months at Pritchard. He then moved to McCann's experimental Center for Advanced Practice, an in-house think tank dedicated to new and innovative marketing techniques. There, he worked closely with Bill Backer and Henry Wolf.

Zachary, a fish out of water, decided to return to *Holiday* as art director in 1969. It was too much too late. *Holiday* had once again hit the skids after he left in 1964, and its popularity continued to decline. Attempts to revive it proved futile, and *Holiday* was sold, with Zachary's assistance, to a businessman named Marty Ackerman. Ackerman also bought *Status* Magazine, and for Zachary's help in acquiring *Holiday* rewarded him with the position of editor. Zachary performed his magic once again, making *Status* a spirited publication.

When his *Status* contract expired, he left to join *Travel & Leisure*. In 1972, after making his imprint there, Frank Zachary came full circle and was offered the plum job of editor-in-chief at *Town & Country* Magazine, a position he has held for 18 years.

Under Zachary, *Town & Country's* focal points have shifted to a very successful combination of high society with emphasis on trends in fashion and graceful living. He also spiced it up with a dash of highbrow satire. When Zachary took over as editor-in-chief in 1972, *Town & Country* had a circulation of 120,000 and $3 million in gross revenues. Today, it boasts a circulation of over 440,000 and gross revenues in excess of $32 million.

At the age of 76, Frank Zachary is the oldest editor-in-chief of any US publication. He remains as vibrant as the magazine he presides over. Zachary's concepts and designs have forever changed the way magazines are produced, read and enjoyed. Blessed with the innate ability and drive to adapt design considerations to societal changes, imbued also with a unique brand of graphic sense, Frank Zachary is truly the gin-in-the-punch of modern day magazine design.

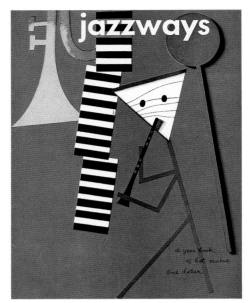

Portfolio, *1948-1950; cover: Herbert Matter*

Jazzways, *1950; cover: Paul Rand*

Holiday, *1951-1964; cover: John Lewis Stage*

Holiday, *1951-1964; cover: George Giusti*

Holiday, *1951-1964; photo: Henri Cartier-Bresson*

Holiday, *1951-1964; photo: Arnold Newman*

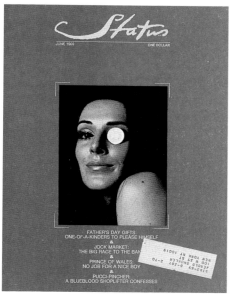

Status, *1969-1971;*
cover: Henry Wolf, Salvador Dali

Travel & Leisure, *1971-1972;*
cover: Ronald Searle

Town & Country, *1972-Present;*
photo: Jerry Salvati

Town & Country, *1972-Present;*
cover: Norman Parkinson

The Kings of Hollywood: Clark Gable, Van Heflin, Gary Cooper & James Stewart, Hollywood, 1958.

Town & Country, *1972-Present; photo: Slim Aarons*

Town & Country, *1972-Present; photo: Victor Skrebneski*

ADC Hall of Fame

Special Award

Robert Weaver

Saul Leiter

Talent runs in Robert Weaver's family. His brother Fritz is the extremely gifted television and Shakespearean actor. Robert is the wonderfully versatile illustrator whose striking images have graced the pages of the country's most respected magazines. His work came to the forefront of American illustration at a time when the country needed a graphic conscience. Robert Weaver, through his cleverly placed brush strokes or pen in ink, was our conscience—whether we knew it or not.

Born in Pittsburgh, Pennsylvania in 1924, Robert Weaver attended the Carnegie Institute of Technology in his hometown and the Art Students League in New York. After serving overseas in the military during World War II, Weaver did not immediately return to his native soil, opting instead to settle in Venice. He spent two years studying at the Academia Delle Belle Arti. Amidst the beauty of Renaissance antiquity and canals dotted with gondolas, Robert Weaver continued to master his drawing technique.

By the mid-fifties, Weaver arrived back in New York armed only with a modicum of confidence and a battered book filled with color mural sketches. He dropped them off at *Town & Country* Magazine. The publication's art director, Tony Mazzola, was intrigued by his work and hired him to illustrate several manuscripts scheduled to appear in subsequent issues of the magazine.

In what has become almost a folklorish tale of naivete, Weaver, knowing little of the technical jargon used to put a magazine together, misunderstood Mazzola when he was asked to "omit bleeding and stay out of the gutter." Weaver took this to mean no violence or harsh visuals! Finally explaining the terminology to Weaver, Mazzola proceeded to use him on a number of occasions. For Robert Weaver, the thrill of seeing his work appear in print and admired by countless people became an "addiction" that lasted four decades.

His work was showcased in every major editorial publication. Readers of *Charm, Esquire, Fortune, Life, Look, Playboy, Seventeen, Sports Illustrated* and *TV Guide* were constantly treated to Weaver's social portraitures. From visually covering the Kennedy campaign in *Esquire* to the last days of Ebbets Field for *Sports Illustrated,* Robert Weaver's work, though commissioned for specific and timely publication, remains timeless.

Because of his vivid visual style, magazine art directors put very little in the way of restrictions on him. Weaver is particularly indebted to ADC Hall of Famers Leo Lionni and Henry Wolf for encouraging him to "break the rules."

Weaver's talent did not stop at illustrating for magazines. His increasing popularity spilled over into the world of promotion and graphics as a record jacket illustrator. Weaver's portrayals of jazz personalities, from traditional to bebop, are especially noteworthy. Whether it was a study of vibrophonist Milt Jackson hunched over his instrument or of alto legend Charlie Parker playing the blues, Robert Weaver captured the true essence of the music through his memorable visuals.

His work has won him a myriad of recognition in the form of articles, awards and gallery exhibits. Weaver was inducted into the Society of Illustrators Hall of Fame in 1985. He's been a visiting professor at Syracuse University and for over 30 years has taught illustration at New York's School of Visual Arts. Silas H. Rhodes, chairman of the board of SVA, characterized Weaver's unmistakable style by saying, "In a triumph of principle, Robert Weaver's art *is* the fine art of illustration."

A typical class will no doubt hear Weaver talk about his craft and wax philosophical on a variety of topics, be it the preservation of our environment or the beauty of baseball. He encourages his students to split from the ordinary and take chances. Weaver regularly brings in people for his students to study and draw. They range from street people and ordinary people to dancers and Guardian Angels, all representing the fabric of our society depicted via the sketch pad.

As tribute to his dynamic body of work, the School of Visual Arts has had two very successful Weaver exhibitions: a retrospective in 1977 and a more recent show encompassing his extraordinary dimensional collages.

Realizing that times change and magazines can no longer provide a forum for his talents, Weaver has turned to the book format, which offers him a wider canvas with which to express himself. A variety of projects, his dimensional collages and teaching duties keep him busy.

A close friend of Weaver's, and one of the nation's best illustrators, Jim McMullan paid tribute to him this way:

> Perhaps it is impossible to speak of Weaver's drawing as a quality distinct from the special kinds of connections he makes in his work; for that same synthesis of surface and subject occurs in the ideas that animate his paintings. They are ideas which remind you always of the immutability of the two dimensional surface while taking you simultaneously on a wild mental journey of associations. The way in which he manipulates your view of the surface in the painting and of the idea "surface" in the objects painted is very much the way a magician shows you the handkerchief; 'Here it is, this flimsy piece of cloth—I wave it about—It is all rather insubstantial—But, presto! A bouquet of flowers.' In Weaver's case, the handkerchief might be the paper he is drawing on, or the paper he draws. He insists on its paperness only to prestidigitate the effect of some other reality and finally to return you to the paper.

A very gentle, soft spoken man, Robert Weaver speaks and creates with great emotional eloquence. For his great contributions and achievements, changing the direction of illustration and publishing while sharing his vision with hundreds of grateful students, the Art Directors Club Hall of Fame takes great pride in presenting him with this recognition. Leave it to Weaver...

ADVERTISING

Zoo visitors, please remember: ugly animals like being looked at, too.

When you take a look at some of our not-exactly-what-you'd-call-cuddly animals here at the Zoo, always try to remember one thing.

Ugliness is in the eye of the beholder.

Please keep this in mind when you first behold the warthog.

The bat is one of the most misunderstood mammals. Nature needs fruit bats to help pollinate plants.

The warthog may look a little odd to you. But, in nature, almost everything has its purpose.

Take those lumpy bumps on the sides of a warthog's head (it's not called a warthog for nothing, you know). They protect the warthog as it digs up the ground

Don't think of it as a large nose. Think of it as a small air filter and heater.

looking for tasty roots.

And they also protect the males when they bang their heads together to compete for a female.

The warthog also has a stringy, scraggly tail that sticks up in the air when it runs. Some people think that it acts like a little flag to the other warthogs running behind in the tall grasses.

So you see?

Ugly to you, maybe.

Very useful to a warthog.

WARTHOG
Weight: up to 200 lbs.
Length: 5' Height: 28" at shoulder
Tusks: Upper pair can curl upward to 12" or more in length.

After you've seen all you want to see of the warthog, walk over to Hoof and Horn Mesa and look for an animal called the Russian saiga (you can't miss it, just look for a big nose).

In Siberia where the saiga lives, it's bitter cold in the winter and very dusty in the summer. When the saiga breathes, the large nose works as a heater and air filter.

TWO-HEADED SKINK

If you're a skink's enemy, you're never really sure which end to attack first.

Over on the other side of the Zoo, stop by Reptile Mesa where we have the tortoises and alligators. And check out the two-headed skink.

So named because its back end looks like its front end, and vice versa.

In the wild, this tends to confuse a skink's enemy, at least long enough for the skink to get both of its ends out of there.

Why don't you come and see some of these things for yourself?

When you find out why some animals are different-looking, maybe you'll start looking at them a little differently. And then you'll feel the way we do. That there's really no such thing as an ugly animal.

Although the warthog comes very, very close.

What big eyes a gecko has. All the better to see you with at night, my dear.

Just when you thought you'd seen everything.
The San Diego Zoo

Pygmy hippos. Isn't that like saying jumbo shrimp?

Is this some sort of zookeeper joke? How can there be such a thing as a pygmy hippo?

Well, as you walk out the east of Tiger River, take a look at the enclosure right in front of you.

There you go. It's a mini-hippo, all right.

The elephant shrew has a nose like an anteater. But its name is from the ears.

The pygmy hippo, even when fully grown, is about one-eighth the size of the river hippo.

The best time to see them (we've got two, a lovely couple) is early in the morning, after they've had breakfast.

They're most active then, and maybe you'll see them doing laps in their pool. (Sometimes they cheat and walk along the bottom. Wouldn't you, if you were a hippo?)

Some of the most interesting animals at the Zoo are on the small side.

If you can call a hippo small.

Over in the Children's Zoo, you can see the lesser panda.

Much smaller than the giant panda we're all familiar with, the lesser panda is about the size of a raccoon. In fact, it's actually related to the raccoon, with a masked face to prove it.

You know, we try not to play favorites here, but we

have to admit the lesser panda is right up there on the list of the cutest animals at the Zoo.

(Speaking of small and cute, don't forget to see the new baby tiger in the Children's Zoo Nursery.)

Then, when you leave the Children's Zoo, walk over to the Klauber-Shaw Reptile House and look for the poison arrow frogs. They're small—the drawing on this page is about actual size—but these little fellas are big-time dangerous.

They secrete a poison that's so powerful, natives in South America use it on the tips of their arrows.

Well, we still haven't mentioned the dwarf mongoose, the pygmy chimp, the mouse deer or the dwarf crocodile. You won't want to miss those.

But enough small talk for now.

Come on out to the Zoo, and take a look at all kinds of animals. Big. Small. And in-between.

There's always something amazing to see, just when you thought you'd seen everything.

Small wonder, isn't it?

Just when you thought you'd seen everything.
The San Diego Zoo

Visit our convenient new location in the jungles of Asia.

You won't need a passport, any of those painful shots or that insect repellent that smells like turpentine.

Just come and visit new Sun Bear Forest at the Zoo.

LION-TAILED MACAQUE
Macaca silenus
Height: 22-30 inches
Weight: 15-20 pounds
Tail: 10-15 inches

We've re-created an Asian rain forest complete with more than 4,000 plants. A lush aviary. Cascading waterfalls and quiet pools of water.

And it's the new home for some of the most mysterious, elusive animals in the world.

The sun bears from Malaysia. And the lion-tailed macaques from India.

The sun bear is the smallest bear in the world. It gets its name from the mark on its chest that resembles a setting sun.

Maybe you'll see them climbing on the fallen logs in their new home.

There's even a big tree with a honey dispenser timed to release honey, as a special treat for the bears (and

a treat for you, to watch).

And speaking of trees, see the trees in Sun Bear Forest are mysterious.

There's one called the sacred ho-tree. Also called the strangler fig of Asia. As it grows, it wraps its branches around other plants, strangling them.

If you walk around the corner, you'll see some of the rarest monkeys in the world.

No more than 2,000 lion-tailed macaques are thought to be alive in the wild.

We're very proud to be able to give ours a big, new home like this.

We've designed it to fit their playful nature, with trees and vines to swing on, tall grasses to hide in, and cool, rushing streams for wading.

As you can probably tell, we're pretty excited about Sun Bear Forest. And the best part is, you don't have to go to Asia to see it.

SUN BEAR
Helarctos malayanus
Height: 3 1/2-4 1/2 feet
Weight: 60-145 pounds

It's right here, at the always-changing, always-amazing, just-when-you-thought-you'd-seen-everything Zoo.

Sun Bear Forest At The San Diego Zoo.
Just when you thought you'd seen everything.

When people at work ask what you did over the weekend, you can always tell them you helped save the planet.

If you've always wanted to help endangered animals, but never knew what you could do to help, we have a very simple suggestion.

Get everyone into the car, and come out to the Wild Animal Park.

Here, you can not only have a good time, you can spend your time doing some good.

That's because your attendance and support helps us help the animals.

We provide a haven where endangered animals can live their lives and raise their families, safe from a world that's closing in fast.

As you ride an electric monorail through two valleys, you'll see good things happening out here. You'll watch hundreds of animals living as they would in the wild. Animals sharing the land, babies that have just been born, herds that have room to run.

Later, take in the serenity of a waterfowl lagoon. Enjoy our animal shows. Pet a Persian gazelle. Or observe the antics of a gorilla troop.

And when the day's over, you won't just leave the Wild Animal Park. You'll leave it a little better off.

The San Diego Wild Animal Park. The rarest of animals. In the rarest of places.

To visit us, take I-15 to the Via Rancho Parkway exit and follow the signs. Or call 747-8702 for more information.

The San Diego Wild Animal Park

Most amusement parks offer a pleasant escape from life. We offer a pleasant return to it.

Come to the San Diego Wild Animal Park, and come back to life.

You'll see rhinos and zebras and wildebeests and animals you don't even know the names of (don't worry, we'll tell you) roaming the landscape.

As a silent, electric monorail carries you on a five-mile trip through two valleys, you'll see things rarely seen outside Africa or Asia.

Maybe you'll watch two giraffes "sparring" with their necks. A newborn gazelle, looking at its mother for the first time. A water buffalo, its head poking above the water, looking at you.

Or you can set out on your own, and walk down a hiking trail, through an Australian rain forest, over a suspension bridge, past African flowers.

Maybe you'll just stand there. Fascinated. For longer than you'd ever imagine, as you see a gorilla troop equally fascinated with a newborn family member.

You can pet a blackbuck antelope. Take home a tillandsia plant. Or watch animal shows with everything from eagles to bears, opossums to kangaroos.

If you want to get away from life for a little while, start by coming back to it.

At the San Diego Wild Animal Park. The rarest of animals. In the rarest of places.

To visit us, take I-15 to the Via Rancho Parkway exit. Or call (619) 480-0100 for more information.

The San Diego Wild Animal Park

If the Serengeti had a backyard, this is what it would be like.

Come to the Wild Animal Park, and you can go on a remarkable trip.

During our 50-minute monorail tour, you'll see the wildlife of Africa and Asia.

And you'll see more wild animals in those 50 minutes than many people see in a lifetime.

They're everywhere you look.

Herds of wildebeest, blackbucks and deer. All running free in our 1,800-acre preserve.

As you ride, and look, and listen, you'll begin to understand why we're here. To provide a sanctuary where endangered animals can live and breed in peace. So, even though the animal world keeps getting smaller and smaller, there will always be a place, a safe place, for them to live.

After you take the monorail tour, there's still plenty to do and see. A gorilla mother playing with her baby. You can take in the new Australian Show and African Marsh exhibit. Or just explore things on your own as you walk along the Kilimanjaro Trail.

Later, you can take home an exotic artifact from our gift shop. And you'll take home something else, too.

An unforgettable picture of what life must be like in the wild. At the San Diego Wild Animal Park. The rarest of animals. In the rarest of places.

To visit us, take I-15 to the Via Rancho Parkway exit. Or call (619) 747-8702 for more information.

The San Diego Wild Animal Park

Perception.

Reality.

For a new generation of Rolling Stone readers, a mouse is not a furry little animal that processes cheese. The mouse we're talking about processes information. And last year, the mouse population, especially among Rolling Stone readers, was on the rise. Rolling Stone readers purchased more than $657 million worth of personal computer equipment and software during 1988. That ain't cheese. If you want to catch your share of that action, bait your trap in the pages of Rolling Stone.

Perception.

Reality.

For a new generation of Rolling Stone readers, it ain't necessary to munch on magic mushrooms to appreciate contemporary American literature. Rolling Stone readers turn the pages of America's best sellers at the rate of 13 million books a year. If you're looking for a highly educated, discerning audience for your advertising message, you'll get great reviews in the pages of Rolling Stone.

Perception.

Reality.

Bummer, Bullwinkle. For a new generation of Rolling Stone readers, mousse is a hair care product, not the star of a Saturday morning cartoon. Last week, Rolling Stone readers used mousse and other hair care products more than 76 million times. If you've got health and beauty products to sell, rack up the sales with your ad in the pages of Rolling Stone.

4 Gold

Art Director: Houman Pirdavari

Creative Director: Pat Burnham

If the Serengeti had a backyard, this is what it would be like.

Come to the Wild Animal Park, and you can go on a remarkable trip.

During our 50-minute monorail tour, you'll see the wildlife of Africa and Asia.

And you'll see more wild animals in those 50 minute than many people see in a lifetime.

They're everywhere you look.

Herds of wildebeest, blackbucks and deer. All runnin free in our 1,800-acre preserve.

As you ride, and look, and listen, you'll begin to understand why we're here. To provide a sanctuary where endangered animals can live and breed in peace So, even though the animal world keeps getting smalle and smaller, there will always be a place, a safe place, for them to live.

After you take the monorail tour, there's still plenty to do and see. A gorilla mother playing with her baby. You can take in the new Australian Show and African Marsh exhibit. Or just explore things on your own as you walk along the Kilimanjaro Trail.

Later, you can take home an exotic artifact from ou gift shop. And you'll take home something else, too.

An unforgettable picture of what life must be like ir the wild. At the San Diego Wild Animal Park. The rares of animals. In the rarest of places.

To visit us, take I-15 to the Via Rancho Parkway exi Or call (619) 747-8702 for more information.

The San Diego Wild Animal Park

5 Silver

Art Director: John Vitro

Last Year Wendee Weichel Beat A Competitor That Tried To Kill Her.

On May 25, 1988, Steven And Barbara Crofts Had A Baby They Weren't Expecting.

The Day Maryanne Blake Took A $75,000 Bike Ride.

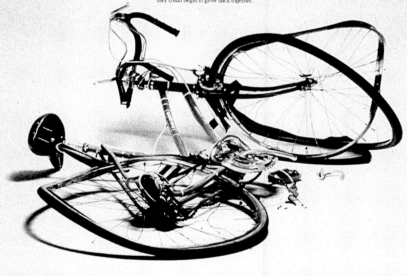

TO GET HIRED THESE DAYS, YOU HAVE TO FILL MORE THAN THE JOB REQUIREMENTS.

SPECIMEN CONTAINER
AFTER DRAWING SPECIMEN,
CLOSE LID AND ATTACH LABEL
NAME
ROOM NO.   DATE
DOCTOR
BIOHAZARD

Many companies across Ohio are instituting mandatory drug testing procedures, such as urinalysis, for screening job applicants.

Starting Wednesday, Tom Beres will show you what it means when they tell you they want to see a sample of your work. Watch "The Test That Could Mean Your Job," all this week on Channel 3 News at 11.

CHANNEL3NEWS

THIS WEEK, FIND OUT HOW CIGARETTE SMOKING CAN AFFECT SEXUAL PERFORMANCE.

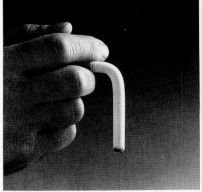

Medical researchers have found a definite connection between cigarette smoking and impotence in men.

Starting Thursday, Eileen Korey will tell you another reason why your loved ones want you to quit smoking. Watch "Smoking & Impotence" on WKYC-TV, Channel 3 News at 11. **3NEWS**

Eileen Korey

THANKS TO VIDEO STORES, KIDS HAVE A WHOLE NEW REASON TO CALL TELEVISION THE BOOB TUBE.

Many video stores in this area will rent adult movies to minors—movies that contain explicit sex and violence.

Starting Wednesday, Jill Beach will tell you how these stores are giving the term "boob tube" a whole new meaning. Watch "Sex-'N-Guns To Go" on WKYC-TV, Channel 3 News at 11. **CHANNEL3NEWS**

7 Silver

Art Director: Don Fibich
Creative Director: Tom Smith
Chuck Withrow
Designer: Don Fibich
Photographer: Ladd Trepal
Martin Reuben

8 Silver

Art Director: Steve Beaumont

Nan Hutchison

Dennis Lim

Can you spot the Range Rover in this picture?

Goodbye road. Goodbye traffic. Goodbye 5 m.p.h.

A Range Rover does something far more impressive than get you through a traffic jam in air-conditioned, arm-chaired, stereo-surrounded comfort.

A Range Rover takes you where there are no jams. Because there is no traffic.

Through the woods. Along the beach. Across the desert. Range Rovers, after all, are so extraordinary, they drive for years in places

ordinary cars couldn't drive a quarter of a mile.

So it's not surprising that to many a Range Rover's most luxurious feature isn't its elegant interior, optional sunroof, or the

RANGE ROVER

security of 24 hour roadside assistance.

Its most luxurious feature is its ability to provide an experience a bit more exhilarating than a highway to the suburbs at six p.m.

Why not call 1-800-FINE 4WD for the Range Rover dealer nearest you?

We won't deny that at somewhat above $34,000 a Range Rover is hardly inexpensive.

But after all the time you've spent in trafficlikethis, what could be nicer than going off on your   own?

9 Silver

Art Director: Roy Grace
Creative Director: Roy Grace
Diane Rothschild
Photographer: Carl Furuta
Copywriter: Diane Rothschild

WE DESIGN EVERY VOLVO TO LOOK LIKE THIS.

You're looking at a perfect Volvo. A Volvo that performed exactly as our safety engineers designed it to.

Its front and rear ends, for example, collapsed on impact. As a result, much of the crash energy was absorbed instead of being passed on to the passengers.

The car's middle section, however, didn't collapse. That's because the entire passenger compartment is surrounded by Volvo's unique "safety cage." Made of six box section steel pillars, this protective housing is strong enough to support the weight of six Volvos.

But the passengers of this car were also protected in ways you can't see. Because inside are such standard features as a driver's side Supplemental Restraint System, a collapsible steering column and, of course, 3-point seat belts, front and rear.

Every Volvo is designed to help protect its passengers in all these ways. And, as a result, will look remarkably similar to this one after being in the same type of accident.

If you're concerned about safety, you can't find a more beautiful car.

VOLVO
A car you can believe in.

Many boots are waterproof. Few are water proven.

Of all the tests a bootmaker can use, none is more valuable than the test of time. A test which clearly proves no boot on earth is as warm, dry and comfortable as any in the Timberland Sport Series. Each stands for two decades of leadership in the science of waterproofing. Each goes through a double waterproofing process, which combines advanced silicone-impregnation with the best Gore-Tex fabric bootie construction. And each has our lightweight polyurethane sole for comfort and durability.

Timberland. Still the driest after twenty years in the water.

Boots, shoes, clothing wind, water, earth and sky.

If you want to walk to heaven, wear a boot that can go through hell.

Boots, shoes, clothing
wind, water, earth and sky.

Proof that the world's most seaworthy vessels are still built by hand.

Boots, shoes, clothing
wind, water, earth and sky.

James Clavell. Cardmember since 1967.

*Membership
Has Its Privileges*

Don't leave home without it.
Call 1-800-THE CARD to apply

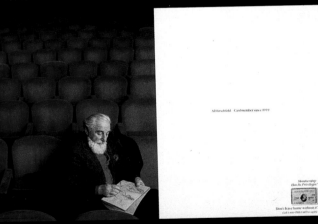

Al Hirschfeld. Cardmember since 1959.

*Membership
Has Its Privileges*

Don't leave home without it.
Call 1-800-THE CARD to apply

Catherine Deneuve. Cardmember since 1978.

*Membership
Has Its Privileges*

Don't leave home without it.
Call 1-800-THE CARD to apply

12 Silver
Art Director: Parry Merkley
Rick Rabe
Creative Director: Gordon Bowen
Photographer: Annie Leibovitz
Copywriter: Gordon Bowen
Agency: Ogilvy & Mather
Client: American Express

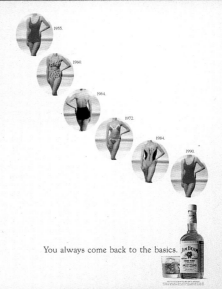

13 Silver
Art Director: Bob Barrie
Creative Director: Pat Burnham
Designer: Bob Barrie
Photographer: Rick Dublin
Kerry Peterson
Copywriter: Jarl Olsen
Agency: Fallon McElligott
Client: Jim Beam

CHINA, BY WAY OF SHANGRI-LA.

THE PEAKS OF GUILIN RISE ALARMINGLY FROM THE GUANGXI PLAIN, LIKE THE MOUNDS OF BURROWING ANIMALS ABOUT TO SURFACE. "OUR POET ZHANG GU," SAYS YOUR GUIDE, "WROTE

that these mountains cross the space from earth to heaven." And for more than a minute, your normally garrulous group falls silent, transfixed. There is only the sound of the wind.

A vacation is not so much a continuous journey as it is a series of moments that you will carry with you and return to for years to come. You never know what

apparently insignificant detail, what tiny thing taken care of just so, will one day be the key to such a memory.

Victoria Harbor, Hong Kong. From the sweep of the Promenade Deck, we look down upon an armada of three-masted junks, quilt-rigged and bobbing like toys in our wake. Astonishingly, pigs and chickens roam their decks. From

an unseen stewpot: a whiff of ginger.

With a gloriously white Royal Viking ship as your base of operations, you will see a China that few other visitors ever uncover.

As the world's most experienced cruise line to The People's Republic, we have been officially designated an "Honored Guest," and accorded special privileges like visitation to Chinese homes, warm welcomes from local officials, and swift, supervised passage for our land excursions.

It is the last nation on earth to continue the manufacture of steam locomotives. Gasping, thunderous, they storm out of the middle distance, casting a dreamy feeling over whatever's going on at the moment.

Our ship is your sanctuary, your home after a busy day. Here you will find the highest crew to passenger ratio

You have never tasted a hamburger until you've savored one on the fantail, calmly overlooking the hustle and bustle of the harbor at Dalian.

name. You will dine, in splendid single seating, on the creations of chefs trained at Roger Vergé and Le Notre.

Wanlichangcheng, they call it, The Great Wall— 4000 miles long and wide enough to accommodate five horsemen side by side. Once, on this very spot, a network of bonfires warned the emperor of his approaching fate, sealed in the swords of Mongols thousands of miles distant.

The breeze in your hair. High tea at four. Ahead, The Forbidden City.

And so it is that a vacation, in the best sense, can last forever.

ROYAL VIKING LINE

This is a delicate transaction, however, and one that does not brook compromise. At Royal Viking we know this. We charge a bit more for knowing it. But then, what we are doing may be nothing less than priceless.

Eight trips to China are planned this year. Isn't it time you joined us? For more information and a copy of our colorful 1989 Cruise Atlas, please visit your trusted travel agent or call us at (800) 426-0821.

As always, we look forward to seeing you on board.

in the world. You will find breezy, strollable decks and staterooms worthy of the

PLAYA DEL CARMEN NAPLES MANILA KETCHIKAN LAS PALMAS OCHO RIOS MELBOURNE PUERTO VALLARTA SHANGHAI CARTAGENA BRISBANE ST... ...PICTON FORT-DE-FRANCE SANTAREM CAPRI SAN BLAS ISLANDS BOMBAY SINGAPORE ROME

Bahamian Registry

IT IS ONE OF THE WORLD'S GREAT WONDERS.
SOON, IT WILL BE MAKING ITS WAY TO THE AMAZON.

ROYAL VIKING LINE

A TRULY GREAT SHIP IS SOMETHING OF
A DESTINATION IN ITSELF.

ROYAL VIKING LINE

Perception.

Reality.

For a new generation of Rolling Stone readers, a mouse is not a furry little animal that processes cheese. The mouse we're talking about processes information. And last year, the mouse population, especially among Rolling Stone readers, was on the rise. Rolling Stone readers purchased more than $657 million worth of personal computer equipment and software during 1988. That ain't cheese. If you want to catch your share of that action, bait your trap in the pages of Rolling Stone.

Sporting Hush Puppies.

Allow us to point out our new look. Soft leather men's casuals and women's Body Shoes—with the Comfort Curve* sole to flex where your foot flexes. In a flush of spring colors.

For twenty years they've been insulated from snow, oblivious to rain, impervious to competition.

Before the Timberland Company existed, only one kind of boot was truly waterproof. The kind you don't like to wear. Because it's made of something other than leather, something plastic or rubber that doesn't breathe.

Relief came two decades ago, when Timberland craftsmen hand-built a full-grain leather boot that was guaranteed waterproof. And insulated.

It was a concept the world was waiting for. No sooner did our boot hit the stores than it sold out. And today it still sells out, even though imitations abound both here and abroad.

The fact is, copying the look of our classic tan buck boot is far easier than copying the workmanship. The meticulous silicone impregnation of the leather, the four-row nylon stitching, the direct bonding of upper to midsole for a guaranteed waterproof seal, and the unbeatable warmth of Thinsulate® insulation.

You live on an earth that's two-thirds water. Can you afford a lesser boot than ours?

Timberland

Boots, shoes, clothing, wind, water, earth and sky.

Boat shoes that have conquered every adverse sailing condition imaginable, including a sea of competition.

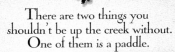

The headline on this page isn't something you should accept without substantiation. So let us hasten to provide it.

Timberland boat shoes are stronger because our construction is superior. You will never see one of our soles flapping loose in the breeze, unstitched from its moccasin upper. We eliminate such stitching altogether in favor of permanent bonding, so shoe and sole stay married until the day they die.

And unlike boat shoes of a lesser quality, ours have premium natural leathers that won't crack, impregnable nylon stitching that won't rot, and solid brass eyelets that won't chip.

This year, we're pleased to introduce the high-performance Ultra Boat Shoe, companion to our Super and Classic Boat Shoe. The Ultra combines the grip and stability of a double density outsole with the comfort and cushioning of a double density midsole. For maximum dryness, the stain-resistant, waterproof leathers have a Hydrofil® lining to wick away moisture.

Water, water, it's everywhere. So is Timberland.

Timberland

Boots, shoes, clothing, wind, water, earth and sky.

There are two things you shouldn't be up the creek without. One of them is a paddle.

The other is a pair of boots from the Timberland Sporting Collection. Because even though we can't keep water out of your boat, we guarantee it won't get through your boots.

Consider the construction of our Super Guide Boot. Comfortable. Dry. Lightweight. Protected by an exclusive Timberland Gore-Tex Leather™ laminate that combines a glove leather lining with a waterproof, breathable Gore-Tex® fabric bootie. The result is a level of comfort and dryness you won't find in any other field boot.

Yet another Super Guide exclusive is a sole of triple density polyurethane permanently bonded to the upper. Compared to boots with traditional rubber soles this lessens weight, adds insulation, expands flexibility and increases slip resistance. Giving you a whole new level of performance.

In fact, every single boot in the Timberland Sporting Collection is built to be warm, dry and comfortable, and the reason is our two-step waterproofing process. Step one is direct bonding of silicone-impregnated waterproof leathers to the sole. Step two is Gore-Tex fabric bootie construction.

Timberland. Not just waterproof. Water-proven.

Timberland

Boots, shoes, clothing, wind, water, earth and sky.

17 Silver

Art Director: John Doyle
Creative Director: Paul Silverman
Photographer: Clint Clemens
Copywriter: Paul Silverman
Agency: Mullen
Client: Timberland Co.

24 Distinctive Merit
Art Director: Roy Grace
Creative Director: Roy Grace
Diane Rothschild
Photographer: Carl Furuta
Copywriter: Diane Rothschild
Client: Range Rover of North America

Lots of people use their Range Rovers just to run down to the corner.

Want to drive where there are no people? No pressures? No pavement? No problem.

With its formidable power and superb engineering, a Range Rover can get you up, over, around or across terrain that would have other 4-wheel drive vehicles waiting for a tow truck.

And what's all the more remarkable is that this same Range Rover is also ideal for such other off-road locales as shopping malls and drive-through banks.

Surprisingly nimble and responsive, the Range Rover is as exceptional on-road as it is off-road.

It out-does a host of luxury cars in posh, polish, and luxury amenities.

It has enough room in back for a refrigerator's worth of food—plus a small refrigerator.

And should you run into anything from a rainstorm to a blizzard, a Range Rover can get you through it with a feeling of comfort and security no ordinary car can approach.

This year, in fact, a Range Rover does that even better. With a new, highly advanced, four-years-in-the-developing, anti-lock braking system that many experts consider the most sophisticated in the world.

All in all, there just isn't a car on the road, or off it, as assuredly rugged, as unstintingly luxurious, as eminently practical and as supremely versatile as a Range Rover.

So whether you're interested in the standard, extravagantly appointed Range Rover, or the even more opulent County model, why not call 1-800 FINE 4WD for the name of a dealer near you?

We won't deny that there are considerably less expensive vehicles than a Range Rover.

But then, people don't simply buy Range Rovers just to run down to the corner.

They also buy them to be sure they'll get back.

RANGE ROVER

Catherine Deneuve. Cardmember since 1978.

Membership Has Its Privileges.

Don't leave home without it.
Call 1-800-THE CARD to apply.

Creative Director: Paul Silverman
Photographer: Gavin Creedon
Copywriter: Paul Silverman
Agency: Mullen
Client: Timberland Co.

For those who accept turbulence as a fact of life.

Although Timberland gear gives you a great look in the flattering sunlight of a calm day at sea, its true worth shines through when the sky blackens and the water opens its jaws to bare on anything afloat. We build our clothing and footwear to meet the needs of people whose serious love of the sea exposes them to all its moods. People who will not or cannot cling to land until turbulence no longer threatens and the coast is clear. For these individuals, shelter is made of three things. Their boat, their skill, their Timberland gear.

Boots, shoes, clothing, wind, water, earth and sky.

Mikhail Baryshnikov Cardmember since 1975

*Membership
Has Its Privileges.*

Don't leave home without it.
Call 1-800-THE CARD to apply.

27 Distinctive Merit

Art Director: Parry Merkley
Rick Rabe
Creative Director: Gordon Bowen
Photographer: Annie Leibovitz
Copywriter: Gordon Bowen
Agency: Ogilvy & Mather
Client: American Express

Art Director: Chris Graves
Creative Director: Roy Grace
Diane Rothschild
Copywriter: Craig Demeter
Agency: Roy Grace
Client: Paddington

J&B Blended Scotch Whisky, 43% Alc. by Vol., Imported by The Paddington Corporation, Ft. Lee, NJ © 1989.

ingle ells,
ingle ells.

The holidays aren't the same without

J&B Scotch Whisky. Blended and bottled in Scotland by Justerini & Brooks, fine wine and spirit merchants since 1749.
To send a gift of J&B anywhere in the U.S., call 1-800-528-6148. Void where prohibited.

For twenty years they've been insulated from snow, oblivious to rain, impervious to competition.

Before the Timberland Company existed, only one kind of boot was truly waterproof. The kind you don't like to wear. Because it's made of something other than leather, something plastic or rubber that doesn't breathe.

Relief came two decades ago, when Timberland craftsmen hand-built a full-grain leather boot that was guaranteed waterproof. And insulated.

It was a concept the world was waiting for. No sooner did our boot hit the stores than it sold out. And today it still sells out, even though imitations abound both here and abroad.

The fact is, copying the look of our classic tan buck boot is far easier than copying the workmanship. The meticulous silicone impregnation of the leather, the four-row nylon stitching, the direct bonding of upper to midsole for a guaranteed waterproof seal, and the unbeatable warmth of Thinsulate® insulation.

You live on an earth that's two-thirds water. Can you afford a lesser boot than ours?

Timberland ⊛

Boots, shoes, clothing, wind, water, / earth and sky.

In time, even these shoes will succumb to the sea. But chances are you'll replace the boat first.

The headline on this page isn't something you should accept without substantiation. So let us hasten to provide it.

Timberland boat shoes are stronger because our construction is superior. You will never see one of our soles flapping loose in the breeze, unstitched from its moccasin upper. We eliminate such stitching altogether in favor of permanent bonding, so shoe and sole stay married until the day they die.

And unlike boat shoes of a lesser quality, ours have premium natural leathers that won't crack, impregnable nylon stitching that won't rot, and solid brass eyelets that won't chip.

This year, we're pleased to introduce the high-performance Ultra Boat Shoe, companion to our Super and Classic Boat Shoe. The Ultra combines the grip and stability of a triple density outsole with the comfort and cushioning of a double density midsole. For maximum dryness, the stain-resistant, waterproof leathers have a Hydrofil® lining to wick away moisture.

Water, water, it's everywhere. So is Timberland.

Timberland ⊛

Boots, shoes, clothing, wind, water, / earth and sky.

There are two things you shouldn't be up the creek without. One of them is a paddle.

The other is a pair of boots from the Timberland Sporting Collection. Because even though we can't keep water out of your boat, we guarantee it won't get through your boots.

Consider the construction of our Super Guide Boot. Comfortable. Dry. Lightweight. Protected by an exclusive Timberland Gore-Tex Leather™ laminate that combines a glove leather lining with a waterproof, breathable Gore-Tex® fabric bootie. The result is a level of comfort and dryness you won't find in any other field boot.

Yet another Super Guide exclusive is a sole of triple density polyurethane permanently bonded to the upper. Compared to boots with traditional rubber soles this lessens weight, adds insulation, expands flexibility and increases slip resistance. Giving you a whole new level of performance.

In fact, every single boot in the Timberland Sporting Collection is built to be warm, dry and comfortable, and the reason is our two-step waterproofing process. Step one is direct bonding of silicone-impregnated waterproof leathers to the sole. Step two is Gore-Tex fabric bootie construction.

Timberland. Not just waterproof. Water-proven.

Timberland ⊛

Boots, shoes, clothing, wind, water, / earth and sky.

---

29 Distinctive Merit

Art Director: John Doyle
Creative Director: Paul Silverman
Photographer: Clint Clemens
Copywriter: Paul Silverman
Agency: Mullen
Client: Timberland Co.

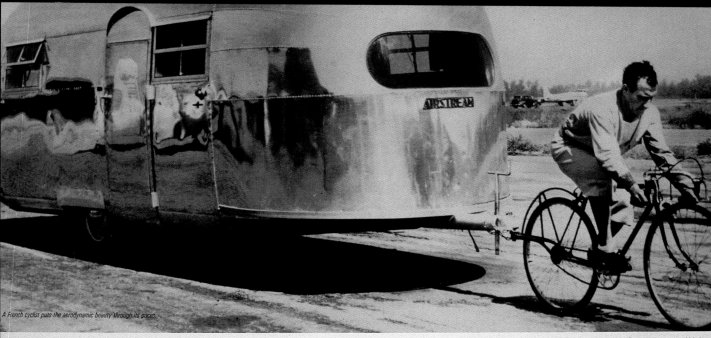

A French cyclist puts the aerodynamic beauty through its paces.

How fuel-efficient is the Airstream?

Way back in the depths of the Depression, our founder Wally Byam happened upon a trailer shape that Airstreamers have since come to know and love.

55 years later, precious little has changed.

Oh, we've added creature comforts all right. Like a deluxe four-burner range. A two-way refrigerator. And almost three dozen other modern-day conveniences.

But our now-familiar fuselage is still honed from the same high-strength, lightweight aluminum. Which, combined with its low center of gravity, means far less vibration. Greater stability in crosswinds. And 30% fewer trips to the gas pump.

(Mileage may vary, depending upon your tow vehicle.)

We'd like to tell you more about our classic trailers, but first you'll need to call: 1 513 596-6111. Or write to Mr. Steve Krivian, 419 W. Pike Street, Jackson Center, OH 45334.

The 1990 Airstream Excella

Dr. H.W. *Holman and his wife Thelma* have been attached to Airstream trailers just about as long as they've been attached to each other. Over half a century, bless them.

Together, they've lugged their custom-made campers across the United States, to Europe, Russia, Africa and Asia. Down ice-encrusted highways, through wind-swept trackless deserts.

And you can bet your beret that they weren't alone.

Owner loyalty like this doesn't surprise us much. After all, our trailers are built for the long haul.

Some 9,000 rivets make sure of that. Along with an exhaustive 95-point quality check on the assembly line. And an unblinking attention to good old Yankee craftsmanship.

A lasting relationship since 1935.

Of course, there may be newer ways to make travel trailers. Faster ones, too. But none that protects your investment better. Or guarantees happier trails.

We'd like to tell you more about our classic trailers, but first you'll need to call: 1 513 596-6111. Or write to Mr. Steve Krivian, 419 W. Pike Street, Jackson Center, OH 45334.

The 1990 Airstream Excella

The happy campers with their Airstream "Argosy".

HORNET + 3

July 24, 1969. The Apollo crew is welcomed home.

Shortly after Neil Armstrong, "Buzz" Aldrin and Michael Collins landed on the silver moon, they landed in a silver Airstream.

Had to, you see. Government regulations.

For 17 days, they enjoyed captivity in the climate-controlled coziness of that 35-foot coach.

Savoring real food, prepared in a real kitchen. Stretching out in a cabin furnished with amenities fit for a king.

A lot like our motorhomes today.

Except today, they come with plush carpeted floors and hand-rubbed hickory cabinets. (Our premier model, the 345, is even stocked with a built-in microwave, a color TV and VCR.)

You'd smile too if you had to be quarantined in an Airstream.

Since 1983, Airstream has built Astrovans for NASA's shuttle program. It gives our boys something to look forward to after a hard day in space.

We'd like to tell you more about our classic motorhomes, but first you'll need to call: 1 513 596-6111. Or write to Mr. Steve Krivian, 419 W. Pike Street, Jackson Center, OH 45334.

The 1990 Airstream Motorhome

Perception.

Reality.

For a new generation of Rolling Stone readers, it isn't necessary to munch on magic mushrooms to appreciate contemporary American literature. Rolling Stone readers turn the pages of America's best sellers at the rate of 13 million books a year. If you're looking for a highly educated, discerning audience for your advertising message, you'll get great reviews in the pages of Rolling Stone.

31 Distinctive Merit

Art Director: Houman Pirdavari
Creative Director: Pat Burnham
Photographer: Rick Dublin
Copywriter: Bill Miller
Agency: Fallon McElligott
Client: Rolling Stone

OUR SHIPS GO PLACES OTHERS DON'T.

If you long leave the paradox of passengers traveling with Royal Viking line to begin or end their cruise with a land package, fine, exchange. But should your client want an all-out land adventure, we have over 1,300 different land get prices in store. Leading him to dozens places in the Australian Outback, Leningrad's Hermitage Museum and the Himalayas. In fact if we don't get him, it's quite possibly there isn't any there there. For sales assistance call (800) 346-8000, for reservations (800) 422-8000.

ROYAL VIKING LINE

FOR THOSE WISHING TO BOOK THE SUN: A RAY OF HOPE.

After gracing the Seven Seas during a much-heralded 100-day inaugural cruise, The Royal Viking Sun returns to Europe and North America for the summer. There, she'll begin passages of slightly shorter duration—two and three weeks—but of no less splendor. At last, all your clients can truly reach the sun. For reservations call (800) 422-8000, for sales assistance dial (800) 346-8000.

ROYAL VIKING LINE

WE RELEASE THIS RATHER EMBARRASSING PHOTO ONLY TO DEMONSTRATE A POINT.

This otherwise elegant place setting diverges from Royal Viking at-sea specifications in one telling aspect: the upper fork and spoon are, lamentably, both pointing the wrong way. The attention to detail that keeps our passengers from ever seeing this sort of thing is one reason our travel agents enjoy the highest of all passenger return rates. For more information, call sales assistance (800) 346-8000 or reservations (800) 422-8000.

ROYAL VIKING LINE

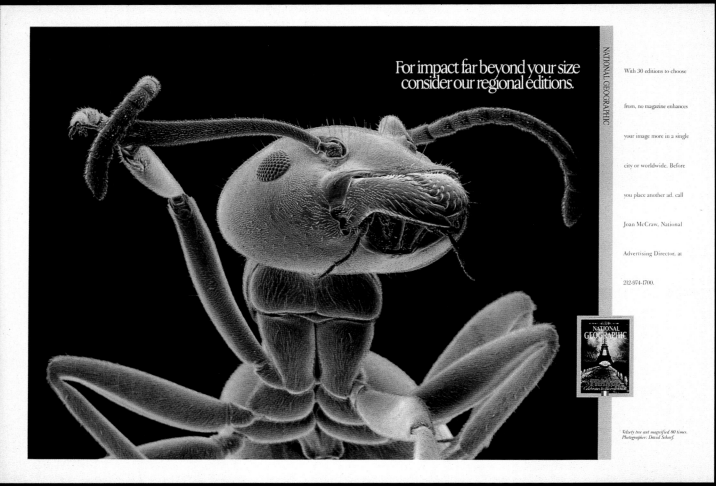

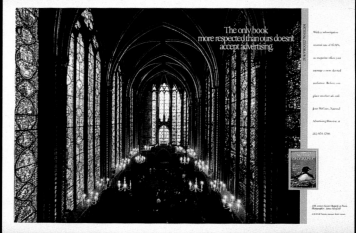

33 Distinctive Merit
Art Director: Cristina Creager
Creative Director: Jim Kingsley
Brett Robbs
Photographer: David Scharf
Mitsuaki Iwago
James Stanfield
Agency: DDB Needham
Client: National Geographic Society

THIS.

FROM OCTOBER UNTIL APRIL, THE ROYAL VIKING STAR WILL OFFER FIVE TO ELEVEN - DAY CRUISES TO BARBADOS, WITH CALLS THROUGHOUT THE SUNSWEPT SOUTHERN CARIBBEAN.

PARADISE.

HEAVEN.

Some abused children grow up to become famous.

Abused children grow up to become abusing adults. Not in every case, but in too many. Nine out of ten murderers, rapists and drug addicts suffered from physical or emotional abuse as a child. So did the four people pictured above. That's something worth thinking about—even if you don't have kids.

Child Abuse. It hurts all of us.

Citizens for the Prevention of Child Abuse

36

Art Director: Marcia Gabor
Creative Director: Terry Burris
Designer: Marcia Gabor
Copywriter: Terry Burris
Agency: Conrad, Phillips & Vutech
Client: Bellantoni Bros. Market

37

Art Director: Bob Brihn
Creative Director: Pat Burnham
Designer: Bob Brihn
Photographer: Kerry Peterson
Copywriter: George Gier
Agency: Fallon McElligott
Client: Porsche

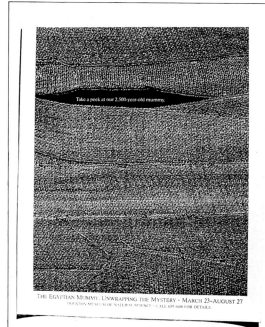

38

Art Director: Bob Brihn
Creative Director: Pat Burnham
Designer: Bob Brihn
Photographer: Kerry Peterson
Copywriter: George Gier
Agency: Fallon McElligott
Client: Porsche

39

Art Director: Dean Narahara
Creative Director: Dick Smith
Designer: Dean Narahara
Copywriter: Laurie Ripplinger
Agency: Taylor, Brown, Smith & Perrault
Client: Houston Museum of Natural Science

Drive Drunk And We'll See You Real Soon.

If you saw drinking and driving from our point of view, you wouldn't drink and drive.

Goodwine
Funeral Homes
Caring For Families The Way Only A Family Can.

Flat Rock 584-3200
Palestine 586-2067
Robinson 544-2131

40
Art Director: David Straka
Creative Director: Pat Fagan
Copywriter: Pat Fagan
Agency: Keller-Crescent
Client: Goodwine Funeral Homes

It wasn't the sun that burned everybody in Baja.

It was Jack Johnson. The man who drove his V6-powered Nissan Hardbody 4x4 against a whole desert full of V8 trucks in this year's SCORE Baja 1000 race.
And won. By over an hour. Hauling off with the 1988 HDRA/SCORE Class 4 championship at the same time.
All of which turned November 11th into one of the hottest days of the year for Nissan.
While turning the competition extremely red in the face.

Built for the Human Race.

41
Art Director: Richard Bess
Creative Director: Bob Kuperman
Copywriter: Julie Curtis
Agency: Chiat/Day/Mojo
Client: Nissan

With the right oil, this Century could last another ten years.

Whether you drive a Buick Century or a Suzuki Samurai, Amoco LDO is the right oil for your car. That's because LDO meets manufacturers' performance requirements for every car made today. So why not drive over to Amoco and change your oil now? On second thought, if you're not using LDO, you'd better take a cab.

LDO Motor Oil. $15 a case, $1.25 a quart.

Self-service pumps. Open seven days a week.

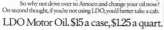

With so many ways to get pumped up, you'll find that a YMCA membership is a real gas. So join today and start increasing your personal mileage.
Free trial membership during September.
YMCA

42
Art Director: Arty Tan
Creative Director: Pat Burnham
Photographer: Kerry Peterson
Copywriter: Jamie Barrett
Agency: Fallon McElligott
Client: Amoco

43
Art Director: Craig Tanimoto
Creative Director: Jac Coverdale
Designer: Craig Tanimoto
Photographer: Jim Arndt
Copywriter: Joe Alexander
Jerry Fury
Agency: Clarity, Coverdale, Rueff
Client: Metro-YMCA

44

Art Director: Bob Brihn
Creative Director: Pat Burnham
Designer: Bob Brihn
Photographer: Kerry Peterson
Copywriter: George Gier
Agency: Fallon McElligott
Client: Porsche

45

Art Director: Bob Barrie
Creative Director: Pat Burnham
Designer: Bob Barrie
Copywriter: Jamie Barrett
Agency: Fallon McElligott
Client: Continental Bank

Spend your European vacation in these luxurious accommodations.

Buy a new Porsche from us and we can arrange for you to pick it up in West Germany. Use it to see Europe, then we'll ship it back to you. Come in for details.

PORSCHE

Good (Huff!) luck to all of our fellow (Puff!) competitors in today's (Gulp!) Chicago Sun-Times (Gasp!) Triathlon.

Continental Bank
Employee Triathlon Team

Use the wrong oil and it won't be a Legend for long.

Whether you drive an Acura Legend or a Pontiac LeMans, Amoco LDO is the right oil for your car. That's because LDO meets manufacturers' performance requirements for every car made today.
So why not drive over to Amoco and change your oil now? On second thought, if you're not using LDO, you'd better take a cab.

LDO Motor Oil. $15 a case, $1.25 a quart.

Now if you have an emergency in your 911, you don't have to call 911.

No matter where you are in North America, if you need gas, help or towing just call the number on your roadside assistance card. It's free with any new Porsche. Call or come in for details.

Porsche 24 Hour Road Service.

46

Art Director: Arty Tan
Creative Director: Pat Burnham
Photographer: Kerry Peterson
Copywriter: Jamie Barrett
Agency: Fallon McElligott
Client: Amoco

47

Art Director: Bob Brihn
Creative Director: Pat Burnham
Designer: Bob Brihn
Photographer: Jim Arndt
Copywriter: George Gier
Agency: Fallon McElligott
Client: Porsche

48
Art Director: Arty Tan
Creative Director: Pat Burnham
Copywriter: Jamie Barrett
Agency: Fallon McElligott
Client: Quick Lube

49
Art Director: Arty Tan
Creative Director: Pat Burnham
Photographer: Kerry Peterson
Copywriter: Jamie Barrett
Agency: Fallon McElligott
Client: Quick Lube

Come to Quick Lube and we'll grease your palms.

Get $2 off your next oil change.
In twenty minutes or less, Amoco service technicians will give you a complete oil and lube job. There's no appointment necessary. Plus, with this coupon, you'll get $2 off.

Amoco Quick Lube

Expiration date ____ Not good in conjunction with other Amoco coupon offers.

We're so good at oil changes, we can do them in the dark.

NOW OPEN UNTIL 10PM

At Amoco Quick Lube, we're open from 7AM to 10 PM. Just stop by at your convenience and our service technicians will give you a complete oil and lube job in twenty minutes or less.

Amoco Quick Lube

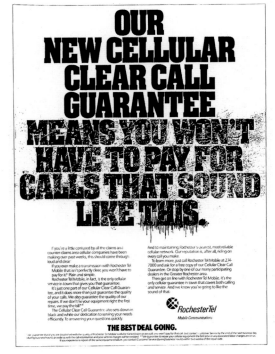

OUR NEW CELLULAR CLEAR CALL GUARANTEE MEANS YOU WON'T HAVE TO PAY FOR CALLS THAT SOUND LIKE THIS.

THE BEST DEAL GOING.

Make fiber part of every meal.

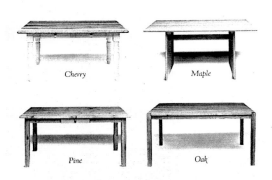

Cherry   *Maple*

Pine   *Oak*

Check out our attractive wooden tables on sale for a limited time. With prices starting at $99, you'll never come away with an upset stomach.

HomePlace

50
Art Director: Bob Wisner
Creative Director: Bob MaHarry
                Sharon Kirk
Designer: Bob Wisner
Illustrator: Bob Wisner
Copywriter: Joel MaHarry
Agency: Hutchins/Young & Rubicam
Client: RTMC

51
Art Director: Bryan Buckley
                Tom DeCerchio
Copywriter: Tom DeCerchio
                Bryan Buckley
Agency: Buckley/DeCerchio
Client: Homeplace

52

Art Director: Larry Jarvis
Ted Gornick
Creative Director: Lloyd Wolfe
Illustrator: Jack Ohman
Copywriter: Rob Rosenthal
Agency: Cole & Weber, Portland
Client: The *Oregonian*

53

Art Director: Chris Graves
Creative Director: Roy Grace
Diane Rothschild
Copywriter: Craig Demeter
Agency: Roy Grace
Client: Paddington

When a politician steps out of line, our man rearranges his face.

How much damage can one man do with his hands? Plenty. If they belong to Jack Ohman, The Oregonian's resident political cartoonist.
Even the slickest political rope-a-dope can't stop his jabs. Then he hits 'em where it hurts: just above that fine line that divides low blow from high comedy. Be on the lookout for Jack Ohman. And see who gets a facial this week.

Jack Ohman Six Days A Week In Forum. The Oregonian

ingle ells, ingle ells.

The holidays aren't the same without J&B

J&B Scotch Whisky. Blended and bottled in Scotland by Justerini & Brooks, fine wine and spirit merchants since 1749. To send a gift of J&B anywhere in the U.S., call 1-800-528-6148. Void where prohibited.
J&B Blended Scotch Whisky 43% Alc. by Vol., imported by The Paddington Corporation, Ft. Lee, NJ © 1989.

With a resale value of 99.43%, this is a true economy car.

You don't buy a new Porsche, you invest in one. That's because with a resale value of nearly 100%, you'll not only keep your money, you'll get to enjoy it.

PORSCHE

Clean Up Around The House.
GARAGE Sale, turn., much misc. & collect-ibles, $1-$600. 5745 W. Mar
Republic/Gazette Classifieds

54

Art Director: Bob Brihn
Creative Director: Pat Burnham
Designer: Bob Brihn
Photographer: Kerry Peterson
Copywriter: George Gier
Agency: Fallon McElligott
Client: Porsche

55

Art Director: Judy Smith
Creative Director: Chris Poisson
Photographer: Tony Hernandez
Copywriter: Gregg Bergan

56
Art Director: Bryan Buckley
         Tom DeCerchio
Copywriter: Tom DeCerchio
         Bryan Buckley
Agency: Buckley/DeCerchio
Client: Homeplace

57
Art Director: Arty Tan
Creative Director: Pat Burnham
Photographer: Kerry Peterson
Copywriter: Jamie Barrett
Agency: Fallon McElligott
Client: Amoco

Come out of the closet.

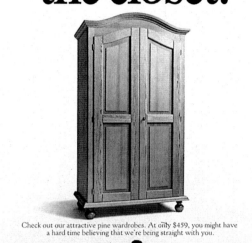

Check out our attractive pine wardrobes. At only $459, you might have
a hard time believing that we're being straight with you.

HomePlace

Isn't it time Celebrities got a little more attention?

Whether you drive a Chevy Celebrity or a Subaru Brat,
Amoco LDO is the right oil for your car. That's because LDO meets
manufacturers' performance requirements for every car made today.
So why not drive over to Amoco and change your oil now?
On second thought, if you're not using LDO, you'd better take a cab.

LDO Motor Oil. $15 a case, $1.25 a quart.

"EVERYONE NEEDS A HERO.
OR AT LEAST
A GRILLED CHEESE SANDWICH."
Sherri Krull, Owner.

SGT. PRESTONS
Saloon and Eatery.

221 Cedar Ave. So. at Seven Corners in Minneapolis. 338-6146.

Free rear end alignment.

If your rear end is starting to shimmy and shake, don't sit on it.
Join the YMCA. We also do complete body work and fix spare tires.
Free trial membership during September.

YMCA

58
Art Director: Bob Brihn
Creative Director: Pat Burnham
Copywriter: Jamie Barrett
Agency: Fallon McElligott
Client: Sgt. Preston's

59
Art Director: Craig Tanimoto
Creative Director: Jac Coverdale
Designer: Craig Tanimoto
Photographer: Joe Michl
Copywriter: Joe Alexander
         Jerry Fury
Agency: Clarity, Coverdale, Rueff
Client: Metro-YMCA

60

Art Director: Arty Tan
Creative Director: Pat Burnham
Copywriter: Jamie Barrett
Agency: Fallon McElligott
Client: Quick Lube

61

Art Director: Ray Fesenmaier
Jessica Welton
Creative Director: Tommy Thompson
Designer: Ray Fesenmaier
Jessica Welton
Photographer: Anthony Sylvestro
Copywriter: Tommy Thompson
Agency: Siddall, Matus & Coughter
Client: Ramada Techworld

You can always count on an Amoco station to give you good directions.

1. Cut out this coupon.
2. Bring it to Amoco Quick Lube.
3. Get $2 off on your oil change.

At Amoco Quick Lube, our service technicians will give you a complete oil and lube job in twenty minutes or less. No appointment necessary.

Expiration date: _____ Not good in conjunction with other Amoco coupon offers.

Avoid the usual Thanksgiving dishes.

RAMADA RENAISSANCE. TECHWORLD

999 9th St. NW, Washington, D.C.

This car comes equipped with central air.

Whether you have the top down or up, you'll be cool no matter how hot it is. Test drive the new 944 S2 Cabriolet today. It's a breath of fresh air.

PORSCHE

Expect light, moderate and heavy winds through the weekend.

In fact, powerful performances are forecast from every section of The Minnesota Orchestra for the new season. We have the turbulence of Rachmaninoff. The gentle airs of Mozart and Debussy. The brisk pacing of Beethoven. And much more. All waiting for you weekends from September through May, when you subscribe.

Enjoying the season is a breeze with the many exciting series we offer. Tickets are available for Wednesday, Friday or Saturday evenings at Orchestra Hall. Or for Thursday or Saturday evenings at the Ordway Music Theatre in St. Paul. And there are plenty of good seats left for the weekend, including our popular Friday night series.

Choices range from five and six concert Mini Series to the 24 concert Imperial Series. With a subscription you can save up to 36% over single ticket prices. And what is more important, you get the richness of experience that comes with repeated attendance, as well as the one-of-a-kind moments that happen only in a live performance.

Best seats go fast, so call 371-5656. And subscribe while conditions are still favorable.

The Minnesota Orchestra 1989/90 Subscription Series.
Edo de Waart, Music Director

62

Art Director: Bob Brihn
Creative Director: Pat Burnham
Designer: Bob Brihn
Photographer: Kerry Peterson
Copywriter: George Gier
Agency: Fallon McElligott
Client: Porsche

63

Art Director: Richard Page
Photographer: Paul Sinkler
Copywriter: Corinne Mitchell
Agency: McCool & Co.
Client: Minnesota Orchestra

64
Art Director: Lisa Rettig-Falcone
Creative Director: Sam Scali
Photographer: Robert Ammirati
Copywriter: Karen Sultz
Agency: Scali, McCabe, Sloves
Client: Perdue

65
Art Director: Craig Tanimoto
Jac Coverdale
Creative Director: Jac Coverdale
Designer: Craig Tanimoto
Copywriter: Joe Alexander
Jerry Fury
Agency: Clarity, Coverdale, Rueff
Client: Metro-YMCA

WHEN YOU BUY THE PERDUE OVEN STUFFER ROASTER,
ASK FOR DOUBLE BAGS.

**Burn dinner
tonight.**

With the food processors at the YMCA, you can get rid of unwanted
leftovers. So join today. And start burning food in the gym, instead of the kitchen.
Free trial membership during September.

YMCA

WHERE IS YOUR CAR PARKED?

ACURA

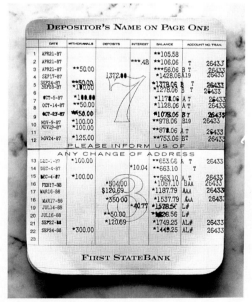

AT THIS RATE, YOU'LL NEVER GET A HOUSE.

Dreyfus
The right fund at the right time.

66
Art Director: Steve Beaumont
Nan Hutchison
Creative Director: Brent Bouchez
Photographer: Gary McGuire
Copywriter: Brent Bouchez
Agency: Ketchum, Los Angeles
Client: American Honda Motor Corp.

67
Art Director: Leslie Sweet
Creative Director: Tony DeGregorio
Copywriter: Pamela Sullivan
Agency: Levine, Huntley, Schmidt & Beaver
Client: Dreyfus

68
Art Director: John Vitro
Creative Director: Jim Winters
Illustrator: Dugald Stermer
Photographer: Ron Garrison
Copywriter: John Robertson
Agency: Franklin & Associates
Client: San Diego Zoo

69
Art Director: John Vitro
Creative Director: Jim Winters
Photographer: Jim Brandenberg
Copywriter: John Robertson
Agency: Franklin & Associates
Client: San Diego Wild Animal Park

Pygmy hippos. Isn't that like saying jumbo shrimp?

Just when you thought you'd seen everything,
The San Diego Zoo

When people at work ask what you did over the weekend, you can always tell them you helped save the planet.

The San Diego Wild Animal Park

With the wrong oil, the end of the road comes much too soon.

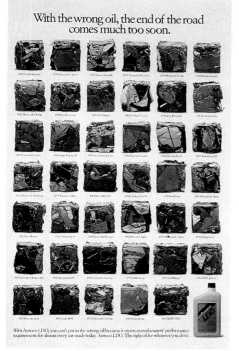

Most amusement parks offer a pleasant escape from life.
We offer a pleasant return to it.

The San Diego Wild Animal Park

70
Art Director: Arty Tan
Creative Director: Pat Burnham
Photographer: Kerry Peterson
Copywriter: Phil Hanft
Agency: Fallon McElligott
Client: Amoco

71
Art Director: John Vitro
Creative Director: Jim Winters
Photographer: Jim Brandenberg
Copywriter: John Robertson
Agency: Franklin & Associates
Client: San Diego Wild Animal Park

72
Art Director: Mark Hriciga
Creative Director: Jim Durfee
Copywriter: Jerry Della Femina
Agency: Della Femina, McNamee WCRS
Client: Isuzu

74
Art Director: Tracy Wong
Creative Director: Gary Goldsmith
Photographer: Steve Hellerstein
Copywriter: Dean Hacohen
Agency: Goldsmith/Jeffrey
Client: EL AL Israel Airlines

BUSINESS WEEK ADMIRES JOE ISUZU SO MUCH THAT IN THEIR JUNE 12ᵀᴴ ISSUE, THEY "LIED" ABOUT ISUZU'S SALES.

American Isuzu Motors, Inc.
Della Femina, McNamee WCRS, Inc.

75
Art Director: Aki Seki
Designer: Aki Seki
Illustrator: Mary Ann Lasher
Copywriter: Augie Cosentino
Agency: Ammirati & Puris Inc.
Client: W.L. Landau's Ethan Allen

76
Art Director: Leslie Sweet
Creative Director: Tony DeGregorio
Designer: Leslie Sweet
Photographer: Cailor/Resnick
Copywriter: Nat Russo
Agency: Levine, Huntley, Schmidt & Beaver
Client: Dreyfus

Every Furniture Maker Starts With The Same Material. So Why Do Some Pieces Still Look Better Than Others?

JUNK HAS ALWAYS HAD A PLACE IN OUR COMPANY, JUST NOT IN OUR PORTFOLIO.

77

Art Director: Ann Rhodes
Creative Director: Larry Asher
Photographer: Darrell Peterson
Copywriter: Larry Asher
Agency: Borders, Perrin & Norrander
Client: King County Medical Blue Shield

78

Art Director: James Offenhartz
Lee Garfinkel
Photographer: Jeff Zwart
Copywriter: Lee Garfinkel
Agency: Levine, Huntley, Schmidt & Beaver
Client: Subaru of America

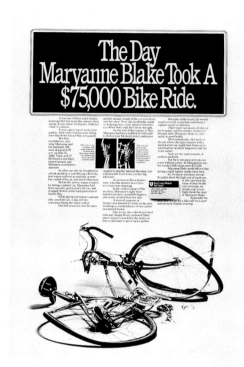

79

Art Director: Ernest Neira
Creative Director: Tony DeGregorio
Photographer: Cailor/Resnick
Copywriter: Jerry Confino
Ernest Neira
Agency: Levine, Huntley, Schmidt & Beaver
Client: Dreyfus

80

Art Director: Leslie Sweet
Ernest Neira
Creative Director: Tony DeGregorio
Designer: Leslie Sweet
Ernest Neira
Photographer: Mike Newler
Copywriter: Nat Russo
Agency: Levine, Huntley, Schmidt & Beaver
Client: Dreyfus

81
Art Director: Ronald Rosen
Creative Director: Roy Grace
Diane Rothschild
Copywriter: Craig Demeter
Client: Whittle Communications

82
Art Director: Leslie Sweet
Creative Director: Tony DeGregorio
Photographer: William Hines
Copywriter: Nat Russo
Agency: Levine, Huntley, Schmidt & Beaver
Client: Dreyfus

83
Art Director: Paul Jervis
Creative Director: Paul Jervis
Designer: Paul Jervis
Photographer: Dan Barba
Copywriter: Mitchell Wein
Agency: Backer, Spielvogel, Bates
Client: Prudential-Bache

84
Art Director: John Vitro
Creative Director: Jim Winters
Illustrator: Dugald Stermer
Photographer: Ron Garrison
Copywriter: John Robertson
Agency: Franklin & Associates
Client: San Diego Zoo

85
Art Director: John Vitro
Creative Director: Jim Winters
Illustrator: Dugald Stermer
Photographer: Ron Garrison
Copywriter: John Robertson
Agency: Franklin & Associates
Client: San Diego Zoo

86
Art Director: Amy Watt
Creative Director: Paul Silverman
Photographer: Peter Noel
Copywriter: Paul Silverman
Agency: Mullen
Client: Manchester League of Women Voters

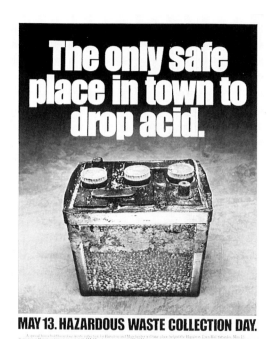

87
Art Director: Cristina Creager
Creative Director: Jim Kingsley
                    Brett Robbs
Photographer: Cary Wolinsky
Copywriter: Andy Dumaine
Agency: DDB Needham
Client: National Geographic Society

88
Art Director: Larry Jarvis
Creative Director: Lloyd Wolfe
Photographer: Greg Leno
Copywriter: Rob Rosenthal
Agency: Cole & Weber, Portland
Client: The *Oregonian*

89
Art Director: David Fox
Creative Director: Jac Coverdale
Designer: David Fox
Photographer: Mark LaFavor
Copywriter: Joe Alexander
Agency: Clarity, Coverdale, Rueff
Client: City of Minneapolis Recycling

90
Art Director: Bernie Hogya
Creative Director: Jay Schulberg
Photographer: Jim Arndt
Copywriter: Ronald Wachino
Agency: Bozell
Client: Illinois Power

It's time more people believed in reincarnation.

Recycle, Minneapolis.

THIS CHRISTMAS, UNWRAP A PERSON FOR A CHANGE.

ILLINOIS POWER

You can see the holiday spirit in all of us.

BANK ONE.

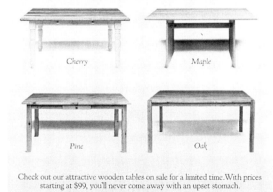

Make fiber part of every meal.

Cherry   Maple

Pine   Oak

Check out our attractive wooden tables on sale for a limited time. With prices starting at $99, you'll never come away with an upset stomach.

HomePlace

91
Art Director: Ray Redding
Creative Director: Glenn Dady
                        Mike Malone
Designer: Ray Redding
                  Bruce Perry
Copywriter: David Culp
Agency: The Richards Group
Client: Bank One

92
Art Director: Bryan Buckley
                        Tom DeCerchio
Copywriter: Tom DeCerchio
                        Bryan Buckley
Agency: Buckley/DeCerchio
Client: Homeplace

93
Art Director: Gary Rozanski
Creative Director: Mike Rogers
Photographer: Jim Hall
Copywriter: Mitchell Wein
Agency: DDB Needham Worldwide
Client: Volkswagen

94
Art Director: Bernie Hogya
Creative Director: Jay Schulberg
Copywriter: Ronald Wachino
Agency: Bozell
Client: Illinois Power

The sun you've always wanted.

THIS CHRISTMAS, GIVE A GIFT THAT SOMEONE WILL OPEN UP AND HIDE IN THE ATTIC.

ILLINOIS POWER

The Meadowlands, 1985. The Giants buried the Eagles.

The Meadowlands, 1979. The Giants buried the Falcons.

The Meadowlands, 1975. The Mafia buried Jimmy Hoffa.

Find out exactly where, why and by whom. In our November issue, on sale now.

PLAYBOY

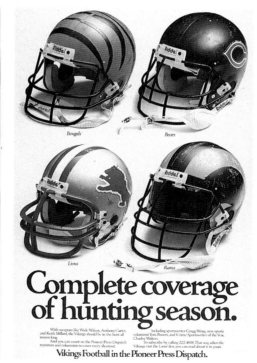

Bengals *Bears*

Lions *Rams*

Complete coverage
of hunting season.

Vikings Football in the Pioneer Press Dispatch.

95
Art Director: Tod Seisser
　　　　　　　Jay Taub
Creative Director: Tod Seisser
　　　　　　　Jay Taub
Designer: Tod Seisser
Photographer: Stock
Copywriter: Jay Taub
　　　　　　　Tod Seisser
Agency: Keye/Donna/Pearlstein

96
Art Director: Jac Coverdale
Creative Director: Jac Coverdale
Designer: Jac Coverdale
Photographer: Paul Sinkler
Copywriter: Joe Alexander
Agency: Clarity, Coverdale, Rueff
Client: St. Paul Pioneer Press Dispatch

97
Art Director: Kevin Grimsdale
Creative Director: Mike Hughes
Photographer: Wayne Gibson
Copywriter: Ed Cowardin
Agency: The Martin Agency
Client: Bath Plus

98
Art Director: Jac Coverdale
Creative Director: Jac Coverdale
Designer: Jac Coverdale
Photographer: Steve Umland
Copywriter: Joe Alexander
Agency: Clarity, Coverdale, Rueff
Client: St. Paul Pioneer Press Dispatch

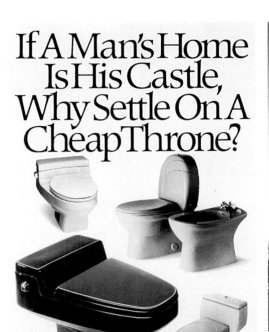

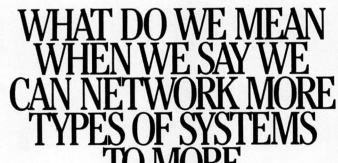

99
Art Director: Mike Moser
Creative Director: Ross Van Dusen
Photographer: Ernie Friedlander
Hunter Freeman
Bob Mizono
Copywriter: David O'Hare
Agency: Chiat/Day/Mojo
Client: 3COM Corp.

100
Art Director: Fred Hammerquist
Creative Director: Rod Kilpatrick
Copywriter: Bob Moore
Agency: Cole & Weber
Client: Safeco

101
Art Director: Ed Evangelista
Creative Director: Ron Berger
Copywriter: Charlie Tercek
Agency: M.V.B.C.S.
Client: Schering Plough

102
Art Director: Gary Yoshida
Creative Director: Larry Postaer
Copywriter: Bob Coburn
Client: American Honda Motor Corp.

103
Art Director: David Rauch
Creative Director: Ron Louie
Photographer: Larry Sillen
Copywriter: Julie Schireson Ralphs
Agency: DDB Needham Worldwide
Client: Crown Royal

104
Art Director: Don Harbor
Creative Director: Bruce Mansfield
Photographer: Kathy Kemp
Copywriter: Sue Fay
        Bruce Mansfield
Agency: Lawler Ballard
Client: Birmingham *Post-Herald*

105
Art Director: Peggy Fields
Creative Director: Sam Scali
Photographer: Hing-Norton
Copywriter: Barbara Hamilton
Agency: Scali, McCabe, Sloves
Client: Western Union

106
Art Director: Dennis D'Amico
Photographer: Kevin Logan
Copywriter: David Metcalf
Agency: Lowe, Tucker, Metcalf
Client: Volvo Penta

How to get President Bush to read your lips.

Send him a Western Union Telegram telling him exactly how you feel.

Just call 1-800-257-4900, ext. 7713 and tell our operator what you want to say or visit any of our 12,500 locations nationwide. Within minutes a telegram will be on its way from your house to the White House.

We even offer a special rate for telegrams to elected officials, including Senators and Representatives, that won't tax your fiscal budget.

And because Western Union sends telegrams 24 hours a day you can have words with the President anytime you want.

Which just goes to show you don't have to be someone special to have influence in the White House.

WESTERN UNION

FISH FOR SALMON, NOT PARTS.

We're using the same bait as last year. Throughout the salmon season we'll have experienced Volvo Diesel dealers, diesel service technicians and an on-site warehouse of genuine Volvo Penta parts and engines in Dillingham. Call George at our warehouse, 907-842-5375, from May 15 to July 31, 1989 for assistance. Good luck on the fishing. If you're powered by Volvo Penta you won't need it on parts.

THE VOLVO PENTA BRISTOL BAY ON-SITE PARTS SERVICE.

Two Hours Ago A Man Applied For A Loan To Buy This Corvette.

Obviously the answer was "yes". Obviously the bank was First Interstate. Because First Interstate is the only bank in town that will process your consumer loan application within two hours. There's no need to even put on your best suit. We'll take your application over the phone and call you back with a response.
The next time you need money, come to First Interstate. We'll put you right back out on the streets.

First Interstate *Bank*
We go the extra mile for you.™

107
Art Director: Clifford Goodenough
Creative Director: Roger Livingston
Photographer: Larry Gilpin
Copywriter: Norah Delaney
Agency: Livingston & Co.
Client: First Interstate Bank of New Mexico

108

Art Director: Chuck Anderson
Creative Director: Jay Schulberg
Copywriter: Judy Johnson
Agency: Bozell
Client: Better Business Bureau NAD

MISLEADING ADS CAN RUN BUT THEY CAN'T HIDE.

Member of Congress
Signature
Address

Name of Advertiser
When Advertising Appeared
Where Advertising Appeared (TV, Magazine, Etc.)

Why You Consider the Advertising Misleading

Mail to: The Director, NAD, 845 Third Avenue, New York, N.Y. 10022

The National Advertising Division of the Council of Better Business Bureaus continues to invite members of Congress to help us identify national advertisers who run misleading or false advertising.

Since 1971, the NAD has resolved more than 2,500 complaints. In over half of the cases, the advertising investigated has been modified or discontinued as a result.

If the NAD fails to achieve a resolution, the case is appealed to the National Advertising Review Board. In almost 20 years of operation, the NARB has never failed to resolve a case.

If you encounter an ad you believe is misleading, send us the information in writing.

Your complaint will receive a quick reply and will be handled at no cost to the taxpayer. You will be informed of the results.

Let's continue to work together to protect the public. And to protect advertisers who tell the truth.

THE NATIONAL ADVERTISING DIVISION OF THE COUNCIL OF BETTER BUSINESS BUREAUS

THE BUNK STOPS HERE.

Member of Congress
Signature
Address

Name of Advertiser
When Advertising Appeared
Where Advertising Appeared (TV, Magazine, Etc.)

Why You Consider the Advertising Misleading

Mail to: The Director, NAD, 845 Third Avenue, New York, N.Y. 10022

The National Advertising Division of the Council of Better Business Bureaus is dedicated to helping you protect the public from false and misleading advertising.

Since 1971, the NAD has resolved more than 2,500 complaints against national advertisers. In over half of the cases, the advertising investigated has been modified or discontinued as a result.

If the NAD fails to achieve a resolution, the case is appealed to the National Advertising Review Board. In almost 20 years of operation, the NARB has never failed to resolve a case.

The NAD invites members of Congress to join us in stopping unruthful advertising. If you have a complaint, send us the information in writing.

Your complaint will receive a quick reply and will be handled at no cost to the taxpayer. You will be informed of the results.

Let's work together to give the public what it deserves—truth, accuracy and no bunk in advertising.

THE NATIONAL ADVERTISING DIVISION OF THE COUNCIL OF BETTER BUSINESS BUREAUS

FREEDOM OF SPEECH DOESN'T MEAN FREEDOM TO LIE.

Member of Congress
Signature
Address

Name of Advertiser
When Advertising Appeared
Where Advertising Appeared (TV, Magazine, Etc.)

Why You Consider the Advertising Misleading

Mail to: The Director, NAD, 845 Third Avenue, New York, N.Y. 10022

Advertising that steps beyond the bounds of truth and accuracy hurts all of us. It misleads the consumer and creates unfair competition for the vast majority of advertisers who play by the rules.

Since 1971, the National Advertising Division of the Council of Better Business Bureaus has resolved more than 2,500 complaints against national advertisers. In over half of the cases, the advertising investigated has been modified or discontinued as a result.

If the NAD fails to achieve a resolution, the case is appealed to the National Advertising Review Board. In almost 20 years of operation, the NARB has never failed to resolve a case.

The NAD invites members of Congress to join us in protecting the public from misleading advertising. If you have a complaint, send us the information in writing. Your complaint will receive a quick reply and will be handled at no cost to the taxpayer. You will be informed of the results.

Let's stick up for our free speech and freedom of speech. Let's make sure they're only the truth.

THE NATIONAL ADVERTISING DIVISION OF THE COUNCIL OF BETTER BUSINESS BUREAUS

109

Art Director: John C. Jay
Creative Director: John C. Jay
Designer: John C. Jay
Photographer: Lance Stadler
Copywriter: Brian Leitch
Client: Bloomingdale's

110
Art Director: Ronald Rosen
Creative Director: Roy Grace
Diane Rothschild
Copywriter: Craig Demeter
Agency: Grace & Rothschild
Client: Whittle Communications

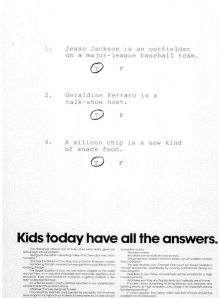

111
Art Director: James Howe
Steve Stith
Designer: James Howe
Dirk Mitchell
Copywriter: Dirk Mitchell
Agency: Thompson/Marince
Client: Barry's Auto

112

Art Director: Bob Brihn
Creative Director: Pat Burnham
Designer: Bob Brihn
Photographer: Kerry Peterson
Copywriter: George Gier
Agency: Fallon McElligott
Client: Porsche

Presenting a Porsche for the open minded.

The Porsche 944 S2 Cabriolet. Just try to top this. Come in for a test drive and open it up.

This car comes equipped with central air.

Whether you have the top down or up, you'll be cool no matter how hot it is. Test drive the new 944 S2 Cabriolet today. It's a breath of fresh air.

Ride it bare back.

Put the top down on the new 944 S2 Cabriolet, start it up and wind it out through all five gears on your favorite stretch of road. This is your moment in the sun.

Isn't it time Celebrities got a little more attention?

Whether you drive a Chevy Celebrity or a Subaru Brat, Amoco LDO is the right oil for your car. That's because LDO meets manufacturers' performance requirements for every car made today. So why not drive over to Amoco and change your oil now? On second thought, if you're not using LDO, you'd better take a cab.

LDO Motor Oil. $15 a case, $1.25 a quart.

Use the wrong oil and it won't be a Legend for long.

Whether you drive an Acura Legend or a Pontiac LeMans, Amoco LDO is the right oil for your car. That's because LDO meets manufacturers' performance requirements for every car made today. So why not drive over to Amoco and change your oil now? On second thought, if you're not using LDO, you'd better take a cab.

LDO Motor Oil. $15 a case, $1.25 a quart.

With the right oil, this Century could last another ten years.

Whether you drive a Buick Century or a Suzuki Samurai, Amoco LDO is the right oil for your car. That's because LDO meets manufacturers' performance requirements for every car made today. So why not drive over to Amoco and change your oil now? On second thought, if you're not using LDO, you'd better take a cab.

LDO Motor Oil. $15 a case, $1.25 a quart.

113

Art Director: Arty Tan
Creative Director: Pat Burnham
Photographer: Kerry Peterson
Copywriter: Jamie Barrett
Agency: Fallon McElligott
Client: Amoco

114
Art Director: Gary Goldsmith
Tracy Wong
Creative Director: Gary Goldsmith
Photographer: Steve Hellerstein
Copywriter: Dean Hacohen
Agency: Goldsmith/Jeffrey
Client: NYNEX Information Resources

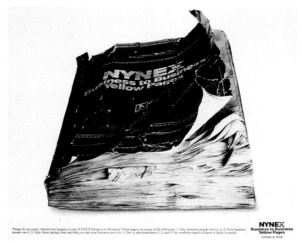

115
Art Director: Dan Scarlotto
Terri Barrett
Creative Director: Tommy Thompson
Photographer: Richard Hoflich
Anthony Sylvestro
Copywriter: John Schmidt
Agency: Siddall, Matus & Coughter
Client: FCEDA

116

Art Director: Tracy Wong
Gary Goldsmith
Creative Director: Gary Goldsmith
Photographer: Susan Goldman
Steve Hellerstein
Stock
Copywriter: Dean Hacohen
Agency: Goldsmith/Jeffrey
Client: EL AL Israel Airlines

117

Art Director: Richard Martino
Creative Director: Steven Cohen
Copywriter: Shen Henricks
Agency: Martino & Co.

118
Art Director: Jordin Mendelsohn
Creative Director: Jordin Mendelsohn
Copywriter: Perrin Lam
Agency: Mendelsohn/Zien
Client: Acura

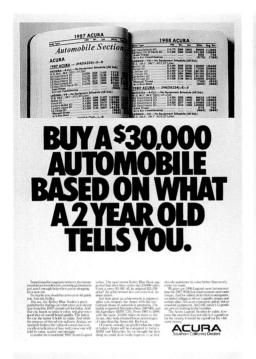

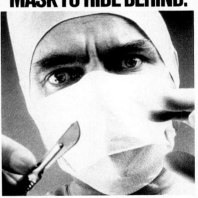

119
Art Director: Don Fibich
Creative Director: Tom Smith
                    Chuck Withrow
Designer: Don Fibich
Photographer: Ladd Trepal
Copywriter: Laura Owen
                    Chuck Withrow
Agency: Wyse Advertising
Client: WKYC-TV3

120

Art Director: Bob Brihn
Creative Director: Pat Burnham
Designer: Bob Brihn
Photographer: Rick Dublin
          Jim Arndt
Copywriter: George Gier
Agency: Fallon McElligott
Client: Porsche

It's about as fast as you can go without having to eat airline food.

The all wheel drive system in the 911 Carrera 4 distributes 247 horsepower to the road at once giving it incredible acceleration. Come in for a test drive. And, then fasten your seatbelts. **PORSCHE**

How to put a little distance between you and the rest of society.

If you're in the market for a luxury car, you don't have to sacrifice performance. The Porsche 928 has more luxury than you'd expect, plus the kick of 326 horses. Visit us for a closer look. **PORSCHE**

Take a 6.9 second test drive.

With 208 horsepower, the Porsche 944 S2 accelerates to 60 mph in a mere 6.9 seconds. Take one for a test drive. You'll fall in love with it very fast. **PORSCHE**

"WE WILL SELL NO WINE BEFORE 11:00 AM."

Steve Mularky, Owner.

SGT. PRESTONS
Saloon and Eatery.

Open at 11:00 AM daily. 221 Cedar Ave. So. at Seven Corners. 338-6146.

"AT OUR BAR YOU WON'T FEEL LIKE A PIECE OF MEAT. YOU'LL FEEL LIKE AN ENTIRE SANDWICH."

Keith Henneberg, Chef.

SGT. PRESTONS
Saloon and Eatery.

221 Cedar Ave. So. at Seven Corners in Minneapolis. 338-6146.

"A LOT OF BARS HAVE A HAPPY HOUR. OURS IS ECSTATIC."

Kristen Young, Waitress.

SGT. PRESTONS
Saloon and Eatery.

221 Cedar Ave. So. at Seven Corners in Minneapolis. 338-6146.

121

Art Director: Bob Brihn
Creative Director: Pat Burnham
Designer: Bob Brihn
Copywriter: Jamie Barrett
Agency: Fallon McElligott
Client: Sgt. Preston's

122

Art Director: Clifford Goodenough
Creative Director: Roger Livingston
Photographer: Larry Gilpin
Copywriter: Norah Delaney
Agency: Livingston & Co.
Client: First Interstate Bank of New Mexico

123

Art Director: Mike Sellers
Creative Director: David Terrenoire
Photographer: Tony Pearce
Copywriter: David Terrenoire
Agency: On Your Own Time Advertising
Client: Durham County Literacy Council

124

Art Director: Jeff Tresidder
Creative Director: Bruce Mansfield
Photographer: Rick Dublin
Copywriter: Scott Mackey
Agency: Lawler Ballard
Client: United Way

125
Art Director: Mike Sellers
Creative Director: David Terrenoire
Photographer: Tony Pearce
Copywriter: David Terrenoire
Agency: On Your Own Time Advertising
Client: Durham County Literacy Council

126
Art Director: John Follis
Creative Director: John Follis
Copywriter: John Follis
Agency: Follis & Verdi, Inc.
Client: Citizens for Prevention of Child Abuse

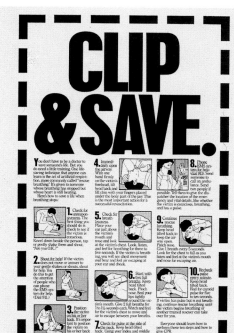

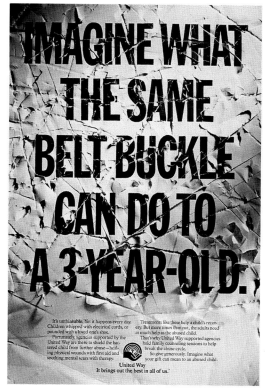

127
Art Director: Clark Lamm
Creative Director: Rick Gibson
Designer: Clark Lamm
Copywriter: Glen Wachowiak
Agency: Grant & Palombo
Client: Red Cross

128
Art Director: Chuck Finkle
Creative Director: Bob Neuman
Designer: Chuck Finkle
Photographer: Susan Goldman
Copywriter: Jerry Giordano
Client: United Way of Tri-State

129
Art Director: Ron Fisher
　　　　　　April Norman
Creative Director: Ron Fisher
　　　　　　　　Virgil Shutze
Photographer: Glenn Bewley
Copywriter: Ron Fisher
　　　　　　Ralph McGill
Agency: HutchesonShutze
Client: Atlanta's Table

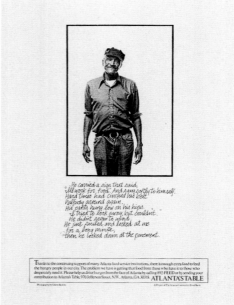

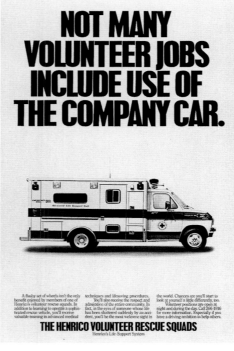

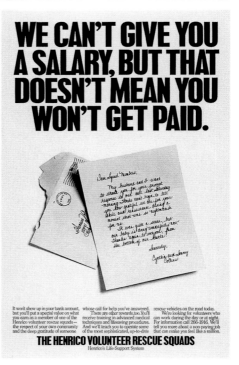

130
Art Director: Jim Brock
Creative Director: Ed Jones
Designer: Jim Brock
Photographer: Pat Edwards
Copywriter: Mac Calhoun
Client: Henrico Volunteer Rescue Squads

131
Art Director: Tom Marcantel
Creative Director: Bob Whitmore
Designer: Tom Marcantel
Photographer: Gordon Myhre
Copywriter: Mike Caughill
Agency: Tampa Art Directors Club
Client: United Way

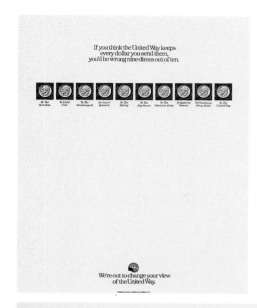

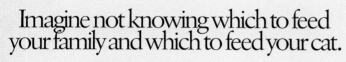

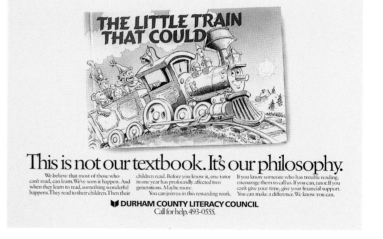

132
Art Director: Mike Sellers
Creative Director: David Terrenoire
Illustrator: Jackie Pittman
Photographer: Tony Pearce
Copywriter: David Terrenoire
Agency: On Your Own Time Advertising
Client: Durham County Literacy Council

THE PRICE OF FREEDOM IS A LOT HIGHER THAN TWO TRAIN TICKETS TO VIENNA.

134
Art Director: Bryan Nimeth
Creative Director: Mark H. Davis
Designer: Bryan Nimeth
Photographer: Charlie Co.
Copywriter: Mark H. Davis
Agency: Marcus Advertising
Client: Cleveland Jewish Federation

CONSIDERING WHAT YOU COULD SPEND ON LIFE'S LUXURIES THIS YEAR, THE NECESSITIES COME PRETTY DARN CHEAP.

LET FREEDOM BRING.

After Years Of Major Exhibits, We Now Present A Miner One.

The Gold Exhibit at The Museum Of Science.

Presenting An Exhibit That's A Lot More Than Just A Flash In The Pan.

The Gold Exhibit at The Museum Of Science.

We Can't Show You Everything In Our New Gold Exhibit, But Here Are A Few Nuggets.

The Gold Exhibit at The Museum Of Science.

135
Art Director: R. Smith
               K. Allensmith
Creative Director: Ron Lawner
Photographer: Stock
Copywriter: Fred Bertino
Agency: Della Femina, McNamee WCRS
Client: Museum of Science

136
Art Director: Craig Hadorn
Creative Director: Ken Hines
Designer: Craig Hadorn
Photographer: John Hood
Copywriter: Ken Hines
            Linda Whitmire
Agency: Lawler Ballard
Client: United Way

For what it costs to watch a horror story, you could keep a child from living one.

Imagine what it would be like if the terror didn't stop when you turned off the VCR. For hundreds of abused children, it doesn't.

But when you donate as little as $2.00 per week to the United Way, you can help organizations like Family And Children's Service provide intensive short-term counseling for abused children and their families. Or help Richmond Aftercare treat two recovering substance abusers.

Or your money could be used to support more than 80 other good causes.

So please give. Because with your help, all these stories could have happy endings.

UNITED WAY

This is the only coupon in today's paper that lets you redeem yourself.

1989 UNITED WAY CAMPAIGN
In support of human services provided for our community, I contribute $_____ to United Way.
☐ Payment Enclosed. ☐ Bill Me Quarterly. ☐ Bill Me Annually.
Name _____
Address _____
City _____ State _____
Zip _____ Telephone( ) _____
Signature _____ Date _____
Mail coupon to: United Way Services, 4001 Fitzhugh Avenue, P.O. Box 6648, Richmond, VA 23230. Or call (804) 353-2900 for more information.

Sure you can save money with those other coupons, but can you save lives? Your donation helps provide shelter for homeless families. Meals for the hungry and undernourished. And medical care for the sick who couldn't otherwise afford it.

It helps provide counseling and support services for rape victims. A place for battered women and children to stay. And support for many other worthwhile causes.

And besides that, it makes you feel good. So if you haven't already, please give.

UNITED WAY

Once a year, the idea of placing a dollar value on human life makes a lot of sense.

When you give to the United Way, your money helps support organizations right here in the Richmond and Tri-Cities area.

Organizations that provide a warm, dry place for homeless families to stay. That conduct daily telephone checks on seniors living alone. Organizations that provide both health and rehabilitative services for patients in their homes. And volunteer rescue squad and ambulance services for those who need help in a hurry.

In fact, your money could help support more than 80 potentially lifesaving services.

So please give. Your contribution really could mean the difference between life and death.

UNITED WAY

Last Year, This Was Larry Tormey's Thanksgiving Dinner.

This Year, He May Not Be So Lucky.

Thanksgiving is almost here. But for thousands of people in Maryland, it will be just another day without food. Unless you help.

Look for your Bags of Plenty bag inside today's Baltimore Sun. Fill it with non-perishable foods and bring it to your neighborhood Giant store, Provident Bank or a Baltimore City fire station by November 27.

If you can, give cash. We will accept cash contributions until December 5. But that leaves us very little time. To make a very big difference.

Bags of Plenty

This Don't Have To Cook A Thing To Make A Memorable Thanksgiving For A Hungry Family.

I want to help with cash.
Name _____ Address _____
City _____ State _____ Zip _____
Here's my check for ☐ $100 ☐ $50 ☐ $35 ☐ Other _____
Make your check payable to Maryland Food Committee and mail to: Maryland Food Committee, Trawlridge, Calvert Savings & Loan, P.O. Box 37434, Baltimore, MD 21208.

At Thanksgiving, the only thing some people think about is food, food, food.

Bags of Plenty

"Gee, Mom, that turkey smells great. I can have a drumstick, right? And lots of mashed potatoes and stuffing? I'll even eat those yukky peas if I can have tons of whipped cream on my pumpkin pie. And can we please eat soon? 'Cause I'm really hungry."

"Gee, Mom, ~~that turkey smells great. I can have a drumstick, right? And lots of mashed potatoes and stuffing? I'll even eat those yukky peas if I can have tons of whipped cream on my pumpkin pie. And can we please eat soon?~~ 'Cause I'm really hungry."

I want to help with cash.

Bags of Plenty

137
Art Director: Sharon Brady
Creative Director: James Dale
Photographer: Steve Longley
Copywriter: Sara Slater
            Sharon Brady
Agency: W.B. Doner
Client: The *Baltimore Sun*

138
Art Director: Debby Lucke
Creative Director: Ron Lawner
Photographer: John Holt
Copywriter: David Abend
Agency: Della Femina, McNamee WCRS
Client: Stanley

139
Art Director: Debby Lucke
Creative Director: Ron Lawner
Photographer: John Holt
Copywriter: Fred Bertino
Agency: Della Femina, McNamee WCRS
Client: Stanley

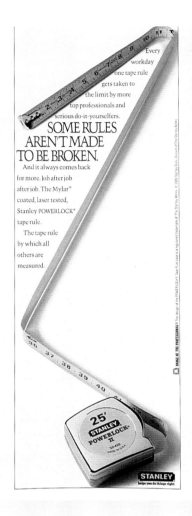

140
Art Director: Bob Brihn
Creative Director: Pat Burnham
Designer: Bob Brihn
Photographer: Jeff Zwart
Copywriter: Bruce Bildsten
Agency: Fallon McElligott
Client: Porsche

141
Art Director: Tom Lichtenheld
Creative Director: Pat Burnham
Designer: Tom Lichtenheld
Copywriter: George Gier
Agency: Fallon McElligott
Client: Time-Life Books

190
Art Director: Ed Evangelista
Creative Director: Ron Berger
Designer: Ed Evangelista
Copywriter: Ron Berger
Agency: M.V.B.C.S.
Client: Windstar Sail Cruise

191
Art Director: Bob Brihn
Creative Director: Pat Burnham
Designer: Bob Brihn
Photographer: Mark LaFavor
Copywriter: Jamie Barrett
Agency: Fallon McElligott
Client: Porsche

THE DIFFERENCE BETWEEN FEELING LIKE A TOURIST WHO HAS INVADED AN ISLAND AND A GUEST WHO HAS BEEN INVITED.

WINDSTAR SAIL CRUISES' WERE CREATED WITH A DRAMATICALLY DIFFERENT IDEA IN MIND.

AN IDEA THAT WORKS LIKE THIS: YOU WAKE UP ONE MORNING AND YOU ARE ANCHORED IN THE LAGOON SURROUNDING BORA BORA, ON BOARD WIND SONG, THE MOST MODERN, STATE-OF-THE-ART SAILING SHIP EVER BUILT.

AFTER BREAKFAST, YOU WALK ALONG A SEEMINGLY ENDLESS WHITE-SAND BEACH. YOU SEE THE SHIP'S CREW GRILLING LOBSTERS, FRESHLY CAUGHT THAT MORNING. FOR LUNCH ON THE BEACH, YOU SIT DOWN, ENJOY A WONDERFUL MEAL, AND REALIZE YOU ARE IN A SETTING YOU WERE CONVINCED EXISTED ONLY IN SOME TRAVEL WRITER'S IMAGINATION.

IN THE VIRGIN ISLANDS, THE IDEA WORKS VIRTUALLY THE SAME, AS IT DOES EVERYWHERE WE SAIL TO: THE LEEWARD ISLANDS, THE DALMATIAN COAST, AS WELL AS THE FRENCH AND ITALIAN RIVIERAS.

WHICH IS, QUITE SIMPLY, THE WHOLE IDEA BEHIND A WINDSTAR CRUISE, TO ALLOW JUST 74 COUPLES TO EXPERIENCE SOME OF THE MOST UNUSUAL PLACES IN THE WORLD ON BOARD THREE 440-FOOT SHIPS THAT OFFER THIS RARE COMBINATION: THE TRANQUILITY AND ROMANCE OF A SAILING SHIP WITH THE FREEDOM AND REFINED LUXURY OF A PRIVATE YACHT.

THE RESULT? 7-DAY CRUISES THAT AS ONE WRITER SAID, "COME CLOSER TO FULFILLING THE FANTASY WE HAVE OF A VACATION AT SEA THAN ANYTHING ELSE."

WINDSTAR SAIL CRUISES

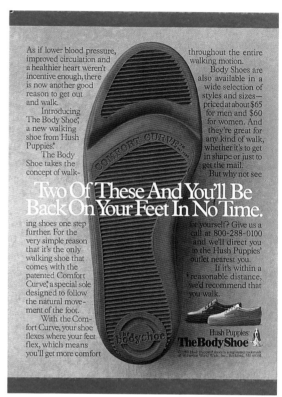

As if lower blood pressure, improved circulation and a healthier heart weren't incentive enough, there is now another good reason to get out and walk.

Introducing The Body Shoe, a new walking shoe from Hush Puppies.

The Body Shoe takes the concept of walk-

Two Of These And You'll Be Back On Your Feet In No Time.

ing shoes one step further. For the very simple reason that it's the only walking shoe that comes with the patented Comfort Curve, a special sole designed to follow the natural movement of the foot.

With the Comfort Curve, your shoe flexes where your feet flex, which means you'll get more comfort

throughout the entire walking motion.

Body Shoes are also available in a wide selection of styles and sizes— priced at about $65 for men and $60 for women. And they're great for any kind of walk, whether it's to get in shape or just to get the mail.

But why not see for yourself? Give us a call at 800-288-0100 and we'll direct you to the Hush Puppies' outlet nearest you.

If it's within a reasonable distance, we'd recommend that you walk.

Hush Puppies.
The Body Shoe

Public phone. Private moment. Lee jeans.

Lee
Easy Rider

192
Art Director: Mark Johnson
Creative Director: Pat Burnham
Photographer: Kurt Markus
Copywriter: Bill Miller
Agency: Fallon McElligott
Client: Lee Jeans

NIKE
AIR

THE JACKSON 5.

See Bo cross-train. See Bo cross-train in a shoe with Nike-Air cushioning and plenty of support. See Bo cross-train in the Air Trainer SC. See it you can do everything Bo can do in it.

193
Art Director: Rick McQuiston
Creative Director: Dan Wieden
  David Kennedy
Copywriter: Jim Riswold
Agency: Wieden & Kennedy
Client: Nike

194
Art Director: John Staffen
Creative Director: Mike Rogers
Photographer: Aaron Jones
Copywriter: Mike Rogers
Agency: DDB Needham
Client: Cigna

195
Art Director: Bill Spewak
Designer: Bill Spewak
Copywriter: Bill Spewak
  John Barker
Agency: Grey Entertainment & Media
Client: ABC Entertainment

The pencil costs 14¢.
The eraser, millions.

Mistakes make products late, more expensive and inferior. Leaving customers dissatisfied, reputations damaged. Since there are no quick fixes, only costly ones, what's a business to do?

At the CIGNA Property and Casualty Companies, we have a very basic goal: Get it right the first time.

Granted, nobody's perfect. But it's surprising how many mistakes can be prevented.

By working to find the best solution, rather than the most expedient one.

Whether we're providing protection for small and medium-size businesses, or meeting the risk management needs of the largest corporations, the benefits are the same: Answers that are fast and accurate. Service that is responsive. Value that is real. And customers who are satisfied. Anything less would be a big mistake.

For more about our business insurance for commercial banks, sponsored by the American Bankers Association, call MarketDyne International, a CIGNA company, at 1-800-523-2710. After all, anyone can pay for lots of pencils. But who can afford all the erasers?

We get paid for results. CIGNA

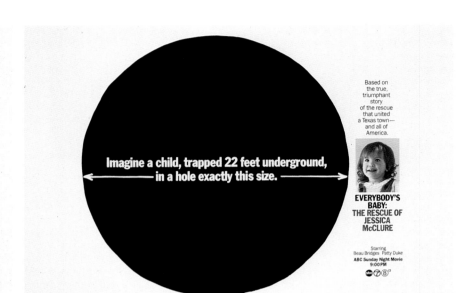

Based on the true, triumphant story of the rescue that united a Texas town— and all of America.

Imagine a child, trapped 22 feet underground, in a hole exactly this size.

EVERYBODY'S BABY: THE RESCUE OF JESSICA McCLURE

Starring
Beau Bridges Patty Duke
ABC Sunday Night Movie
9:00 PM

The magazine to read from the time you leave the cradle.

When you're a new arrival into the world of sailing, your first excursions across the bay are as important as your first unaided steps across your parents' kitchen floor. For it's a time to develop new skills, discover your potentials and widen your horizons.

Which is why we publish Sail: to instruct, inform and inspire novices, as much as we write it to stimulate performance sailors and engage bluewater cruisers.

It's an editorial commitment exemplified in columns like Learning to Sail, Offshore Racing and Cruisewise Cruising. As well as special sections on everything from buying a new boat to commissioning a used one.

No other sailing magazine offers so much to help launch you on your way. Which is probably why no other sailing magazine has so much in the way of dedication from its readership. So whether you're leaving the cradle for the first time or the fifty-first, there's only one word you really need to know—Sail.

SAIL

1960.

1968.

1975.

1980.

1986.

1990.

You always come back to the basics. JIM BEAM

196
Art Director: Bob Barrie
Creative Director: Pat Burnham
Designer: Bob Barrie
Photographer: Rick Dublin
Copywriter: Jarl Olsen
Agency: Fallon McElligott
Client: Jim Beam

197
Art Director: Steve Haesche
Photographer: Christopher Cunningham
Copywriter: Peter Pappas
Agency: Mullen
Client: Sail

198
Art Director: Mike Mazza
Creative Director: Lee Clow
Copywriter: Brian Belefant
Agency: Chiat/Day/Mojo
Client: Nissan

199
Art Director: Bob Barrie
Creative Director: Pat Burnham
Designer: Bob Barrie
Photographer: Robin Moyer
Copywriter: Jamie Barrett
Agency: Fallon McElligott
Client: Federal Express

200
Art Director: Donna Weinheim
Creative Director: Donna Weinheim
Photographer: David Langley
Copywriter: Cliff Freeman
                Jane King
Agency: Cliff Freeman & Partners
Client: Conde Nast

201
Art Director: John Vitro
Creative Director: Jim Winters
Photographer: Jim Brandenberg
Copywriter: John Robertson
Agency: Franklin & Associates
Client: San Diego Wild Animal Park

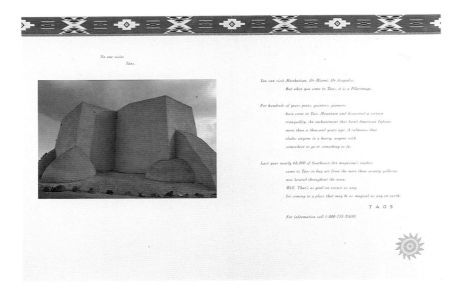

202
Art Director: Steven Sessions
Creative Director: Steven Sessions
Designer: Steven Sessions
Illustrator: Steven Sessions
Copywriter: John Hartmann
Agency: Steven Sessions, Inc.
Client: Southwest Art Magazine

203
Art Director: John Staffen
Creative Director: Mike Rogers
Photographer: Lamb & Hall
Copywriter: Giff Crosby
Agency: DDB Needham
Client: Michelin

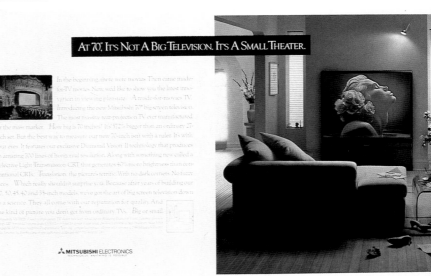

204
Art Director: James Offenhartz
Creative Director: Lee Garfinkel
Photographer: Ken Nahoum
Copywriter: Marian Allen Godwin
Agency: Levine, Huntley, Schmidt & Beaver
Client: Technics

205
Art Director: Rick Boyko
Creative Director: Bob Kuperman
Copywriter: Steve Rabosky
Agency: Chiat/Day/Mojo
Client: Mitsubishi

Big enough to hold a meeting. Fast enough to keep it short.

206
Art Director: Jerry Gentile
Mike Mazza
Creative Director: Bob Kuperman
Copywriter: Jerry Fields
Agency: Chiat/Day/Mojo
Client: Nissan

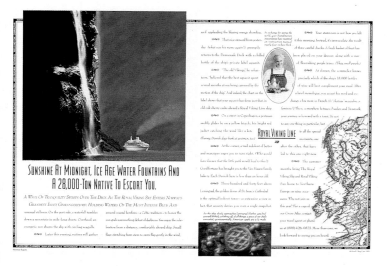

207
Art Director: Jeremy Postaer
Creative Director: Jeffrey Goodby
Rich Silverstein
Photographer: Harvey Lloyd
Hank Benson
Copywriter: Amy Krouse
Agency: Goodby, Berlin & Silverstein
Client: Royal Viking Line

208
Art Director: Larry Martin
Creative Director: Guy Bommarito
Copywriter: Guy Bommarito
Agency: GSD&M Advertising
Client: Texas Department of Commerce

209
Art Director: Steve Stone
Creative Director: Jeffrey Goodby
Rich Silverstein
Photographer: Loren McIntyre
Jay Maisel
Dan Escobar
Copywriter: Rob Bagot
Agency: Goodby, Berlin & Silverstein
Client: Royal Viking Line

210
Art Director: Leslie Sweet
Creative Director: Tony DeGregorio
Designer: Leslie Sweet
Photographer: Cailor/Resnick
Copywriter: Pamela Sullivan
Agency: Levine, Huntley, Schmidt & Beaver
Client: Dreyfus

211
Art Director: Rick Boyko
Creative Director: Steve Rabosky
Copywriter: Rob Feakins
Agency: Chiat/Day/Mojo
Client: Mitsubishi

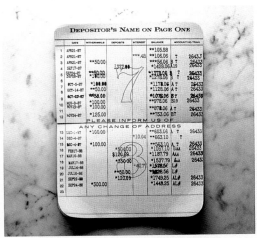

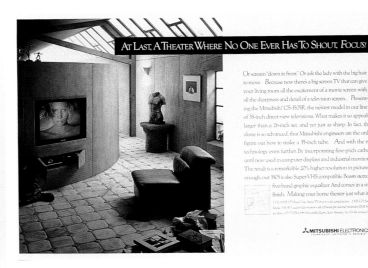

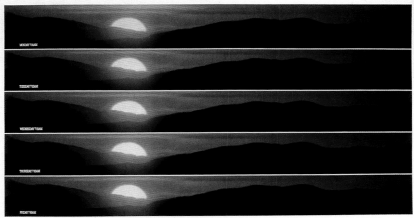

212
Art Director: Leslie Sweet
Creative Director: Tony DeGregorio
Copywriter: Pamela Sullivan
Agency: Levine, Huntley, Schmidt & Beaver
Client: Dreyfus

213
Art Director: Leslie Sweet
                Sal DeVito
Creative Director: Tony DeGregorio
Designer: Leslie Sweet
Photographer: Cailor/Resnick
Copywriter: Nat Russo
                Sal DeVito
Agency: Levine, Huntley, Schmidt & Beaver
Client: Dreyfus

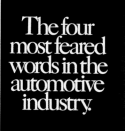

218
Art Director: Roy Grace
Creative Director: Roy Grace
Diane Rothschild
Photographer: Elizabeth Heyert
Copywriter: Diane Rothschild
Client: Century Furniture

219
Art Director: Jud Smith
Creative Director: Jack Supple
Illustrator: Bill Reynolds
Photographer: Rod Pierce
Copywriter: Kerry Casey
Agency: Carmichael Lynch
Client: Federal Cartridge

Why we offer the same sofa in 67 sizes.

Century Furniture

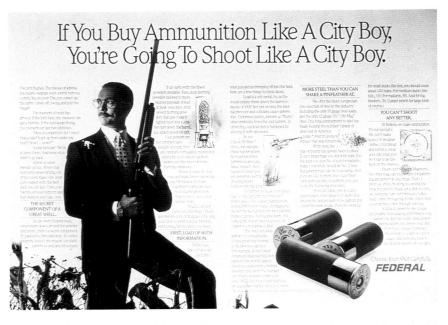

If You Buy Ammunition Like A City Boy, You're Going To Shoot Like A City Boy.

FEDERAL

No other guitar effects processor lets you PLAY up to twelve effects simultaneously.

Send in the clones.

The New Accord

220
Art Director: Kevin McCarthy
Creative Director: Jean Robaire
John Stein
Designer: Kevin McCarthy
Photographer: Paul Gersten
Copywriter: Brian Belefant
Agency: Stein, Robaire, Helm
Client: RolandCorp US

221
Art Director: Gary Yoshida
Creative Director: Larry Postaer
Copywriter: Bob Coburn
Client: American Honda Motor Corp.

222
Art Director: Frank Todaro
Creative Director: Earl Cavanah
Photographer: Gil Smith
Copywriter: Rob Slosberg
Agency: Scali, McCabe, Sloves
Client: Volvo

223
Art Director: Houman Pirdavari
Creative Director: Pat Burnham
Photographer: Rick Dublin
Copywriter: Jarl Olsen
Agency: Fallon McElligott
Client: Penn

224
Art Director: Jay Shields
Creative Director: Bob Warren
Photographer: Parish Kohanim
Copywriter: Pat Wages
Client: Bridgestone Sports

225
Art Director: Sheri Olmon
Creative Director: Marty Cooke
Photographer: David Bailey
Copywriter: Alan Platt
Agency: Chiat/Day/Mojo Advertising Inc.
Client: American Express Gold Card

226
Art Director: John Doyle
Designer: John Doyle
Photographer: Clint Clemens
Copywriter: Paul Silverman
Agency: Mullen
Client: Timberland Co.

227
Art Director: Leslie Sweet
Creative Director: Tony DeGregorio
Photographer: William Hines
Copywriter: Nat Russo
Agency: Levine, Huntley, Schmidt & Beaver
Client: Dreyfus

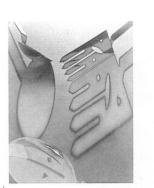

228
Art Director: Gary Johns
Creative Director: Gary Johns
Designer: Gary Johns
Photographer: Mark Coppos
Copywriter: Gary Johns
Agency: Gary D. Johns, Inc.
Client: Bissell & Wilhite Co.

229
Art Director: Pam Cunningham
Creative Director: Bob Kuperman
Copywriter: Steve Bassett
Agency: Chiat/Day/Mojo
Client: Nissan

230
Art Director: Laura Della Sala
Creative Director: Bob Kuperman
Copywriter: Rob Feakins
Agency: Chiat/Day/Mojo
Client: Mitsubishi

231
Art Director: Rod Smith
Creative Director: Ron Lawner
Photographer: Myron
Copywriter: Alan Marcus
Agency: Della Femina, McNamee WCRS
Client: Foot-Joy

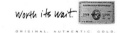

232
Art Director: Sheri Olmon
Creative Director: Marty Cooke
Photographer: David Bailey
Copywriter: Alan Platt
Agency: Chiat/Day/Mojo Advertising Inc
Client: American Express Gold Card

233
Art Director: Jeremy Postaer
Creative Director: Jeffrey Goodby
　　　　　　　Rich Silverstein
Photographer: Duncan Sim
　　　　　　　Hank Benson
Copywriter: Rob Bagot
Agency: Goodby, Berlin & Silverstein
Client: Royal Viking Line

234

Art Director: Jeanne MacDonald
Creative Director: Bob Kuperman
Photographer: Dan Arsenault
Copywriter: Matt Bogen
Agency: Chiat/Day/Mojo Advertising Inc.
Client: Mitsubishi

235

Art Director: Mark Johnson
Creative Director: Pat Burnham
Photographer: Kurt Markus
Copywriter: Bill Miller
Agency: Fallon McElligott
Client: Lee Jeans

Too much road. Too little time. Six miles from home. Lee jeans.

236

Art Director: Patty Thompson
Creative Director: Ron Fisher
                    Virgil Shutze
Photographer: Charles Jameson
Copywriter: Ralph McGill
Agency: HutchesonShutze
Client: American Forest Council

"BY 1945, AMERICA'S FORESTS WILL BE HISTORY."

237

Art Director: Mark Johnson
Creative Director: Pat Burnham
Photographer: Kurt Markus
Copywriter: Bill Miller
Agency: Fallon McElligott
Client: Lee Jeans

22 years. 3 months. 6 days. Lee jeans.

238
Art Director: Ed Evangelista
Creative Director: Ron Berger
Copywriter: Charlie Tercek
Agency: M.V.B.C.S.
Client: Life Magazine

239
Art Director: Fred Hammerquist
Creative Director: Rod Kilpatrick
Photographer: Bruce Wilson
Copywriter: Bob Moore
Agency: Cole & Weber
Client: Raleigh Bicycles

240
Art Director: Bob Barrie
Creative Director: Pat Burnham
Designer: Bob Barrie
Photographer: Kerry Peterson
Copywriter: Jarl Olsen
Agency: Fallon McElligott
Client: Jim Beam

241
Art Director: Bob Barrie
Creative Director: Pat Burnham
Designer: Bob Barrie
Photographer: Kerry Peterson
Copywriter: Jarl Olsen
Agency: Fallon McElligott
Client: Jim Beam

242
Art Director: Parry Merkley
Creative Director: Gordon Bowen
Photographer: Annie Leibovitz
Copywriter: Gordon Bowen
Agency: Ogilvy & Mather
Client: American Express

243
Art Director: John Doyle
Creative Director: Paul Silverman
Photographer: Clint Clemens
Copywriter: Paul Silverman
Agency: Mullen
Client: Timberland Co.

For twenty years they've been insulated from snow, oblivious to rain, impervious to competition.

There are two things you shouldn't be up the creek without. One of them is a paddle.

SOMEBODY UP THERE LIKES US.

AN AIRLINE SEAT SHOULDN'T FEEL LIKE THIS.

244
Art Director: John Doyle
Creative Director: Paul Silverman
Photographer: Clint Clemens
Copywriter: Paul Silverman
Agency: Mullen
Client: Timberland Co.

245
Art Director: Tim Delaney
Creative Director: Jim Copacino
Copywriter: Jim Copacino
Agency: Livingston & Co.
Client: Alaska Airlines

246
Art Director: Tim Delaney
Creative Director: Jim Copacino
Copywriter: Jim Copacino
Agency: Livingston & Co.
Client: Alaska Airlines

247

Art Director: Scott Ballew
        Steve Popp
Creative Director: Stan Richards
Photographer: Ka Yeung
        Brian McWeeney
Copywriter: Chris Sekin
        Kevin Swisher
Agency: The Richards Group
Client: Pier 1 Imports

248

Art Director: Debby Lucke
Creative Director: Ron Lawner
Photographer: John Holt
Copywriter: Fred Bertino
Agency: Della Femina, McNamee WCRS
Client: Stanley

249
Art Director: Dan Scarlotto
Creative Director: Tommy Thompson
Designer: Dan Scarlotto
Illustrator: Ben Marshell
           Greg Ragland
           Allen Garns
Copywriter: John Schmidt
Agency: Siddall, Matus & Coughter
Client: Kettler & Scott

250
Art Director: Roy Grace
           Chris Graves
Creative Director: Roy Grace
           Diane Rothschild
Photographer: Bruno
Copywriter: Diane Rothschild
           Craig Demeter
Client: Paddington

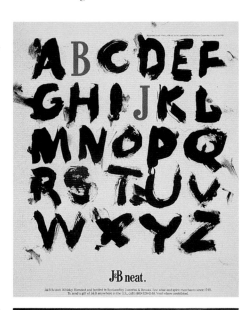

251

Art Director: John Butler
Mike Shine
Creative Director: Bill Hamilton
Designer: Graham Clifford
Photographer: Joe Baraban
Copywriter: Mike Shine
John Butler
Agency: Chiat/Day/Mojo Advertising Inc.
Client: NYNEX Information Resources

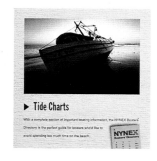

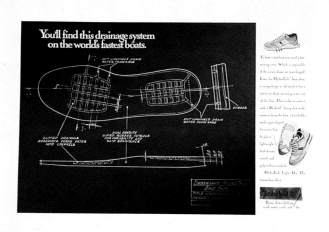

252

Art Director: Brian Fandetti
Creative Director: Paul Silverman
Photographer: Harry DeZitter
Jack Richmond
Copywriter: Paul Silverman
Agency: Mullen
Client: Timberland Co.

253
Art Director: Brian Stymest
Creative Director: Sean Fitzpatrick
Photographer: Diane Padys
　　　　　　　Charles Purvis
Copywriter: Charles Mullen
Agency: McCann-Erickson
Client: Wamsutta/Pacific Home Products

254
Art Director: Roy Grace
Creative Director: Roy Grace
　　　　　　　　Diane Rothschild
Copywriter: Diane Rothschild
Client: Range Rover of North America

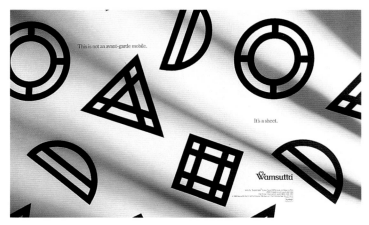

255
Art Director: John Doyle
Designer: John Doyle
Photographer: Clint Clemens
Copywriter: Paul Silverman
Agency: Mullen
Client: Timberland Co.

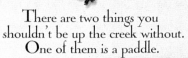

There are two things you shouldn't be up the creek without. One of them is a paddle.

The other is a pair of boots from the Timberland Sporting Collection. Because even though we can't keep water out of your boat, we guarantee it won't get through your boots.

Consider the construction of our Super Guide Boot. Comfortable. Dry. Lightweight. Protected by an exclusive Timberland Gore-Tex Leather™ laminate that combines a glove-leather lining with a waterproof, breathable Gore-Tex® fabric bootie. The result is a level of comfort and dryness you won't find in any other field boot.

Yet another Super Guide exclusive is a sole of triple density polyurethane permanently bonded to the upper. Compared to boots with traditional rubber soles this lessens weight, adds insulation, expands flexibility and increases slip resistance. Giving you a whole new level of performance.

In fact, every single boot in the Timberland Sporting Collection is built to be warm, dry and comfortable, and the reason is our two-step waterproofing process. Step one is direct bonding of silicone-impregnated waterproof leathers to the sole. Step two is Gore-Tex fabric bootie construction.

Timberland. Not just waterproof. Water-proven.

Boots, shoes, clothing, wind, water, earth and sky.

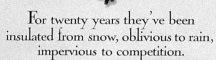

For twenty years they've been insulated from snow, oblivious to rain, impervious to competition.

Before the Timberland Company existed, only one kind of boot was truly waterproof. The kind you don't like to wear. Because it's made of something other than leather, something plastic or rubber that doesn't breathe.

Relief came two decades ago, when Timberland craftsmen hand-built a full-grain leather boot that was guaranteed waterproof. And insulated.

It was a concept the world was waiting for. No sooner did our boot hit the stores than it sold out. And today it still sells out, even though imitations abound both here and abroad.

The fact is, copying the look of our classic tan buck boot is far easier than copying the workmanship. The meticulous silicone impregnation of the leather, the four-row nylon stitching, the direct bonding of upper to midsole for a guaranteed waterproof seal, and the unbeatable warmth of Thinsulate® insulation.

You live on an earth that's two-thirds water. Can you afford a lesser boot than ours?

Boots, shoes, clothing, wind, water, earth and sky.

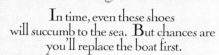

In time, even these shoes will succumb to the sea. But chances are you'll replace the boat first.

The headline on this page isn't something you should accept without substantiation. So let us hasten to provide it.

Timberland boat shoes are stronger because our construction is superior. You will never see one of our soles flapping loose in the breeze, unstitched from its moccasin upper. We eliminate such stitching altogether in favor of permanent bonding, so shoe and sole stay married until the day they die.

And unlike boat shoes of a lesser quality, ours have premium natural leathers that won't crack, impregnable nylon stitching that won't rot, and solid brass eyelets that won't chip.

This year, we're pleased to introduce the high-performance Ultra Boat Shoe, companion to our Super and Classic Boat Shoe. The Ultra combines the grip and stability of a triple density outsole with the comfort and cushioning of a double density midsole. For maximum dryness, the stain-resistant, waterproof leathers have a Hydrofil® lining to wick away moisture.

Water, water, it's everywhere. So is Timberland.

Boots, shoes, clothing, wind, water, earth and sky.

ARE AMERICA'S FORESTS OUT OF THE WOODS?

AMERICAN FOREST COUNCIL

"BY 1945, AMERICA'S FORESTS WILL BE HISTORY."

AMERICAN FOREST COUNCIL

ANOTHER DAY, ANOTHER 6 MILLION TREES.

AMERICAN FOREST COUNCIL

256
Art Director: Patty Thompson
Creative Director: Ron Fisher
　　　　　　　　　Virgil Shutze
Photographer: Charles Jameson
Copywriter: Ralph McGill
Agency: HutchesonShutze
Client: American Forest Council

257
Art Director: Rick Boyko
Creative Director: Bob Kuperman
　　　　　　　　Steve Rabosky
Copywriter: Rob Feakins
　　　　　　　Steve Rabosky
Agency: Chiat/Day/Mojo
Client: Mitsubishi

258
Art Director: Frank Haggerty
Creative Director: Kerry Casey
Photographer: Jim Marvy
Copywriter: Kerry Casey
Agency: Carmichael Lynch
Client: ZEBCO

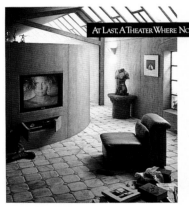

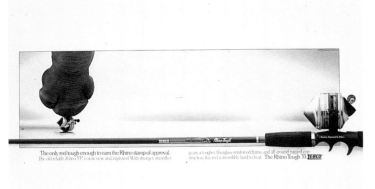

259
Art Director: Fred Hammerquist
Creative Director: Rod Kilpatrick
Photographer: Rod Photo
Copywriter: Hugh Saffel
Agency: Cole & Weber
Client: K2 Corp.

260
Art Director: Ed Evangelista
Creative Director: Ron Berger
Designer: Ed Evangelista
Copywriter: Ron Berger
Agency: M.V.B.C.S.
Client: Windstar Sail Cruise

Eat your vegetables.

Feed them to your dog.

Be home by 10:30.

A.M.

Don't question authority.

Ignore it.

I see a man and a mule in your future.

261
Art Director: Sharon Occhipinti
Creative Director: Charlie Piccirillo
Photographer: Nancy Ney
                Raymond Meier
                James Koepnick
Copywriter: Doug Raboy
Agency: DDB Needham Worldwide
Client: Colombian Coffee

Some people can't wait for their next coffee break.

The perfect Sunday.

262
Art Director: Peter Favat
Photographer: Dwight Olmsted
Copywriter: Don Pogany
Agency: Ingalls, Quinn & Johnson
Client: Converse

263

Art Director: Tom Lichtenheld
Creative Director: Pat Burnham
Illustrator: Sharon Werner
Copywriter: Bruce Bildsten
Agency: Fallon McElligott
Client: Azur

WILD FURNITURE.
WILD MUSIC.
WILD MUSHROOMS.

RESTAURANT · BALLROOM
GAVIIDAE COMMON

BLACK TRUFFLES.
GREEN LENTILS.
PURPLE CHAIRS.

RESTAURANT · BALLROOM
GAVIIDAE COMMON

TOO WEIRD.
TOO NOISY.
TOO DIFFERENT.

RESTAURANT · BALLROOM
GAVIIDAE COMMON

No one visits
Taos.

TAOS

Not all roads lead to
Santa Fe.

SANTA FE

Whisper the name.

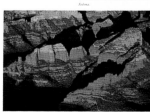

SEDONA

264

Art Director: Steven Sessions
Creative Director: Steven Sessions
Designer: Steven Sessions
Illustrator: Steven Sessions
Copywriter: John Hartmann
Agency: Steven Sessions, Inc.
Client: Southwest Art Magazine

265
Art Director: Rich Silverstein
Photographer: Jay Maisel
Agency: Goodby, Berlin & Silverstein
Client: Royal Viking Line

266
Art Director: Stephen Doyle
Creative Director: Stephen Doyle
Photographer: George Hein
Agency: Drenttel Doyle Partners
Client: Olympia & York/World Financial Center

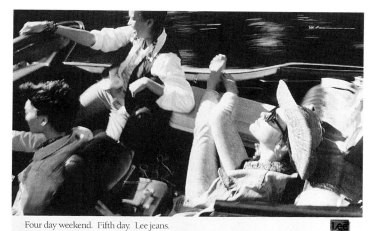

Four day weekend. Fifth day. Lee jeans.

Public phone. Private moment. Lee jeans.

9 O'clock date. 8:55. Lee jeans.

267

Art Director: Mark Johnson
Creative Director: Pat Burnham
Photographer: Kurt Markus
Copywriter: Bill Miller
Agency: Fallon McElligott
Client: Lee Jeans

HAS YOUR AIRLINE LOST ITS PERSONALITY?

Over the last few years, a lot of bright, spunky west coast airlines have been replaced by a few huge, national carriers. Airlines that are very efficient. Very businesslike. And about as interesting as a tax form.

One airline, however, hasn't lost its identity: Alaska Airlines, the one with the smiling Eskimo on the tail.

Hop on an Alaska Airlines flight and you'll still find bright, energetic people who take great pride in doing everything they can to serve their customers. With flair, spirit, and their own individual style. So the next time you're traveling up or down the west coast, fly Alaska Airlines.

And see if our attitude toward flying doesn't change yours.

Alaska Airlines

AT ALASKA AIRLINES, WE BRUSH AFTER EVERY MEAL.

We also dust, sweep, scrub and polish. Whatever it takes to keep our planes neat and tidy.

That's why we not only vacuum the seats, we also vacuum the seat pockets. We don't just sweep our carpets, we regularly steam clean them.

And on a regular basis, we spend 36 worker-hours "deep cleaning" the entire aircraft. Why do we go to all this trouble? Because we know how you feel about messy airplanes. So along with friendlier people, tastier meals and roomier seats, we'll do all we can to make sure you fly in a clean cabin.

Next trip to or from California, the Pacific Northwest, Arizona, Alaska or Mexico, take off on Alaska Airlines. We can promise you a clean getaway.

Alaska Airlines

WHO IN HIS RIGHT MIND EATS AIRLINE FOOD ON THE GROUND?

The Chairman of Alaska Airlines does. So does every other key executive in the company.

It happens during our "officers' lunch"—a twice-weekly meeting where our top managers sink their teeth into important corporate issues. Such as our meal service.

After all, we want to be certain that we're serving our passengers the kind of food that we would want to eat ourselves.

That's why you can look forward to entrees like Chicken Bordelaise and Pasta Alfredo, all prepared with fresh ingredients. And served with crisp green salads and tasty desserts.

So next trip up or down the west coast, or to Mexico, be sure to fly Alaska Airlines.

And try the Chicken Piccata. Our Chairman highly recommends it.

Alaska Airlines

268

Art Director: Tim Delaney
Creative Director: Jim Copacino
Photographer: Hank Benson
Copywriter: Jim Copacino
Agency: Livingston & Co.
Client: Alaska Airlines

269
Art Director: Barbara Simon
Creative Director: Andrew Langer
Copywriter: Ginni Stern
Agency: Lowe Marschalk
Client: Free Press

270
Art Director: Bob Barrie
Creative Director: Pat Burnham
Designer: Bob Barrie
Illustrator: Bob Barrie
Copywriter: Jarl Olsen
Agency: Fallon McElligott
Client: Hush Puppies

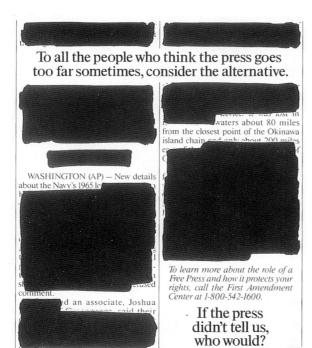

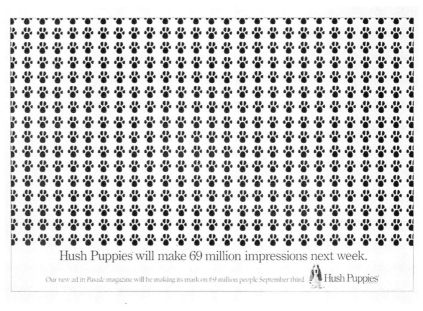

271
Art Director: Dean Hanson
Creative Director: Pat Burnham
Photographer: Eric Saulitis
Agency: Fallon McElligott
Client: Eleanor Moore

272
Art Director: Paul Asao
Creative Director: Jack Supple
Copywriter: Kerry Casey
Agency: Carmichael Lynch
Client: Blue Fox

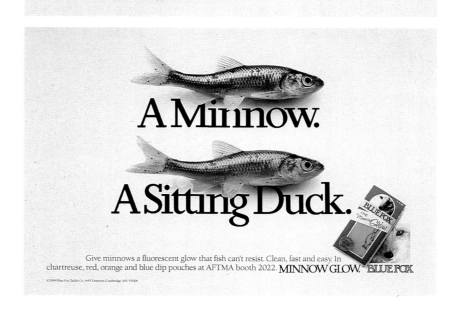

273
Art Director: Houman Pirdavari
Creative Director: Pat Burnham
Photographer: Jim Arndt
Copywriter: Bill Miller
Agency: Fallon McElligott
Client: Rolling Stone

274
Art Director: Brian Fandetti
Creative Director: Paul Silverman
Photographer: Harry DeZitter
Copywriter: Paul Silverman
Agency: Mullen
Client: Timberland Co.

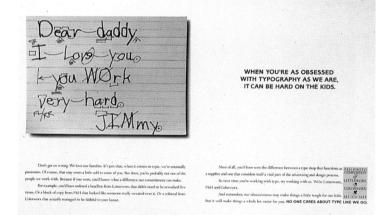

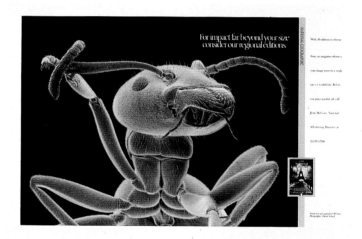

275
Art Director: Bob Brihn
Creative Director: Pat Burnham
Designer: Bob Brihn
Photographer: Rick Dublin
Copywriter: Jamie Barrett
Agency: Fallon McElligott
Client: Letterworx

276
Art Director: Cristina Creager
Creative Director: Jim Kingsley
　　　　　　　　　 Brett Robbs
Photographer: David Scharf
Copywriter: Andy Dumaine
Agency: DDB Needham
Client: National Geographic Society

277
Art Director: Houman Pirdavari
Creative Director: Pat Burnham
Photographer: Dave Jordano
Copywriter: Jarl Olsen
Agency: Fallon McElligott
Client: Penn

278
Art Director: Jac Coverdale
Creative Director: Jac Coverdale
Designer: Jac Coverdale
Photographer: Tom Connors
Copywriter: Joe Alexander
Agency: Clarity, Coverdale, Rueff
Client: Twin Cities Direct Choice

Guess what Penn is coming out with next?

The all new Pro Penn tennis shoe. Timeless styling with high-tech construction, from the world's largest manufacturer of tennis balls. Available exclusively through pro shops and selected tennis specialty stores.

penn

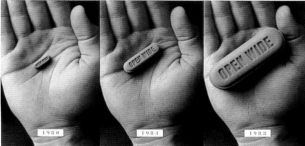

Are your Health Plan costs getting harder and harder to swallow?

279
Art Director: Jeremy Postaer
Creative Director: Jeffrey Goodby
                    Rich Silverstein
Photographer: Duncan Sim
Copywriter: Rob Bagot
Agency: Goodby, Berlin & Silverstein
Client: Royal Viking Line

280
Art Director: Jeremy Postaer
Creative Director: Jeffrey Goodby
                    Rich Silverstein
Photographer: Duncan Sim
Copywriter: Rob Bagot
Agency: Goodby, Berlin & Silverstein
Client: Royal Viking Line

281

Art Director: Mark Ashley
Creative Director: Jim Cole
Dick Henderson
Photographer: Parish Kohanim
Copywriter: Ken Lewis
Agency: Cole Henderson Drake, Inc.
Client: Dunlop Tennis

282

Art Director: Adrian Saker
Creative Director: Andy Berlin
Photographer: Gerry Bybee
Copywriter: Jim Anderson
Agency: Goodby, Berlin & Silverstein
Client: Clark's of England

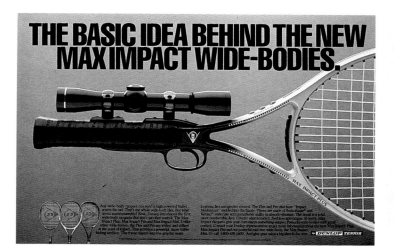

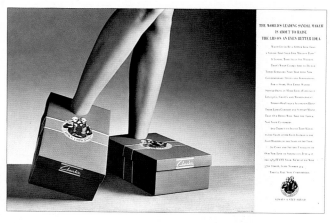

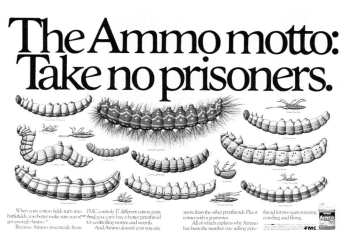

283

Art Director: Shari Hindman
Creative Director: Mike Hughes
Illustrator: Ed Lindlof
Copywriter: Kerry Feuerman
Agency: The Martin Agency
Client: FMC Corp.

284

Art Director: Steve Stein
Creative Director: Jeffrey Goodby
Rich Silverstein
Photographer: Jay Maisel
Dan Escobar
Peter Hendrie
Copywriter: David Fowler
Agency: Goodby, Berlin & Silverstein
Client: Royal Viking Line

285
Art Director: Bob Barrie
Creative Director: Pat Burnham
Designer: Bob Barrie
Photographer: Rick Dublin
Copywriter: Jarl Olsen
Agency: Fallon McElligott
Client: Jim Beam

286
Art Director: Mike Rosen
Creative Director: Gary Goldsmith
Photographer: Nora Scarlet
Copywriter: Mike Rosen
Agency: Goldsmith/Jeffrey
Client: Knoll International

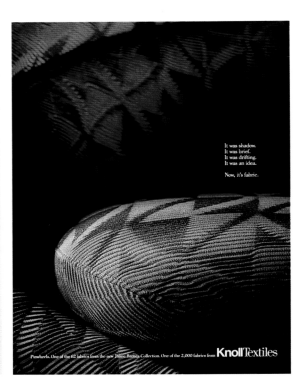

287
Art Director: Dean Hanson
Creative Director: Pat Burnham
Copywriter: Phil Hanft
Agency: Fallon McElligott
Client: Weyerhaeuser

288
Art Director: Bob Brihn
Creative Director: Pat Burnham
Designer: Bob Brihn
Photographer: Rick Dublin
Copywriter: Jamie Barrett
Agency: Fallon McElligott
Client: Letterworx

289
Art Director: Jim Henderson
Creative Director: Lyle Wedemeyer
Photographer: Jim Marvy
Copywriter: Pete Smith
Agency: Martin/Williams
Client: 3M Co.

290
Art Director: Wendy Hansen
Creative Director: Lyle Wedemeyer
Photographer: Rick Dublin
Copywriter: Pete Smith
Agency: Martin/Williams
Client: 3M Co.

What you'd be selling without new ideas.

IF YOU NEED YOUR HEADLINES IN A HURRY,
WE'LL WORK THROUGH LUNCH.

Never underestimate the power of the wrong clinical code.

291
Art Director: Bob Brihn
Creative Director: Pat Burnham
Designer: Bob Brihn
Photographer: Rick Dublin
Copywriter: Jamie Barrett
Agency: Fallon McElligott
Client: Letterworx

OUR RUB-DOWNS WILL EVEN
STICK TO TEFLON.

292
Art Director: Bob Brihn
Creative Director: Pat Burnham
Designer: Bob Brihn
Photographer: Rick Dublin
Copywriter: Jamie Barrett
Agency: Fallon McElligott
Client: Letterworx

293
Art Director: James Offenhartz
Creative Director: Lee Garfinkel
Photographer: Ken Nahoum
Copywriter: Marian Allen Godwin
Agency: Levine, Huntley, Schmidt & Beaver
Client: Technics

294
Art Director: Victor Mazzeo
Creative Director: Kathy Kiely
Photographer: Mark Weiss
Copywriter: Joe Sweet
Agency: Pedone & Partners
Client: Cumberland Packing Corp.

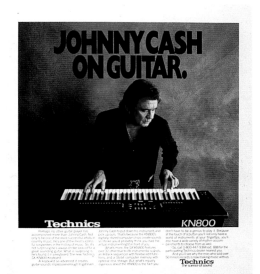

I see a man and a mule in your future.

295
Art Director: Sharon Occhipinti
Creative Director: Charlie Piccirillo
Photographer: Nancy Ney
     Raymond Meier
     James Koepnick
Copywriter: Doug Raboy
Agency: DDB Needham Worldwide
Client: Colombian Coffee

Some people can't wait for their next coffee break.

The perfect Sunday.

296
Art Director: Jeff A. Barnes
Creative Director: Jeff A. Barnes
Designer: Jeff A. Barnes
Photographer: Gina Uhlmann
Copywriter: Jeff A. Barnes
Agency: Barnes Design Office
Client: Johnson Industries

297
Art Director: Steve Haesche
Photographer: Christopher Cunningham
Copywriter: Peter Pappas
Agency: Mullen
Client: Sail

298
Art Director: Adrian Saker
Creative Director: Andy Berlin
Photographer: Gerry Bybee
Copywriter: Jim Anderson
Agency: Goodby, Berlin & Silverstein
Client: Clark's of England

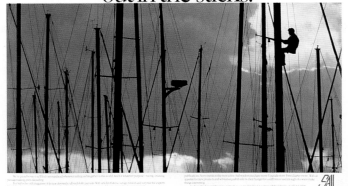

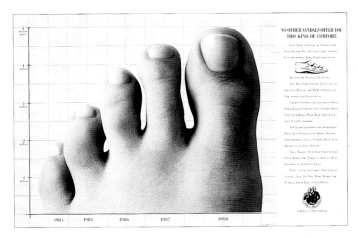

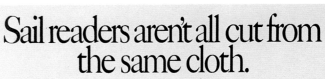

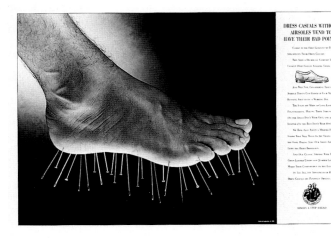

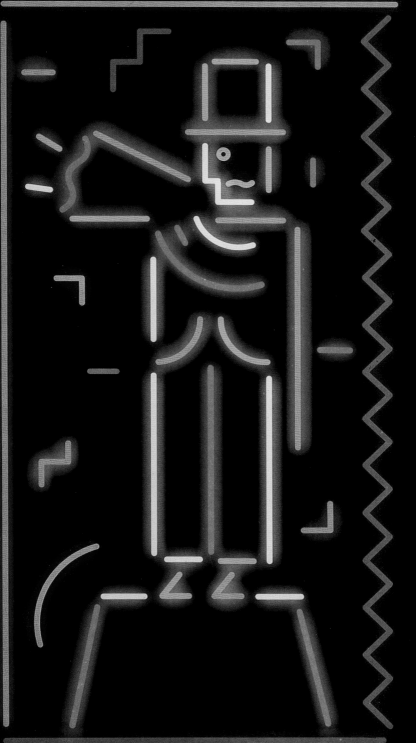

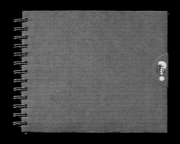

314 Silver
Art Director: Steve Ditko
Creative Director: Steve Ditko
Designer: Steve Ditko
Terry Bliss
Photographer: Kent Knudson
Copywriter: Sarah Harrell
Studio: Ditko Design
Client: Andresen Typographics

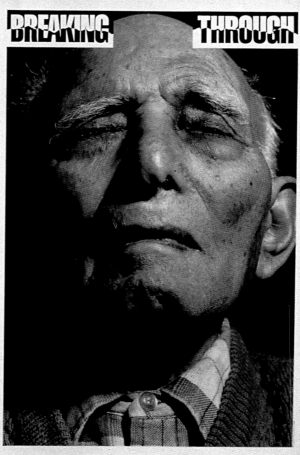

BREAKING THROUGH

315 Silver

Art Director: John Muller
Patrice Eilts
Jane Weeks
Lee Ernst
Photographer: Various
Copywriter: David Marks
Agency: Muller & Co.
Client: Kansas City Art Directors Club

331
Art Director: John Sayles
Designer: John Sayles
Studio: Sayles Graphic Design
Client: Norwest Bank Iowa

332
Art Director: Clive Helfet
Creative Director: Christopher A. Kogler
Designer: Clive Helfet
Producer: Steven Weinstock
Client: Thirteen/WNET

333
Art Director: David Warren
Client: Denver Art Museum

334
Art Director: John Sayles
Designer: Craig Keiran
Studio: Sayles Graphic Design
Client: Iowa Rural Electric Cooperative

335
Art Director: Patrick SooHoo
Creative Director: Harry Kerker
Designer: Katherine Lam
　　　　　Eddie Yip
Studio: Patrick SooHoo Designers
Client: Acapulco Tourism Board

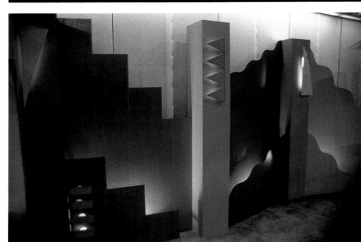

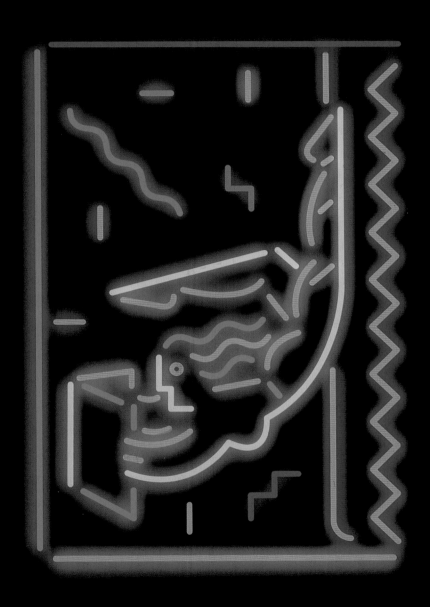

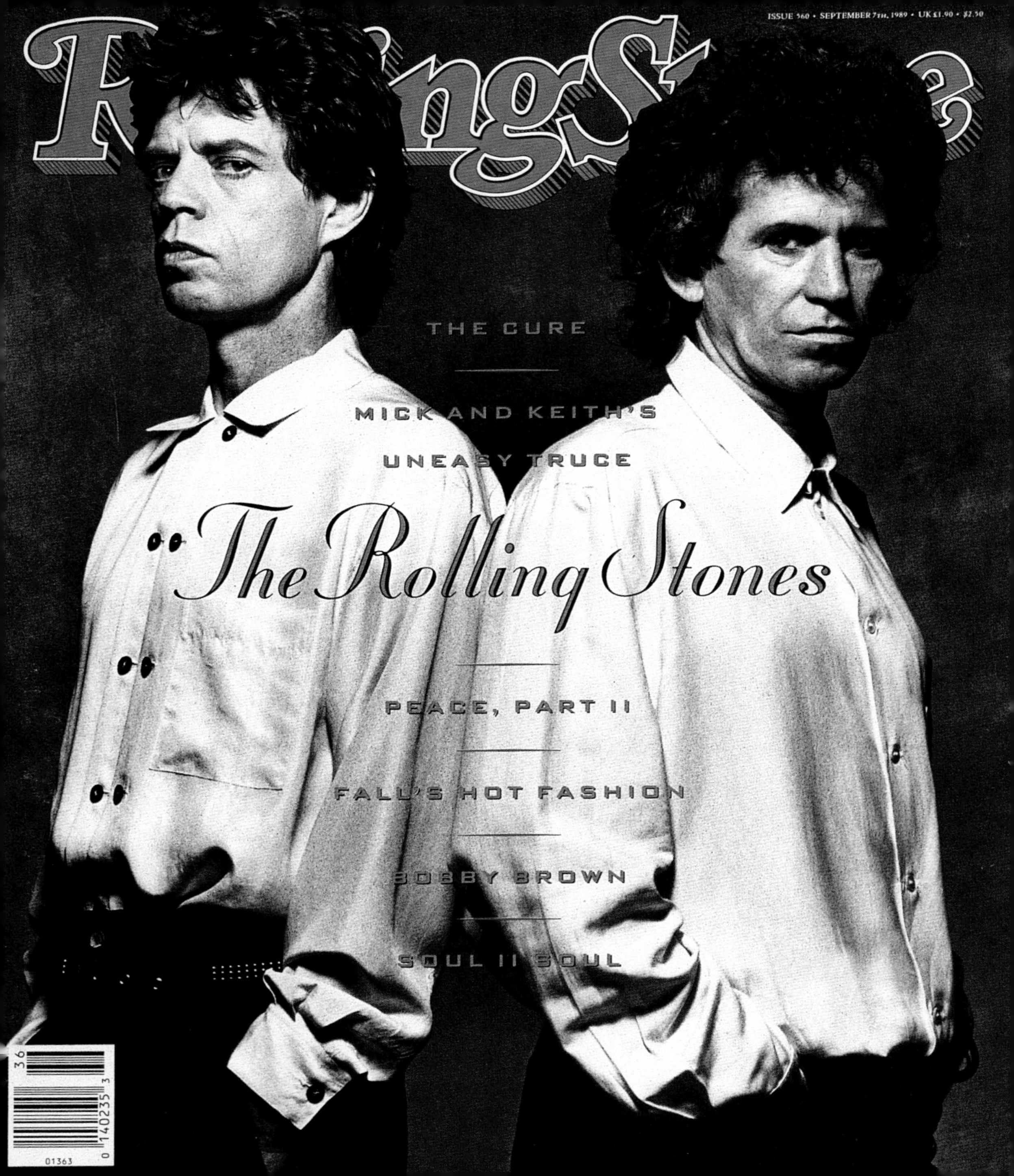

ISSUE 560 • SEPTEMBER 7TH, 1989 • UK £1.90 • $2.50

Rolling Stone

THE CURE

MICK AND KEITH'S
UNEASY TRUCE

The Rolling Stones

PEACE, PART II

FALL'S HOT FASHION

BOBBY BROWN

SOUL II SOUL

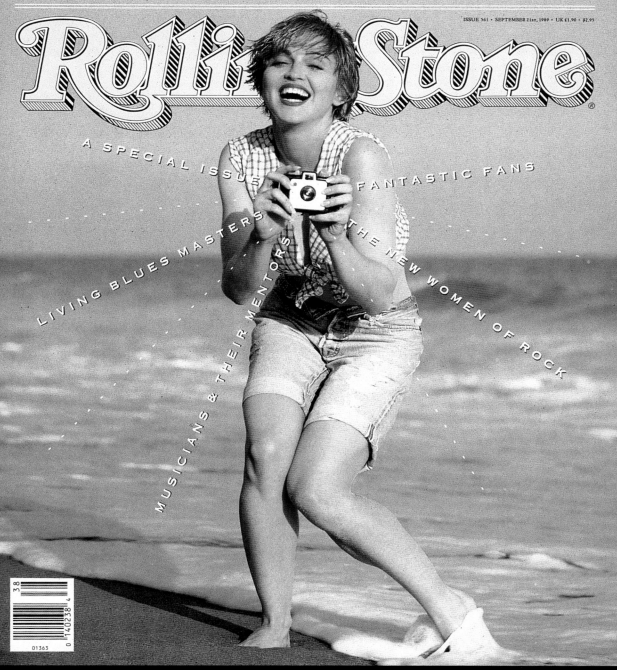

ISSUE 561 • SEPTEMBER 21st, 1989 • UK £1.90 • $2.95

Rock & Roll Photo Album

Rolling Stone

A SPECIAL ISSUE

FANTASTIC FANS

LIVING BLUES MASTERS

THE NEW WOMEN OF ROCK

MUSICIANS & THEIR MENTORS

341 Silver

Art Director: Fred Woodward
Photographer: Herb Ritts
Publication: Rolling Stone

CONVENTIONAL

IN THE 150 YEARS SINCE PHOTOGRAPHY WAS INVENTED, THE PHOTO IMAGE HAS THOROUGHLY INFILTRATED OUR CULTURE. FROM THE BARRAGE OF STILL AND MOVING PICTURES WE CONFRONT DAILY, TO THE MOST ARCANE OF GALLERY FARE, THE RECORDED IMAGE, FOR BETTER OR WORSE, HAS IN LARGE PART SUPPLANTED THE WORD AS THE PRIMARY METHOD OF COMMUNICATION. NOWHERE IS THAT MORE TRUE THAN IN LOS ANGELES, WHERE MANIPULATION OF IMAGE (IN ALL SENSES) IS A CENTRAL ACTIVITY AND A SIGNIFICANT CONTRIBUTION TO THE NATION'S IDENTITY. SO IN CELEBRATION OF THE 150TH ANNIVERSARY OF PHOTOGRAPHY AND THE FOURTH ANNIVERSARY OF L.A. STYLE, WE DECIDED TO EXPLORE THE STATE OF PHOTOGRAPHY IN OUR CITY IN 1989. WE ASKED HISTORIAN AND PHOTOGRAPHER MARK JOHNSTONE TO PROVIDE A CHRONICLE OF LOS ANGELES PHOTOGRAPHY, AND GROUNDBREAKING PHOTOGRAPHER ROBERT HEINECKEN OFFERED HIS PERSPECTIVE ON THE ESSENTIAL PHOTOGRAPHIC IMPULSE AND HOW IT ACTUALLY CHANGED SEEING. WE ASKED A GROUP OF PHOTO INSIDERS FOR THEIR COMMENTS ON THE L.A. PHOTOSCENE. AND ASKED NUMEROUS IMPORTANT PHOTOGRAPHERS TO DISPLAY THEIR WORK. AND WE'VE TAKEN A LOOK AT ROBERT SHAPAZIAN'S EXTRAORDINARY COLLECTION OF EARLY AND AVANT-GARDE IMAGES, PROFILED THE BLACK GALLERY, AND ASSEMBLED A PORTFOLIO OF CONTEMPORARY PHOTOGRAPHS, SOME OF THEM MAKING THEIR DEBUT PUBLIC APPEARANCE IN THESE PAGES. ELSEWHERE IN THE ISSUE, WE OFFER A LOOK AT L.A. PIONEER EDMUND TESKE ("IN CHARACTER"), AT MASTER FRAMER STEVE JOSEFSBERG ("STYLEMAKERS"), AT THE BEST IN EASY-TO-USE CAMERAS ("EQUIPMENT"), AND AT MOCA'S GARRY WINOGRAND ("DATEBOOK"). NATURALLY, OUR SELECTION IS REPRESENTATIVE. WE COULD NOT HAVE INCLUDED ALL THE WORTHY ARTISTS IN A BOOK MANY TIMES THE SIZE OF OUR MAGAZINE. ALSO, IT IS FAIR TO POINT OUT THAT WE HAVE APPROACHED THIS PROJECT WITH AT LEAST TWO CURATORIAL PREJUDICES: FIRST, WE DO NOT BELIEVE THAT THE DISTINCTION BETWEEN "ART" AND "PHOTOGRAPHY" MAKES ANY SENSE AT ALL, BUT OUR SELECTION OF PICTURES, PARTICULARLY IN "THE EMERGING IMAGE" PORTFOLIO, LEANS TO WORK THAT REMAINS FIRMLY ROOTED IN PHOTOGRAPHY (RATHER THAN ART THAT MIGHT BEST BE DESCRIBED AS "PHOTO-DERIVED"). SECOND, WHEN THERE WAS A CHOICE TO BE MADE, WE FREQUENTLY ELECTED TO SHOW LESSER-KNOWN WORK OR PHOTOGRAPHS BY LESSER-KNOWN ARTISTS RATHER THAN FAMOUS IMAGES BY WORLD-RENOWNED PHOTOGRAPHERS THAT ARE ROUTINELY USED TO REPRESENT PHOTOGRAPHY IN LOS ANGELES. WE APOLOGIZE IN ADVANCE TO ALL THOSE WHO ARE OFFENDED BY OUR INCLUSIONS AND EXCLUSIONS. —MICHAEL LASSELL AND GARRETT WHITE

Photography in L.A.

PERSPECTIVES

136

Red Rain

VISIONS FROM FLATLAND, BLEED HEAT #3, 1988-89, WALKER EVANS, 78 x 82 x 92

THE
SOUL
OF
EAST
TEXAS

A land of tall trees and deep roots, where the past still haunts the present.

PHOTOGRAPHY BY

KEITH CARTER

TEXT BY

PRUDENCE MACKINTOSH

WORSHIPER

NEW BETHEL MISSIONARY BAPTIST CHURCH, CHEEK COMMUNITY »

M EARS ARE ATTUNED to the voices of East Texas even though I've lived in the city for twenty years. "I oughta whup the tar outta you," I hear a mother tell her son as I hug the Jacksonville tomatoes at the farmers' market. I linger around the rim, hungrier for the experiences of my childhood than for the produce.

In a doctor's office a man from East Texas tells me about his heart surgery: "Last year I was not to where I couldn't hardly get out of bed." He is clearly enjoying the attention that his failing heart has attracted from important city doctors. "I was brought up hard," he explains.

The black woman championing my

hair summarizes her sister's life and recent death in one confident sentence: "She did what the Lord gave her to do." I scribble the sentence in the margin of a magazine, tear off the scrap of paper, and put it in my purse.

Perhaps I am making up for the inattentiveness of childhood. With no other frame of reference, I, like most children, regarded the landscape of my childhood as ordinary. In 1956, my sixth-grade class celebrated the end of elementary school with a trip to Dallas, where we took in such extravagant sights as Cinerama, the Health and Science Museum at Fair Park, with its shocking planet representations of a baby being born, and

BEECH TREE

HORTON'S MANTEL

MAN WITH BLIND ROOSTER

FAMILY IN GARDEN

MEAGAN

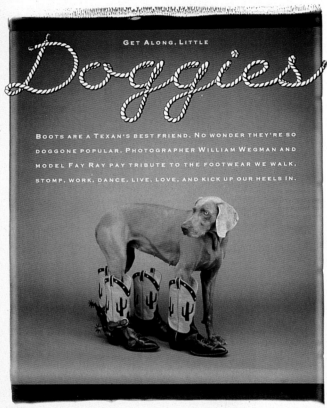

GET ALONG, LITTLE

Doggies

BOOTS ARE A TEXAN'S BEST FRIEND. NO WONDER THEY'RE SO
DOGGONE POPULAR. PHOTOGRAPHER WILLIAM WEGMAN AND
MODEL FAY RAY PAY TRIBUTE TO THE FOOTWEAR WE WALK,
STOMP, WORK, DANCE, LIVE, LOVE, AND KICK UP OUR HEELS IN.

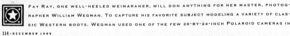

FAY RAY, ONE WELL-HEELED WEIMARANER, WILL DON ANYTHING FOR HER MASTER, PHOTOG-
RAPHER WILLIAM WEGMAN. TO CAPTURE HIS FAVORITE SUBJECT MODELING A VARIETY OF CLAS-
SIC WESTERN BOOTS, WEGMAN USED ONE OF THE FEW 20-BY-24-INCH POLAROID CAMERAS IN

114 · DECEMBER 1999

THE WORLD. PAGE 114: CRUSHED GOATSKIN BOOTS BY LARRY MAHAN ($199), J BAR W WESTERN
WEAR (CLEBURNE, DALLAS, FORT WORTH); SPURS BY RANDY BUTTERS ($275), TWO MOONS
TRADING COMPANY (DALLAS). PAGE 115: CUSTOM CALFSKIN BOOTS ($525), M. L. LEDDY'S BOOT

TEXAS MONTHLY · 115

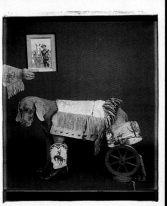

PHOTOGRAPHY BY HERB RITTS PRODUCED BY KATE HARRINGTON

THINLY
VEILED

ISSEY MIYAKE'S SHEER LAME BLOUSE.

AZZEDINE ALAIA'S SLEEK DRESS IN STRETCH KNIT.

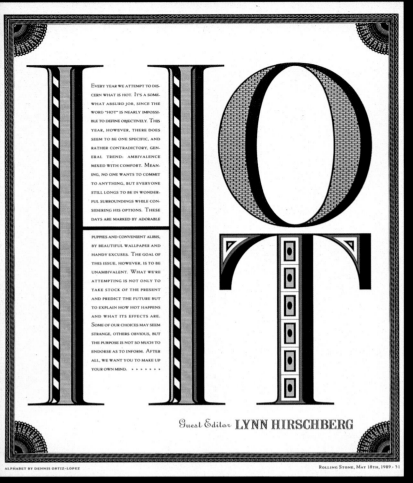

HOT

Every year we attempt to discern what is hot. It's a somewhat absurd job, since the word "hot" is nearly impossible to define objectively. This year, however, there does seem to be one specific, and rather contradictory, general trend: ambivalence mixed with comfort. Meaning, no one wants to commit to anything, but everyone still longs to be in wonderful surroundings while considering his options. These days are marked by adorable puppies and convenient alibis, by beautiful wallpaper and handy excuses. The goal of this issue, however, is to be unambivalent. What we're attempting is not only to take stock of the present and predict the future but to explain how hot happens and what its effects are. Some of our choices may seem strange, others obvious, but the purpose is not so much to endorse as to inform. After all, we want you to make up your own mind. ✦ ✦ ✦ ✦ ✦ ✦

Guest Editor **LYNN HIRSCHBERG**

ALPHABET BY DENNIS ORTIZ-LOPEZ

ROLLING STONE, MAY 18TH, 1989 · 51

HOT COVER Inspiring lust in audiences, Sylvester Stallone and gossip columnists alike, starlet Uma Thurman tries to cope with all the attention while keeping her sense of Uma··· *Photographs by* **MATTHEW ROLSTON**

HOT MOOD These are not the best of times; these are not the worst of times. At the end of the decade, we are turning ambivalent. Maybe.

Nowadays, there are two sides to every answer. We don't face facts and, hell, simply *decide*. No. That would be too instinctual, too easy, too blithe, too unlike us.

Instead, we consider every alternative and feel complete enthusiasm for none of them. We postpone. We fret. We second-guess. Whether it's a matter of deciding what to have for lunch (a sandwich? a salad?) or how to spend the rest of our lives (duplicitous corporate scumbag in New York? bad lyric poet in Seattle?), neither a wholehearted yes nor an unequivocal no comes naturally. We say maybe. We try to act on both impulses, to be unsentimental romantics, to work uptown but live downtown or vice versa, to have it all, foreclosing no option. As individuals, and even as a nation, we grow faint at the prospect of absolute commitment, whether it's marriage, or military intervention in the third world, or thirty-year fixed-rate mortgages. We find it hard to feel unalloyed pleasure (would you say you love Bette Midler's Disney movies?) or unmitigated disapproval (would you say you hate George Bush?). To most of us, every city, every book, practically every way of life is an interesting place to visit, but we wouldn't want to live there. Would we? Ours is a generation comfortably adrift, bobbing on a sea of ambivalence.

But that's not all bad. Probably.

Ambivalence as a defining sensibility, widespread and full-blown, is something new. There is virtually nothing today about which thoughtful people – especially thoughtful younger people – do not feel mixed emotions. Every hankering, whether it's for a policy (like national health insurance), or a commodity (like microwave ovens), or a performer (like David Letterman), comes with disclaimers, a special codicil of qualifiers or qualms.

This is not to say that one's parents and their parents never second-guessed themselves. Despite the upbeat sheen of the official 1950s, the last generation had its own ambivalents: Jack Lemmon, John Updike, John Cheever and, in his thuggish tavern-philosopher way, Frank Sinatra are all about being of two (or more) minds, about the competing seductions of suburb and city, convention and impulse, the familiar and the new.

But Lemmon's discombobulated characters were exceptions, Cheever's and Updike's white-collar Hamlets mere literary creatures. Until rather recently, television was obliged to depict the official dad – Ward Cleaver, Ozzie Nelson, Mike Brady. Today the only remaining official dad is the president of the United States, and TV's most beloved parents, downscale (*Roseanne*) and upscale (*thirtysomething*), are knees-of no-easy-answers ambivalence. *Thirtysomething* is appealing, one of its creators explains, because its stories are untidy, its characters irresolute. "Ambiguity and ambivalence," he says, "are as much a part of life as resolution." And according to *Newsweek*, the film *Broadcast News* was "the first romantic comedy driven by ambivalence." Tell me I'm smart and attractive, yes, but even better, tell me I'm smart, attractive *and* confused.

In 1962, Tom Hayden drafted the Students for a Democratic Society charter, the so-called Port Huron Statement, which launched the New Left. Its jumping-off point was a collective sense of ambivalence, its signatories people privileged enough to harbor mixed feelings about their privilege. "We are people of this generation," Hayden wrote, "bred in at least modest comfort, housed now in universities, looking uncomfortably at the world we inherit." Because they were very young, and because the injustices were more spectacular and more remediable, the New Leftists coped with ambivalence by plunging into unsubtle political commitment, not (as they would later) by wandering away, jaded and flip. It was simple in the Sixties: Once the world came up to snuff – no more war, no more greed, no more lies – ambivalence would be outmoded. And indeed, for most of those who felt it, the thrilling surge of antiwar sentiment was the last moment of absolute certainty about politics.

Today's ambivalence is a post-Vietnam syndrome, civilian shell shock. The war itself was a mess of second thoughts from beginning to end. Presidents Kennedy and Johnson were ambivalent about sending U.S. troops. The war was waged ambivalently by infantrymen ordered to kill and protect the same people by generals ambivalent about strategy and tactics. From 1968 on, the American public was composed not mainly of hawks or doves but of confused, anxious citizens. Even to those who demanded withdrawal, the final spectacle – GIs bashing would-be refugees on the helipad, North Vietnamese tanks rolling through Saigon – was not exactly gladdening. The memorial to Vietnam veterans in Washington, D.C., is a grand, heartbreaking dead end, ambivalence in black granite.

By the time the war ended, a certain "Hey, who cares?" fecklessness had already set in among the young, a rejection of both hippie abandon and conventional so-

Illustration by Etienne Delessert

BY KURT ANDERSEN

58 · Rolling Stone, May 18th, 1989

346 Silver
Art Director: Fred Woodward
Publication: Rolling Stone

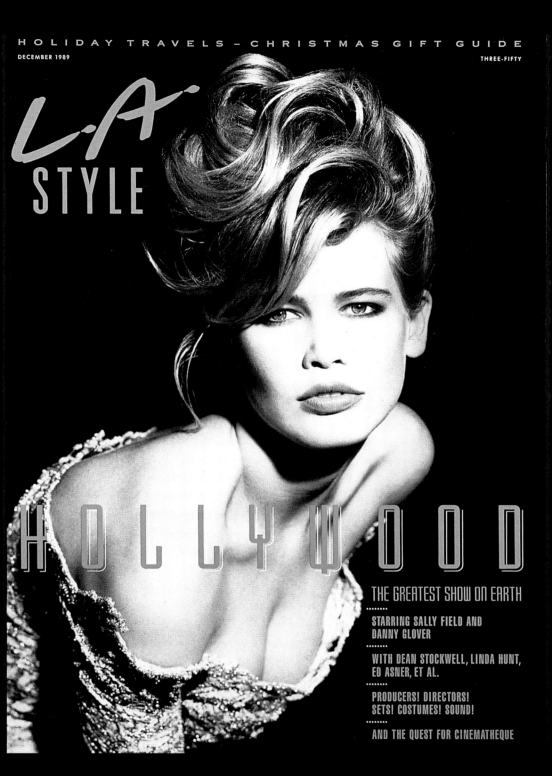

DECEMBER 1989

THREE-FIFTY

L.A STYLE

HOLLYWOOD

THE GREATEST SHOW ON EARTH

STARRING SALLY FIELD AND
DANNY GLOVER

WITH DEAN STOCKWELL, LINDA HUNT,
ED ASNER, ET AL.

PRODUCERS! DIRECTORS!
SETS! COSTUMES! SOUND!

AND THE QUEST FOR CINEMATHEQUE

347 Distinctive Merit

Art Director: Michael Brock
Designer: Michael Brock
Photographer: Herb Ritts
Studio: Michael Brock Design
Client: LA Style

348 Distinctive Merit
Art Director: Fred Woodward
Designer: Fred Woodward
Photographer: Matt Mahurin
Publication: Rolling Stone

PART ONE

Terrorized by her husband's repeated death threats, Renee Linton did everything women are supposed to do to protect themselves under the system. Yet despite her calls for help, her court order of protection, her flights ‹Nowhere to Run› to a shelter for battered women, the system failed to save her.

By Ellen Hopkins

PHOTOGRAPH BY MATT MAHURIN

VENICE

VISIONS

VENICE WAS ALMOST a dream come true. The dreamer was Abbot Kinney, an Easterner who had made his fortune manufacturing Sweet Caporal cigarettes for America's tobacco-addicted millions. When he migrated—in 1880, at the tender age of 30—from Washington, D.C. to unspoiled Los Angeles, he harbored nobler ambitions. By 1902 Kinney had acquired the wherewithal to begin fashioning a fantastic community out of seaside salt marshes in what was then Ocean Park. With his millions he built "Venice of America," a combination amusement park and watery, Italianate village—one of the most strangely charming developments ever to arise on these or any other shores. Along the waterfront and on Abbot Kinney Pier he erected a new dance hall, a handsome opera house, a vast saltwater bathhouse with 1000 dressing rooms, and huge restaurant constructed, to resemble a docked ship. Hotels and more restaurants lined Windward Avenue, which led back to Venice Lagoon [now Windward Circle]. From there canals radiated in three directions. Gondolas plied their waters, propelled by imported Italian gondoliers. Newly built homes and cottages looked out on the waterways between gracefully arched bridges. This was a Disneyland you could live in. • Kinney had thought of himself as a bringer of culture to these frontier beaches. Artists, lecturers and great orchestras were part of this vision, but he lost many thousands of dollars his first year pursuing his aspiration to finer things. So he adjusted, quickly installing the most spectacular amusement area on the West Coast with a high-speed early roller coaster, the Race Thru the Clouds, as its centerpiece. • Early on, the whole project had been referred to as "Kinney's Folly," and perhaps, in a sense, it was. Though the money rolled in, the enterprise became a crass version of the finer dream. The flower of Venice of America really only lasted from its opening in 1905 until the canals were condemned as a public health hazard in 1913. The beachfront midway was still going strong when Kinney died in 1920, but before the year was out his magnificent pier had burned down, practically to the waterline. • So it goes. Though the pier and its amusement area were reconstructed, Venice continued in decline. Most of its canals had been filled in by 1930, and when the pier was finally demolished in 1946, the era of its history was clearly over. • But even in decay, Venice attracted the same. With the '50s came the Beats, a loose band of dropouts, ne'er-do-wells and disaffected artists looking for a place to live cheaply out of reach of the authorities. They evolved into a funky bohemian subculture that would become part of the enduring texture of the place. • Through all of the years before and since, the well-intentioned have tried repeatedly to cleanse and renovate Venice and their successes have ranged from modest to profound. Now they're at it again. The prospects seem better this time—or worse, depending on which Venice you love the most. —The Editors

THE ROLLING STONE INTERVIEW

Elvis Costello may be thought of as the angry young man of the British New Wave, but as he and his wife, Cait O'Riordan, greet me in the elegant piano bar of the Four Seasons Clift Hotel,

BY DAVID WILD

photograph by matt mahurin

Designer: Michael Brock
Photographer: Deborah Turbeville
Studio: Michael Brock Design
Client: LA Style

352 Distinctive Merit

Art Director: Fred Woodward
Designer: Fred Woodward
Gail Anderson

Photography by
Bret Wills

SAFE AT HOME

This summer in Cooperstown, N.Y., the National Baseball Hall of Fame and Museum celebrates its 50th anniversary as the spiritual home of the game and as the repository of its treasures. From the essential (the Babe's bat) to the eccentric (the Babe's bowling ball), the Hall has it all. Enjoy the tour

MAYS STEPPED HERE: ON MAY 30, 1971, WILLIE MAYS CROSSED THIS PLATE AT CANDLESTICK PARK TO SCORE AN NL-RECORD 1,950TH RUN

SIDE BY SIDE

PHOTOGRAPHY BY WILLIAM COUPON

In Mexico "Ay, Chihuahua!" is an expression of amazement and surprise, and for good reason. Chihuahua, Mexico's largest state, is a land of extremes, embracing both the scorching desert that bears its name and the northern Sierra Madre Occidental, a mountain range with the coldest temperatures in Mexico. It is only natural, then, that Chihuahua is also home to two tribes on the extremes of their cultures, the Tarahumara Indians and the German-speaking Altkolonier, or Old Colony Mennonites.

Both groups have agreements with the government that allow them to sidestep two important requirements of Mexican citizenship: education in the Spanish language and mandatory weekend military training for young men. Both groups eschew city life and have settled in the dry triangle created by the towns of Cuauhtémoc, Creel, and Guachóchic. But the similarities between the two tribes halt there.

The Mennonites are an old Anabaptist group whose members migrated from the Alps to the south of Russia in 1789 and fled to Canada in 1874. When the Canadians required them to teach English in their church schools in 1922, the Altkolonier moved to Mexico. As far as historians know, the Tarahumara settled in Chihuahua eons ago, though many of them lived at lower elevations before the tribe's trouble with the Tepehuane and Apache.

Mennonite

Tarahumara

In the mountains and deserts of northern Indians live bound by timeless traditions.

Mexico, Mennonite farmers and Tarahumara They couldn't be more different—or more alike.

Within fifteen years of their arrival, the Mennonites became Mexico's most productive small farmers. They are the country's leading commercial producers of oats and a white cheese called *queso Chihuahua*, a fundamental in dishes like *queso fundido* and *quesadillas*. Part of the Mennonite success is owed to technology; they use tractors because tractors facilitate working, but for transportation they prefer horse-drawn wagons because cars, they say, facilitate sinning.

In their own language, the Tarahumara call themselves Rarámuri, or "foot runners," because their ancestors had little need for bows and arrows: they ran down game on foot. They have never concerned themselves with productivity or technology. They use nineteenth-century implements and draft animals to eke out a subsistence based on corn and squash.

The Tarahumara are as indefatigably festive as the Mennonites are austere. They devote a significant portion of their corn harvest to making *tesgüino* (corn beer) and about one hundred days a year to drinking it and recovering from hangovers.

Despite these apparent differences, the Mennonites and the Tarahumara have a deep spiritual affinity. Passionate about their chosen ways of life, both have found in Chihuahua a place where they can be free of the pressures of the modern world. ❧

DICK J. REAVIS

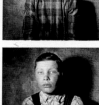

Even as children, the Mennonites and Tarahumara inhabit separate worlds. There is little interaction between them, since each group speaks its own language, not Spanish.

Both the Tarahumara and the Mennonites have been granted exemptions from military service and schooling in Spanish. Centuries after the conquest of Mexico, they remain unassimilated.

A colorful as the Mennonites are plain, the festive Tarahumara love flamboyant clothes and strong drink. Much of their corn harvest goes to the production of a home brew called tesgüino.

Turning their   backs to the world, the Tarahumara long ago took to the hills to escape hostile tribes.

THE MANY RECENT sightings of Elvis Presley have led to a new and illuminating line of inquiry: If Elvis is able to make appearances after his death, shouldn't he have been able to show up before his birth? ∼ He is, after all, the King. ∼ Exhaustive research has uncovered a wealth of evidence previously ignored by scholars who were distracted by events of lesser significance. ∼ Skeptics may choose to pooh-pooh the Peruvian mountain carvings – visible only by aircraft – in the shape of a teddy bear. They may dismiss as coincidence the fact that Inca priests of the period wore chains

Lascaux, France (left): The birth of rock. Not by any means the last time the King will be criticized by Neanderthals. Carvings tell of a benevolent stranger who came out of nowhere, defeated the clan's enemies with martial arts and gave everybody a free horse. Easter Island (right): The audience at the National Geographic Society began to cough and wheeze uncomfortably when forced to confront this picture. Some members of the Memphis Mafia have commented on Elvis's big head.

IN SEARCH of HISTORIC ELVIS

BY ALAN D. MAISLEN · ILLUSTRATIONS BY ANITA KUNZ

around their necks. ∼ The open-minded Elviologist (as opposed to the Prealiquarian, with his amateur faddism) can only sigh with tolerance. ∼ Naysayers cannot so easily abrogate the Rouen tapestry that depicts the martyrdom of Saint Joan of Arc. The figure in the background was assumed to be a Burgundian bishop, chiefly because of his high-collared, gold-sequined robe and the fact that he seems to be sneering at Saint Joan. Embroidered along the bottom: *Je veux un morceau d'amour brûlant.* Loose translation: "I want a hunk, a hunk of burning love." ∼ Compelling evidence of Elvisiation may be seen in any of a thousand Asian jungles, from Cambodia to Japan. There it is commonplace to find great, ornate decaying temples. Should it surprise anyone that, for untold millenniums, these were sites where thousands of worshipers swooned before the imposing centerpiece: a giant statue of a man weighing over 300 pounds? ∼ And is it mere happenstance that these are the same cultures in which originated the art of painting on black velvet? ∼ Why hasn't this proof come to light sooner? A deliberate conspiracy to suppress it! The motive? Scientific ego, unwilling to give credit to the munificent contributions of the preternatural Presley. The most blatant example? The 1900 diaries of Walter Reed, the so-called father of the

cure for yellow fever. He describes his first patient: "Hands: shaking. Knees: weak. Can't seem to stand on own two feet. Lips: hot (like volcano). Patient delirious. Acts wildly, as if he were a bug. Question: Why is he all shook up?" ∼ Is it not curious that, weeks later, Reed should "discover" the cause of yellow fever to be a mosquito? And how peculiar that he should find it in Cuba, a land renowned for its "fuzzy trees." ∼ Only Elvis's characteristic modesty prevented him from taking credit for his many cross-cultural contributions, and even doubters agree it's a good thing Colonel Parker never contemplated the T-shirt rights. ∼ Should you embrace my theory, prepare to suffer the indignities inflicted on all who hold unpopular beliefs: for truly, the unwashed masses have yet to learn the golden rule: Don't be cruel. In fact, this author has been hounded into virtual seclusion, not unlike the post-Vegas Presley. ∼ Nevertheless, I have followed my dream and discovered a promising new course of study. Anybody's grandmother can claim to have seen Elvis sucking down a grape Slurpy at the local Bob's Big Boy years after his "death." Few, however, have bothered to look for the very real appearances of Elvis in inappropriate places while he was still alive. ∼ Just who was that shadowy pompadoured figure lurking on the Grassy Knoll? ∼ I'll never tell.

by JOHN WEST   photography by DAVE G. HOUSER

"DOES ANYONE HERE REMEMBER HOWARD CARTER'S DISCOVERY of King Tut's tomb?" our guide asked as we walked into the Valley of the Kings, across the Nile and west of the city of Luxor, where the lion-colored Theban Hills lie like a clenched fist in the dust. "Of course!" muttered the retired doctor at my shoulder, "it was only sixty-six years ago," and he was off like a shot to join the line waiting to see the smallest, least rewarding and most cramped excavation among the 62 tombs known to exist here—that of King Tutankhamen.

Sixty-six years ago seems as current as your next breath in this land of the Old. If we date our civilization from the Renaissance, Egypt has existed ten times as long; if we count our years from the birth of Christ, the Sphinx was already older than Christianity is now. Spend a few weeks along the Nile and what comes to mind is death and the magnificent opening verse in Ecclesiastes: "The earth abideth for ever. . . and there is no new thing under the sun."

Take, for instance, the most aggressive touts on the planet, who pounce on you at the Pyramids or here, 400 miles south of Cairo, the way mosquitos pounce on bathers in a swamp. Earlier in the day, the spry octogenarian doctor and I had set out from Luxor for the west riverbank and the tombs in a narrow-awninged ferry launch with a clattering motor like a tractor engine, chugging creakily and patiently on across the sprawling surface of the Nile back into the furthest sunstruck silences of antiquity.

The insistent pleas and opened palms instantly begin to nibble at your attention and follow you through every turn, even through car windows, like some siege of piranhas, the unblinking, beseeching stares regarding you calmly, at once unhoping and ravenous. Then comes the entrepreneur, a famished-looking youth with a dull yellow pallor like a nicotine stain and wet black eyes. He captures your attention with scraps of gaiety and jokes snatched up at random over years from fleeing Americans:

THE NILE

ABU SIMBEL, A TEMPLE
DEDICATED TO PHARAOH
RAMSES II, BY THE
SUDANESE BORDER
(ABOVE). THE GRAND AND
IMPOSING NILE (RIGHT).

"What's up doc? Everything copacetic? All A-OK? Mister! *Monsieur!* You know what is a camel with no hump? Make a guess, mister. You couldn't guess? Hubert Humphrey! See? Hump-free. You don't like jokes? Maybe you like to be serious all the time." Wrong. What I liked to be was up the road with the doctor, who had rented a bicycle that ran better than a new policeman. After while, crocodile.

There's nothing new about this. Tourists have flocked to Egypt for 3,000 years, and from the beginning, natives have had a reputation as sarcastic fast-talkers—"witty and ready to abuse," wrote Seneca. However, I could not imagine any one of them telling a worse joke than Hump-free. I was on a two-week tour of Egypt, traveling from Cairo all the way up to Abu Simbel near the Sudanese border and working my way back on a three-day boat trip on the Nile from Aswan to Luxor through the most intense concentration of tombs, temples, treasures, mystic art and ruins in the world.

Cairo was like entering some living many-layered Troy—some old massive millstone still thick with the intermingled pulps and chaff of its slow immense gristings through 4,000 years: Alexander, the Caesars, Napoléon, Europeans. In the seethe of its streets, 14 million people dwelt, most as close to dust as lizards. Five hundred thousand alone lived in a huge necropolis, the "city of the dead" that stretched along Cairo's eastern edge. Down an interminable succession of narrow alleys, I glimpsed milling tunnels of trade in hot tea, tin pots, cabbages and tallow-white chicken carcasses as I sat in a traffic jam so infinite and tangled it brought to mind the Amazonian jungle. The noise was stultifying, the horn being the one part of the estimated one million cabs, 2,300 buses and 780,000 cars that works. Once moving, my driver drove with

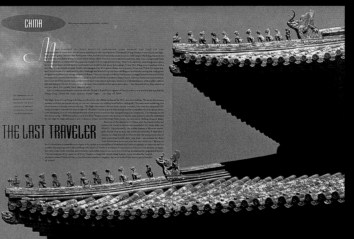

THE LAST TRAVELER

A DRIVE THROUGH O'KEEFFE COUNTRY

356 Distinctive Merit

Art Director: Michael Brock
Designer: Michael Brock
Photographer: Various
Studio: Michael Brock Design
Client: LA Style

357 Distinctive Merit

Art Director: Paul Davis
Designer: Risa Zaitschek
Illustrator: Various
Photographer: Various
Client: Wigwag Magazine Co., Inc.

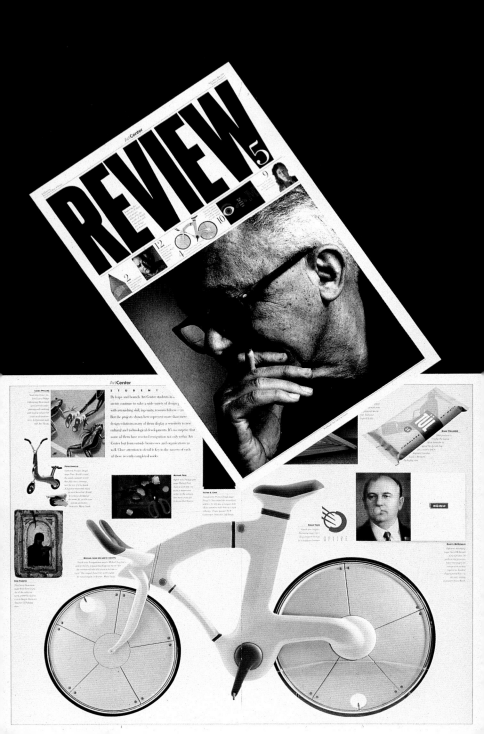

359 Distinctive Merit
Art Director: Kit Hinrichs
Designer: Kit Hinrichs
Illustrator: Terri Driscoll
Photographer: Benoit Jacques
Rick Eskite
Studio: Steven A. Heller
Studio: Pentagram
Art Center College of Design

360
Art Director: Michael Grossman
Designer: Michael Grossman
Illustrator: Philip Burke
Publication: Village Voice

361
Art Director: Nicki Kalish
Creative Director: Tom Bodkin
Designer: Nicki Kalish
Illustrator: Jim Ludtke
Publication: The *New York Times*

362
Art Director: Lynn Phelps
Designer: Lynn Phelps
Illustrator: Theo Rudnak
Publication: Minnesota Guide

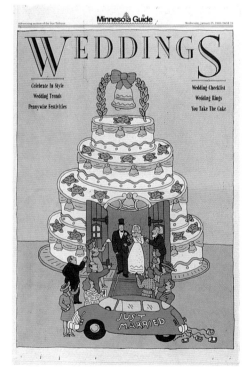

363
Art Director: Lynn Phelps
Designer: Lynn Phelps
Illustrator: Seymour Chwast
Publication: Minnesota Guide

364
Art Director: Francesca Messina
Creative Director: Tom Bodkin
Designer: Francesca Messina
Illustrator: Terry Allen
Publication: The *New York Times*

365
Art Director: Lynn Phelps
Designer: Lynn Phelps
Illustrator: Guy Billout
Publication: Minnesota Guide

366
Art Director: Lucy Bartholomay
Designer: Lucy Bartholomay
Illustrator: John Sibbick
Publication: The *Boston Globe*

367
Art Director: Lynn Phelps
Designer: Lynn Phelps
Illustrator: Peter Lindman
Photographer: Peter Lindman
Publication: Minnesota Guide

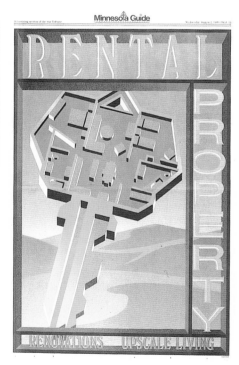

368
Art Director: Lynn Phelps
Designer: Lynn Phelps
Illustrator: Laura Smith
Publication: Minnesota Guide

369
Art Director: Lucy Bartholomay
Designer: Lucy Bartholomay
Illustrator: Tim Carroll
John Hersey
Etienne Delessert
Maira Kalman
Sheldon Greenberg
J. W. Stewart
Publication: The *Boston Globe*

370
Art Director: JoEllen Murphy
Illustrator: Tim Lewis
Publication: The *Washington Post*

371

Art Director: Ed Kohorst
Designer: Ed Kohorst
Illustrator: Carol Zuber
Publication: The *Dallas Morning News*

The Dallas Morning News

HIDDEN
WARS

Nineteen wars are raging in the world. They have claimed the lives of an estimated 3 million people, more than twice as many deaths from war as the United States has suffered in its history. Of those killed, nearly 90 percent have been civilians. Yet most of these wars have escaped public notice.

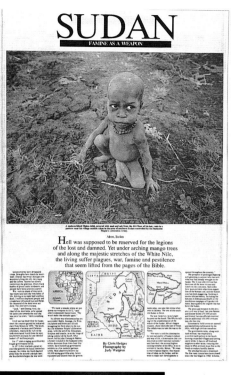

SUDAN
FAMINE AS A WEAPON

Hell was supposed to be reserved for the legions of the lost and damned. Yet under arching mango trees and along the majestic stretches of the White Nile, the living suffer plagues, war, famine and pestilence that seem lifted from the pages of the Bible.

By Chris Hedges
Photography by
Judy Walgren

COLOMBIA & PERU

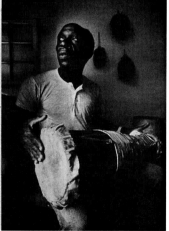

THE NEW MOBSTERS | GLOBAL WARMING | THE PREGNANT PROFESSIONAL

The Boston Globe Magazine

Cuba

PHOTOGRAPHY
BY KEITH JENKINS

The island nation

372

Art Director: Lucy Bartholomay
Designer: Lucy Bartholomay
Photographer: Keith Jenkins
Publication: The *Boston Globe*

373
Art Director: Scott Menchin
Creative Director: Scott Menchin
Designer: Scott Menchin
Photographer: Timothy Greenfield-Sanders
Publication: 7 Days

374
Art Director: Michael Brock
Designer: Michael Brock
Photographer: Herb Ritts
Studio: Michael Brock Design
Client: LA Style

375
Art Director: Ronda Kass
Creative Director: Everett Halvorsen
Publication: Forbes

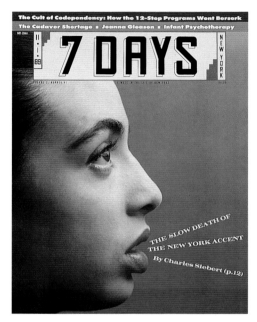

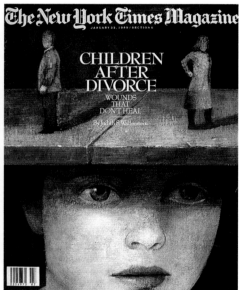

376
Art Director: Janet Froelich
Designer: Janet Froelich
Illustrator: Anita Kunz
Publication: The *New York Times*

377
Art Director: Janet Froelich
Designer: Janet Froelich
Illustrator: Wiktor Sadowski
Publication: The *New York Times*

378
Art Director: D. J. Stout
Designer: D. J. Stout
Photographer: Keith Carter
Publication: Texas Monthly

379
Art Director: Scott Menchin
Creative Director: Scott Menchin
Designer: Scott Menchin
Photographer: William Duke
Publication: 7 Days

380
Art Director: Fred Woodward
Photographer: William Coupon
Publication: Rolling Stone

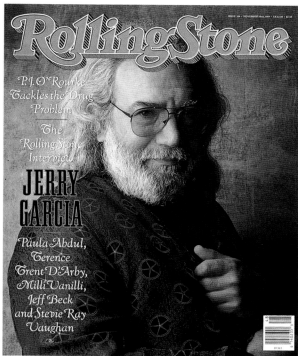

381
Art Director: Fred Woodward
Designer: Jolene Cuyler
Illustrator: Sue Coe
Publication: Rolling Stone

382
Art Director: Mary Workman
Designer: Timothy W. Brown
Photographer: Chip Simons
Publication: Tennessee Illustrated

383
Art Director: Janet Froelich
Photo Editor: Kathy Ryan
Designer: Justine Strasberg
Photographer: Chip Simons
Illustrator: Kam Mak
Publication: The *New York Times*

384
Art Director: Janet Froelich
Photo Editor: Kathy Ryan
Designer: Richard Samperi
Photographer: James Nachtwey
Publication: The *New York Times*

385
Art Director: Robert Best
　　　　　David Walters
Designer: Robert Best
　　　　David Walters
　　　　Mary Ann Salvato
Copywriter: Pete Hamill
Publication: *Premiere*

386
Art Director: Jane Palecek
Designer: Jane Palecek
Illustrator: Alan Cober
Publication: *Hippocrates* Magazine

GARBO
TALKS
(a little)

387
Art Director: Tom Bentkowski
Designer: Nora Sheehan
Publication: Life Magazine

BLOODLINE

Instead of the skid row regulars who sell their
● blood plasma, a doctor sees the new poor: ●
● single mothers, artists, the guy next door. ●

PHOTOGRAPHS BY KEN WILKES

388
Art Director: Jane Palecek
Designer: Jane Palecek
Photographer: Ken Wilkes
Publication: Hippocrates Magazine

1939 ★ 1989

389
Art Director: Tom Bentkowski
Designer: Nora Sheehan
Photographer: Timothy White
Publication: Life Magazine

BODY
And
SOUL

INTERACT IN WAYS WE ARE ONLY
BEGINNING TO UNDERSTAND

BY KEITH C. WATSON

390
Art Director: Mark Geer
Designer: Mark Geer
Illustrator: Gary Kelley
Copywriter: Keith Watson
Studio: Geer Design, Inc.
Client: Memorial Care Systems

391
Art Director: Olivia Badrutt-Giron
Photographer: Tyen
Publication: Elle

392
Art Director: Robert Best
David Walters
Designer: Robert Best
Photographer: Karen Kuehn
Publication: Premiere

393
Art Director: Robert Best
David Walters
Designer: Robert Best
David Walters
Mary Ann Salvato
Copywriter: Peter Biskind
Publication: Premiere

394
Art Director: Robert Best
David Walters
Designer: Mary Ann Salvato
Photographer: Miche Del Sol
Copywriter: Stacy Title
Publication: Premiere

395
Art Director: Robert Best
            David Walters
Designer: Robert Best
            David Walters
Illustrator: Gary Halgren
Copywriter: Jack Barth
            Trey Ellis
Publication: Premiere

396
Art Director: Robert Best
            David Walters
Designer: Robert Best
            David Walters
            Mary Ann Salvato
Photographer: Terry O'Neill
Copywriter: Phoebe Hoban
Publication: Premiere

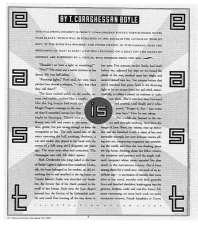

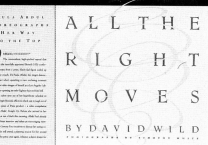

397
Art Director: Fred Woodward
Designer: Debra Bishop
Illustrator: Tom Curry
Publication: Rolling Stone

398
Art Director: Fred Woodward
Designer: Debra Bishop
Photographer: Timothy White
Publication: Rolling Stone

399
Art Director: Robert Best
            David Walters
Designer: Robert Best
            David Walters
            Mary Ann Salvato
Illustrator: Kam Mak
Copywriter: Jon Bowermaster
Publication: Premiere

400
Art Director: Robert Best
            David Walters
Designer: Robert Best
            David Walters
            Mary Ann Salvato
Illustrator: Daniel Torres
Copywriter: Rex Reed
Publication: Premiere

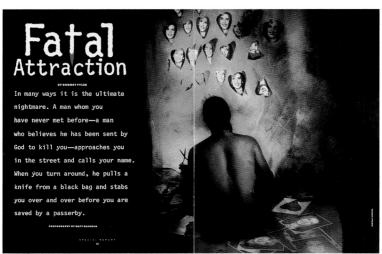

401
Art Director: Doug Renfro
Creative Director: Jim Darilek
Designer: Doug Renfro
Photographer: Matt Mahurin
Publication: Special Report: Personalities

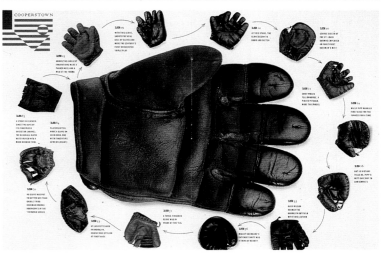

402
Art Director: Steven Hoffman
Designer: Darrin Perry
Photographer: Bret Wills
Publication: Sports Illustrated

403

Art Director: Fred Woodward
Designer: Gail Anderson
Photographer: Deborah Feingold
Publication: Rolling Stone

404

Art Director: Janet Froelich
Designer: Nancy Harris
Illustrator: Douglas Smith
Publication: The *New York Times*

405

Art Director: Janet Froelich
Designer: Janet Froelich
Illustrator: Matt Mahurin
Publication: The *New York Times*

406

Art Director: Mary Workman
Designer: Timothy W. Brown
Illustrator: Steven Madson
Publication: Tennessee Illustrated

407

Art Director: Robert Best
David Walters
Designer: Mary Ann Salvato
Photographer: Terry O'Neill
Publication: Premiere

408

Art Director: Robert Best
David Walters
Designer: Robert Best
David Walters
Mary Ann Salvato
Photographer: Terry O'Neill
Copywriter: Edmund White
Publication: Premiere

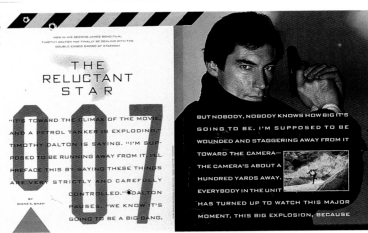

409

Art Director: Robert Best
David Walters
Designer: Robert Best
Photographer: Douglas Kirkland
Copywriter: Diane K. Shaw
Publication: Premiere

410

Art Director: Robert Best
David Walters
Designer: Robert Best
David Walters
Mary Ann Salvato
Photographer: Kobal Collection
Copywriter: Howard Gensler
Publication: Premiere

411
Art Director: D. J. Stout
Designer: D. J. Stout
Photographer: William Coupon
Publication: Texas Monthly

412
Art Director: Tom Bentkowski
Designer: Nora Sheehan
Photographer: Bettina Rheims
              Steven Meisel
Publication: Life Magazine

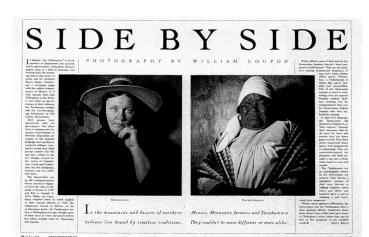

413
Art Director: Andrew Gray
Creative Director: Stephen Doyle
Photographer: Kei Ogata
　　　　　Raymond Meier
Agency: Drenttel Doyle Partners
Client: In Fashion

414
Art Director: Randy L. Dunbar
Photographer: Carin Riley
　　　　　David Riley
Publication: Home Magazine

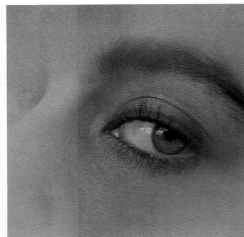

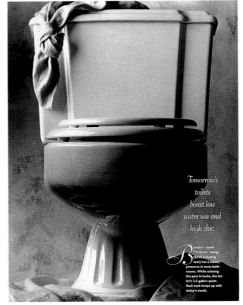

Am
I
Blue?

Everyone is blue now and then.
But this season the blues take on a
colorful mood with a brand new
attitude. Gone are the days of
kitschy, suburban blues and harsh
color applied for shock effect.
Today's blue makeup is applied
with a light touch for a look that's
soft, moody and romantic. "Anyone can wear blue," says makeup
artist Michele Yoyski. "It's the
conventional color for eyes and,
blended properly, can be worn on
lips and cheeks, too. But it has to
be used with care." It's the rebirth
of the blues—sensuous and subtle.

Tomorrow's
toilets
boast low
water use and
high chic.

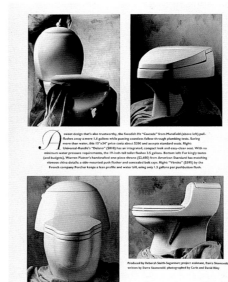

Am
I
Blue?

PORTRAITS IN PORCELAIN
A gallery of new toilet designs from discreet to divine

415
Art Director: Diana LaGuardia
Designer: Chris Gangi
Photographer: Helmut Newton
Publication: Conde Nast Traveler

416
Art Director: Tuan Dao
Creative Director: Mary Russell
Designer: Tuan Dao
Photographer: Jeremy Stitger
Publication: Taxi Magazine

HELMUT NEWTON re-creates in the Tuscan spa town of Montecatini Terme the forbidden romantic drama of his youth, and we mark your card for a visit

The Burning Secret

THE FILMING OF STEFAN ZWEIG'S STORY "The Burning Secret," starring Faye Dunaway and Klaus Maria Brandauer, touched the imagination of photographer Helmut Newton. He writes: "In my parents' apartment in Berlin there was a big library. Some of the books were under lock and key, out of bounds to my twelve-year-old eyes. But I was an avid reader and an adept thief, and always managed to get these forbidden books out of the case and smuggle them into my bedroom, where I read them at night under my blanket by flashlight. My eyesight may have been permanently impaired, but it was all worth the trouble, because those books were the most exciting events in my life. One of the best reads was Stefan Zweig's 'The Burning Secret,' and I still have it by my bedside. Its setting, the spa at Semmering, in Austria, reminds me vividly of the many summers I spent with my parents in just such places, being bored, getting into trouble, ogling the girls, and watching my older brother falling in love with the *gouvernantes* employed by the hotels. Here is my little *photo roman*, photographed before I saw the movie, retelling the story of 'The Burning Secret,' with words from it—only I have set my interpretation in the Italian spa town of Montecatini Terme, in Tuscany. It is early summer. A beautiful woman arrives to take the cure with her young son, Edgar, physically weak and sensitive. She is bored and falls ready victim to another spa guest, a baron from a minor Austrian noble line, a thorough cad and womanizer who befriends the boy in order to make the mother his mistress. Edgar meantime becomes intent on discovering once and for all the forbidden secret of adult life."

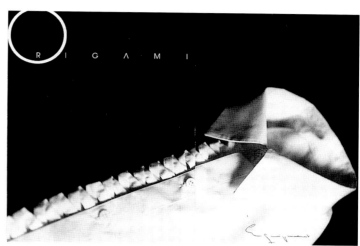

"The hunter in him scented a prey. Provocatively he tried to hold her eye with his, for sometimes she looked past him with a lively but uncertain glance. . . . He thought, too, he could detect the hint of a smile beginning to play around her lips. But he couldn't be certain, and the uncertainty itself excited him"

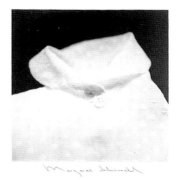

"She jumped up, responding to the initial shock, and realized at once just how far she had rashly ventured. She was, after all, no stranger to playing with fire, but now her awakened instinct told her how close this game had already come to the danger point. She didn't feel sure of her self-control."

HOW TO ENJOY MONTECATINI

417
Art Director: D. J. Stout
Designer: D. J. Stout
Illustrator: Ian Pollock
 Philip Burke
 Anita Kunz
Publication: Texas Monthly

418
Art Director: Diana LaGuardia
Designer: Chris Gangi
Photographer: Helmut Newton
Publication: Conde Nast Traveler

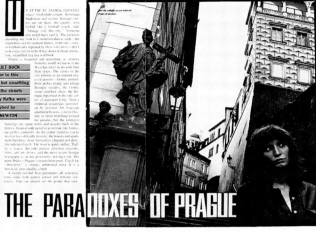

419
Art Director: Tom Bentkowski
Designer: Nora Sheehan
Publication: Life Magazine

420
Art Director: Tom Bentkowski
Designer: Nora Sheehan
Photographer: Mary Ellen Mark
Publication: Life Magazine

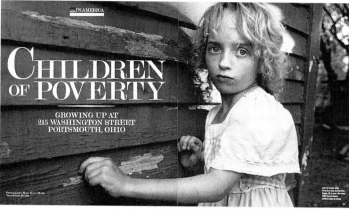

421

Art Director: Roberto Burroni
            Karen Wells Verlander
Creative Director: Regis Pagniez
Photographer: Edouard Sicot
Publication: Elle Decor Magazine

422

Art Director: D. J. Stout
Designer: D. J. Stout
Photographer: Danny Turner
Publication: Texas Monthly

Washington's premier chef goes shopping

BATTERIE DE CUISINE

"Baking has its own basics."

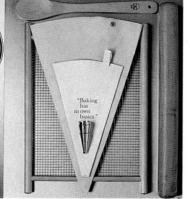

Jean-Louis Palladin chooses nothing but the best

A BRUSH WITH LIFE

WANDA FORD

LYNN WYATT

ROBERT L. B. TOBIN

SARAH LEA

MRS. LEE T. BIVINS

VALENTINE HOBCHOW

423
Art Director: D. J. Stout
Designer: D. J. Stout
Photographer: Matt Mahurin
Publication: Texas Monthly

424
Art Director: D. J. Stout
Designer: D. J. Stout
Photographer: Doug Milner
Publication: Texas Monthly

ABORTION STREET

At a nondescript office building in Dallas, two sides wage endless war over an unresolvable question.

by Mimi Swartz.

PHOTOGRAPHY BY MATT MAHURIN

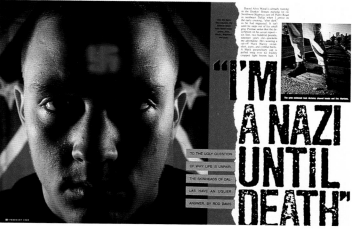

"I'M A NAZI UNTIL DEATH"

TO THE UGLY QUESTION

OF WHY LIFE IS UNFAIR,

THE SKINHEADS OF DAL-

LAS HAVE AN UGLIER

ANSWER. BY ROD DAVIS

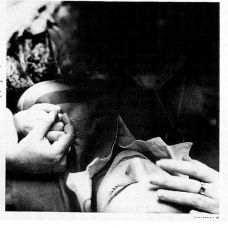

THE ONLY LAW WE GO

BY IS THE GOOD BOOK'S

LAW. I KNOW THAT WE

WILL BE PERSECUTED."

CHOOSE LIFE!

SENTENCED TO DEATH!

ALICE FOUND BASEBALL

BATS, RED SPRAY PAINT,

AND A NAZI FLAG IN THE

BACK OF THE PICKUP.

425
Art Director: D. J. Stout
Designer: D. J. Stout
Photographer: Kurt Markus
Publication: Texas Monthly

426
Art Director: D. J. Stout
Designer: D. J. Stout
Illustrator: Richard Mantel
    Braldt Bralds
    Etienne Delessert
    Marshall Arisman
    Alex Murawski
Publication: Texas Monthly

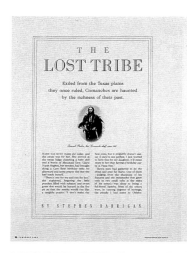

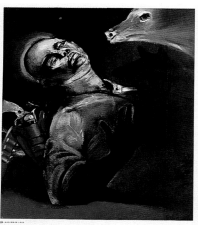

427
Art Director: Steven Hoffman
Designer: Craig Gartner
Publication: Sports Illustrated

428
Art Director: D. J. Stout
Designer: D. J. Stout
Photographer: Sally Gall
Publication: Texas Monthly

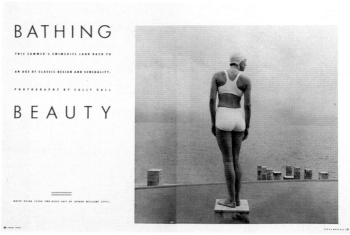

429
Art Director: Steven Hoffman
Designer: Craig Gartner
Photographer: Gregory Heisler
Publication: Sports Illustrated

430
Art Director: Tom Bentkowski
Designer: Nora Sheehan
Publication: Life Magazine

THEY

Five accomplished athletes, disabled while performing

NEVER

their sports, faced their most difficult challenge and

GAVE

succeeded, against enormous odds, in building new lives

UP

*Text
by
RICHARD
HOFFER*

*Photographs
by
GREGORY
HEISLER*

His back broken
from a fall in '78,
Ron Turcotte lives
quietly at his home
in eastern Canada.

THE JOCKEY

DID YOU EVER SEE SECRE-tariat, a shimmer of speed and syncopation, charging out of the backstretch? What would you give to command that kind of locomotion? The ability to walk on your own feet for the rest of your life? The Jockey is weary of such riddles. He got a better deal than most riders. "Jockeys have died," he says. Anyway, to this day he gets a free copy of the *Daily Racing Form* in the mail. Some poor jockey who won only 10 races, he says, wouldn't rate that remembrance. "I'm a lucky man."

Paralyzed in a '88
crash, Bob Hart
still frequents
tracks with friend
Vivien Veerkamp.

THE DRIVER

HE IS INNOCENT OF THE irony involved when he putters along Gasoline Alley in his wheelchair, his own little car. He returns to the Indy 500 as often as he is able, but the sight of him there is neither morbid nor cautionary. Anybody can hit a slick spot, anybody can crash. The Driver is there for the same reason he was 21 years ago, when he backed into the Turn 1 wall. He likes the race, the action, the noise. The hurly-burly around him gives him an idea: "Maybe I could drive the pace car in the parade lap."

THE 1939 CLASSICS

As the Depression drew to an end, a quarter was the going rate for a pound of meat, one and a half gallons of gas, postage for eight letters (with a penny change), or a movie ticket. This last was a treat that America was unwilling to deny itself. Each week two thirds of the country visited the local Bijou to escape into a fresh cavalcade of newsreels, cartoons, previews and, more often than not, double features.

By 1939, 15,000 motion picture theaters (as opposed to 23,000 screens in the current multiplex era) were averaging 85 million paid admissions weekly—four times today's audience, or double the one that sits home to watch *The Cosby Show* for free. Neither the moviegoers nor the studios working overtime to entertain them could have guessed that Hollywood would never have as creative a year again.

The industry cranked out close to 400 movies, many of which were series as predictable as network television fare now: Dr. Kildare vs. diseases, Charlie Chan and Mr. Moto vs. criminals, Gene Autry vs. rustlers, Andy Hardy vs. his hor-

HOLLYWOOD WAS NEVER BETTER

mones. There were even alarums ripped straight from the newspaper headlines—*Confessions of a Nazi Spy*—similar to a modern movie-of-the-week. Yet the studios also crafted an inordinately large number of pictures that still have the power to captivate and enchant us a half century later. They deservedly can be called classics.

Hollywood's wonderful year had its beginnings long before in the breakthrough 1927 picture *The Jazz Singer*, which forced filmmakers to retool for talkies. The soundstages built to ensure quiet on the set also required directors and crews to master new equipment and effects. Writers had to graduate from producing truncated title cards to full-fledged dialogue. Performers could no longer be just pretty faces.

A dozen years later the industry was cruising at top gear. And its production was simply breathtaking: *Destry Rides Again, Gunga Din, The Hunchback of Notre Dame, Young Mr. Lincoln, Of Mice and Men, You Can't Cheat an Honest Man, Beau Geste* and—better still—the 10 evergreens that LIFE revisits on the following pages.

Another shift at the Dream Factory: James Stewart and Jean Arthur make their way to the set of *Mr. Smith Goes to Washington*, a golden oldie from the golden year.

25

431
Art Director: Albert Chiang
Photographer: Frans Lanting
Publication: Islands Magazine

432
Art Director: Michael Brock
Designer: Michael Brock
Photographer: Stuart Watson
Studio: Michael Brock Design
Client: LA Style

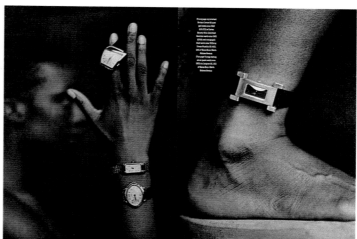

433
Art Director: Mary Workman
Designer: Timothy W. Brown
Photographer: Russell Monk
Publication: Tennessee Illustrated

434
Art Director: Diana LaGuardia
Designer: Catherine Caldwell
                Chris Gangi
                Audrey Razgaitis
Illustrator: Various
Photographer: Various
Publication: Conde Nast Traveler

435
Art Director: Paul Davis
Designer: Risa Zaitschek
Illustrator: Various
Photographer: Various
Client: Wigwag Magazine Co., Inc.

436
Art Director: Fred Woodward
Publication: Rolling Stone

437
Art Director: D. J. Stout
Designer: D. J. Stout
Publication: Texas Monthly

Terrorized by her husband's repeated death threats, Renee Linton did everything women are supposed to do to protect themselves under the system. Yet despite her calls for help, her court order of protection, her flights ‹Nowhere to Run› to a shelter for battered women, the system failed to save her.

By Ellen Hopkins

PHOTOGRAPH BY MATT MAHURIN

HOLY ART!

THE REVEREND HOWARD FINSTER IS SPREADING GOD'S WORD AS FAST AS HE CAN PAINT, AND FOR GALLERY GOERS AND ROCK STARS ALIKE, SEEING IS BELIEVING BY DAVID HANDELMAN

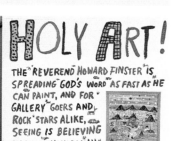

God's brushman can't get his sacred art finished 'cause the phone keeps a-ringing. He's got four paintings going—but there goes that phone again. "Somebody wantin' art!" exclaims Howard Finster. The awg seventy-three-year-old retired minister picks up the receiver and settles into a lumpy, torn vinyl chair in his Summerville, Georgia, studio. A gas heater blazes in the corner, fermenting the room's musty, doggy smell.

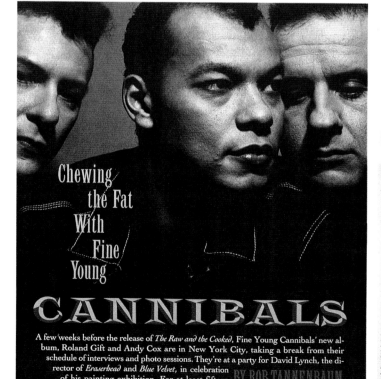

Chewing the Fat With Fine Young CANNIBALS

A few weeks before the release of *The Raw and the Cooked*, Fine Young Cannibals' new album, Roland Gift and Andy Cox are in New York City, taking a break from their schedule of interviews and photo sessions. They're at a party for David Lynch, the director of *Eraserhead* and *Blue Velvet*, in celebration of his painting exhibition. For at least fifteen

BY ROB TANNENBAUM

PHOTOGRAPHS BY NORMAN WATSON

DECEMBER 1989 · $1.95
All-American Crooks: What Went Wrong at Dallas' Carter High

Texas Monthly.

Wild Forever

A Sneak Preview of Big Bend Ranch, Texas' Rugged New Parkland

BY STEPHEN HARRIGAN · PHOTOGRAPHY BY MARK KLETT

THE ALL-

ONCE THEY WERE FOOTBALL

HEROES, BOUND FOR GLORY.

NOW THEY ARE FELONS,

AMERICAN

BOUND FOR PRISON. HERE

IS WHAT WENT WRONG

AT DALLAS' CARTER HIGH.

CROOKS

BY DANA RUBIN

ILLUSTRATION BY MATT MAHURIN

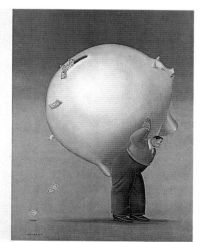

A Fool and his Money

I'VE TAKEN A PERSONAL FINANCE COURSE, SET UP A HOUSEHOLD BUDGET, AND KEPT MY 1972 VOLKSWAGEN. SO HOW COME I'M ALWAYS BROKE?

BY LAWRENCE WRIGHT

438
Art Director: Diana LaGuardia
Designer: Chris Gangi
         Audrey Razgaitis
Illustrator: Various
Photographer: Various
Publication: Conde Nast Traveler

439
Art Director: Fred Woodward
Publication: Rolling Stone

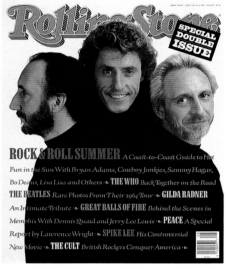

"I don't need this shit!" says *USA Today* gossip columnist Jeannie Williams. It's the morning of May 19th, and Williams has just seen the breakfast press screening of *Do the Right Thing* at the Cannes film festival. Tonight, the film will have its black-tie, red-carpet gala première at the Palais des Festivals, on the Côte d'Azur beach, where it will be competing with films from around the world for the coveted Palm d'Or prize. This morning, the more modest Palais press-confer-

Director Spike Lee's 'Do the Right Thing' Takes a Provocative Look at Race Relations
By David Handelman

PART ONE: THE SHIFT   Most of us have lived our entire lives with the threat of the cold war, the terror of nuclear annihilation. But now, for the first time in memory, peace–not war–is breaking out around the world. From Moscow to Washington, the old assumptions are falling away, and a new and vastly different era is coming into being. After all the darkness and carnage of the twentieth century, is man finally ready to give up his most catastrophic habit– the urge to make war?   BY LAWRENCE WRIGHT

440

Art Director: Shoshanna Sommer
Creative Director: Dan Barron
Designer: Shoshanna Sommer
Illustrator: Philippe Weisbecker
Publication: Art Direction

441

Art Director: Scott Menchin
Creative Director: Scott Menchin
Designer: Scott Menchin
Photographer: Susan Schelling
Publication: How

442

Art Director: Claude Skelton
Designer: Claude Skelton
Illustrator: Anthony Russo
Publication: Warfield's

443

Art Director: Claude Skelton
Designer: Claude Skelton
Photographer: C. Paul Haynes
Publication: Warfield's

444

Art Director: Claude Skelton
Designer: Claude Skelton
Photographer: Tom Wolff
Publication: Warfield's

445

Art Director: David Lerch
Designer: David Lerch
Illustrator: David Lerch
Studio: Peterson & Co.
Client: Southern Methodist University

458 Silver

Art Director: Jose Camejo
Designer: Jose Camejo
Photographer: J. C. Alonso
Client: Turbana Corp.

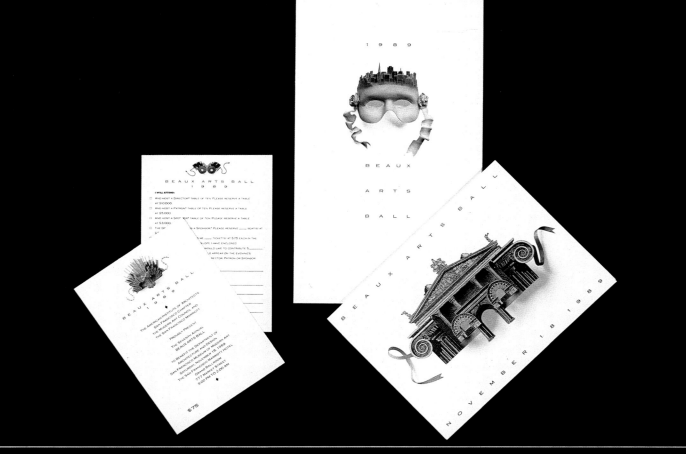

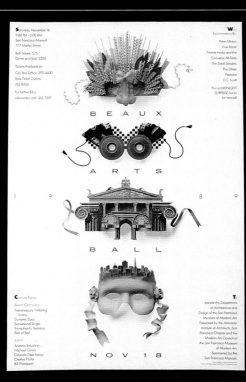

459 Silver

Art Director: **Kit Hinrichs**
Designer: **Kit Hinrichs**
Susan Tsuchiya
Photographer: **Barry Robinson**
Studio: **Pentagram**
Client: **San Francisco Museum of Modern Art**
San Francisco Institute of Architects

460 Silver
Art Director: Dick Lemmon
Creative Director: Jan Zechman
Designer: Dick Lemmon
Client: Illinois Film Office

FILM

461 Distinctive Merit
Art Director: John Van Dyke
Creative Director: John Van Dyke
Designer: John Van Dyke

462 Distinctive Merit
Art Director: Thomas Ryan
Designer: Cathy Wayland
Photographer: McGuire
Copywriter: John Baeder
Studio: Thomas Ryan Design
Client: Cracker Barrel Old Country Stores, Inc.

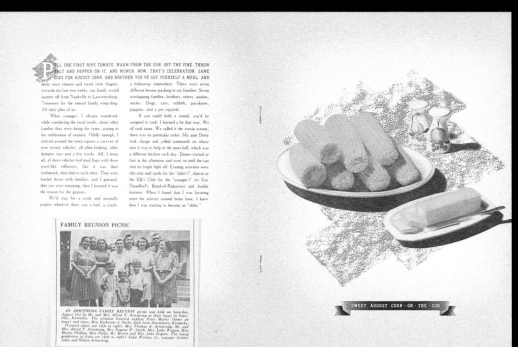

463 Distinctive Merit
Art Director: Linda Hinrichs
Designer: Linda Hinrichs
Natalie Kitamura
Photographer: Barry Robinson
Copywriter: Delphine Hirasuna
Studio: Pentagram
Client: Pentagram

Yee-Ping Cho
Illustrator: Various
Photographer: Various
Copywriter: Jane Arnold
Maxwell Arnold
Studio: Cross Associates, A Siegel & Gale Co.
Client: Simpson Paper Co.

465 Distinctive Merit
Art Director: Stacy Drummond
Designer: Stacy Drummond
Illustrator: Ann Field
Agency: CBS Records

466 Distinctive Merit
Art Director: Jeff Larson
Scott Johnson
Designer: Scott Johnson
Jeff Larson
Agency: Larson Design Associates
Client: Larson Design Associates

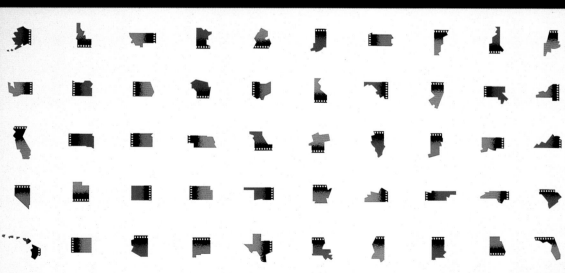

USA FILM FESTIVAL XIX

APRIL 13-19 AMC GLEN LAKES THEATRES DALLAS, TEXAS

467 Distinctive Merit
Art Director: Kenny Garrison
Creative Director: Kenny Garrison
Designer: Kenny Garrison
Studio: Richards Brock Miller Mitchell & Assoc.
Client: USA Film Festival/Dallas

468 Distinctive Merit
Art Director: Minoru Morita
Designer: Minoru Morita

469
Art Director: Barbara Vick
Designer: Barbara Vick
Illustrator: Miro Salazar
Copywriter: Linda Peterson
Agency: SBG Partners
Client: Capital Guaranty

470
Art Director: Bill Tomlinson
Creative Director: Bill Tomlinson
Designer: Bill Tomlinson
Illustrator: Jon Ellis
Copywriter: Cathleen Toomey
　　　　　　Mark Melton
Studio: Tomlinson Advertising Design
Client: Timberland Co.

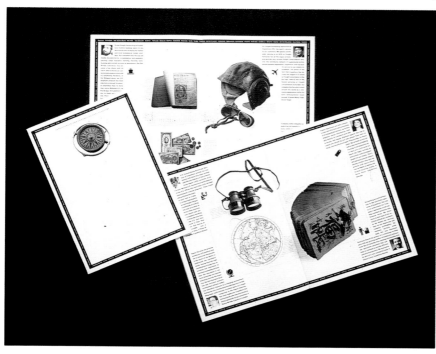

471
Art Director: John Van Dyke
Creative Director: John Van Dyke
Designer: John Van Dyke
Photographer: Cliff Fiess
Copywriter: Rick Moss
Agency: Van Dyke Co.
Client: Expeditors International

472
Art Director: Peter Harrison
　　　　　　Harold Burch
Designer: Harold Burch
　　　　　Peter Harrison
Illustrator: Gene Greif
Copywriter: John Berendt
　　　　　　Warner Communications
Studio: Pentagram Design
Client: Warner Communications Inc.

473
Art Director: Kit Hinrichs
Designer: Kit Hinrichs
    Belle How
Copywriter: Valoree Dowell
Studio: Pentagram
Client: Immunex Corp.

474
Art Director: Brian Boyd
Designer: Brian Boyd
Illustrator: John Craig
Photographer: Robert Latorre
Copywriter: Kevin Orlin Johnson
Studio: Richards Brock Miller Mitchell & Assoc.
Client: Chili's, Inc.

475
Art Director: Dale Lamson
Creative Director: Dale Lamson
Designer: Dale Lamson
Photographer: Greg Grosse
Copywriter: Dale Lamson
Studio: Lamson Design

476
Art Director: Lynn Bernick
    Doug May
Designer: Lynn Bernick
Photographer: Various
Copywriter: Lisa Cobb
Studio: May & Co.
Client: Cobb & Friend

477

Art Director: Tjody Overson
Illustrator: Various
Copywriter: Mike Gibbs
Agency: McCool & Co.
Client: Weyerhaeuser

478

Art Director: Larry Brooks
　　　　　Kosh
Designer: Larry Brooks
　　　　　Kosh
Illustrator: Larry Brooks
　　　　　Kosh
Copywriter: John Timpane
Studio: Kosh/Brooks
Client: Champion International

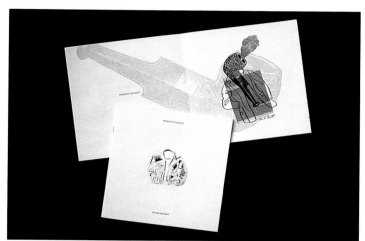

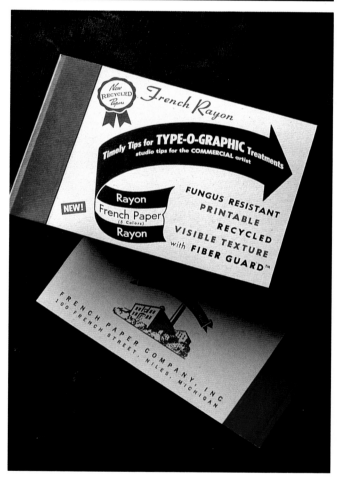

479

Art Director: Charles S. Anderson
　　　　　Dan Olson
Designer: Charles S. Anderson
　　　　　Dan Olson
Illustrator: Randy Dahlk
Copywriter: Lisa Pemrick
Studio: Charles S. Anderson Design
Client: French Paper Co.

480

Art Director: Charles S. Anderson
　　　　　Dan Olson
Designer: Charles S. Anderson
　　　　　Dan Olson
Photographer: Various
Copywriter: Jon Anderson
Studio: Charles S. Anderson Design
Client: Goldsmith, Aigo & Co.

481
Art Director: Andrée Cordella
Creative Director: Andrée Cordella
Designer: Andrée Cordella
Illustrator: Rob Howard
            Andrew Berry
Photographer: Geoffrey Stein
Copywriter: Andrée Cordella
Studio: Cordella Design
Client: Gilbert Paper Co.

482
Art Director: Kevin Prejean
Creative Director: Willie Baronet
Designer: Kevin Prejean
Illustrator: Lynn Rowe Reed
Copywriter: Poppy Sundeen
Agency: Knape&Knape
Client: HCA Medical Center of Plano

483
Art Director: Leslee Avchen
            Laurie Jacobi
Designer: Leslee Avchen
            Laurie Jacobi
Photographer: Terry Heffernan
Copywriter: Cynthia Zwirn
Studio: Avchen & Jacobi, Inc.
Client: Consolidated Papers, Inc.

484
Art Director: John Sayles
Illustrator: John Sayles
Copywriter: LeAnn Koerner
Studio: Sayles Graphic Design
Client: Professional Match Consultants

485
Art Director: Charles S. Anderson
Designer: Charles S. Anderson
Photographer: Gary McCoy
Copywriter: Chuck Carlson
Studio: The Duffy Group
Client: Dorsey & Whitney

486
Art Director: Charles S. Anderson
Designer: Charles S. Anderson
                Dan Olson
Photographer: James Williams
Copywriter: Lisa Pemrick
Studio: Charles S. Anderson Design
Client: Pantone, Inc.

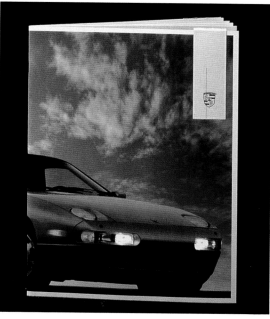

487
Art Director: Brent Croxton
Creative Director: Bob Manley
Designer: Brent Croxton
Illustrator: Brian Cronin
Copywriter: Craig Walker
Agency: Altman & Manley
Client: Group Health Plan

488
Art Director: Joe Duffy
Designer: Joe Duffy
                Haley Johnson
Illustrator: Jan Evans
                Lynn Schulte
Photographer: Jeff Zwart
Copywriter: Chuck Carlson
Studio: The Duffy Group
Client: Porsche

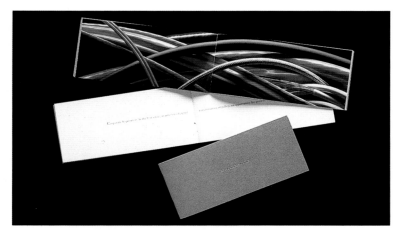

489
Art Director: John Van Dyke
Creative Director: John Van Dyke
Designer: John Van Dyke
Photographer: Doug Evans
Copywriter: Brian McKenna
Agency: Van Dyke Co.
Client: The Northern Group

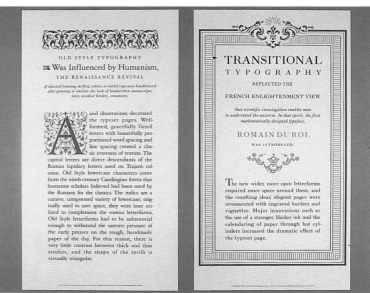

490
Art Director: Leah Toby Hoffmitz
Creative Director: Leah Toby Hoffmitz
Designer: Terry Irwin
        Leah Toby Hoffmitz
Copywriter: Leah Toby Hoffmitz
        Shawn Woodyard
Studio: Letterform Design
Client: Characters & Color

491
Art Director: Jean McCartney
Creative Director: Bryan Dixon
Designer: Jean McCartney
Photographer: Steven Randazzo
Client: West Point Pepperell

492
Art Director: Andrew Gray
Creative Director: Thomas Kluepfel
Photographer: George Hein
Agency: Drenttel Doyle Partners
Client: Arrow Co.

493
Art Director: Vic Cevoli
Creative Director: Vic Cevoli
Designer: John Avery
Photographer: Clint Clemens
Copywriter: Neill Ray
Agency: Hill, Holliday
Client: Nissan Infiniti

494
Art Director: Tyler Smith
Creative Director: Tyler Smith
Designer: Tyler Smith
Photographer: George Petrakes
Copywriter: Steve Battista
Studio: Tyler Smith
Client: Fox River Paper

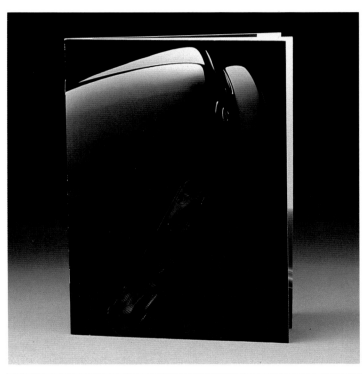

495
Art Director: Jerry Takigawa
Creative Director: Jerry Takigawa
Designer: Jerry Takigawa
      LeAnn Hansen
Photographer: Batista Moon Studio
      Westlight
Copywriter: Gay Machado
Studio: Jerry Takigawa Design
Client: Metricom Inc.

496
Art Director: Jack Byrne
Creative Director: Jack Byrne
Designer: Jack Byrne
Photographer: Symore Mednick
Copywriter: Phil Yadinsky
Studio: Design Resource, Inc.
Client: Design Resource, Inc.

497
Art Director: Karen Kornblum
Creative Director: Kevin Maginnis
Designer: Karen Kornblum
Photographer: Various
Copywriter: Bobbe Kendall
Client: Siemens Medical Systems

498
Art Director: Sharon Werner
Designer: Sharon Werner
Illustrator: Sharon Werner
Photographer: James Williams
Copywriter: Chuck Carlson
Studio: The Duffy Group
Client: D'Amico Cucina

499
Art Director: Martin Stevers
Designer: Martin Stevers
Illustrator: Jennifer Hewitson
Photographer: Dave Harrison
Copywriter: Ken Alfrey
Studio: Grayson
Client: The Baldwin Co.

500
Art Director: Janet Odgis
Creative Director: Janet Odgis
Designer: Janet Odgis
          Elizabeth Bakacs
          Richard Manville
Illustrator: Various
Photographer: Various
Copywriter: Paul Rosenthal
Client: Champion International

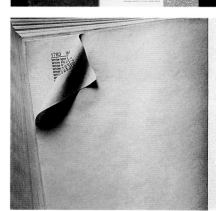

501

Art Director: Sharon Werner
Designer: Sharon Werner
Illustrator: Charles Burns
Copywriter: Chuck Carlson
Studio: The Duffy Group
Client: Fox River Paper

502

Art Director: Janis Koy
Designer: Janis Koy
            Michelle Freisenhahn
Photographer: Bob Cardellino
            Jim Keller
Client: Bexar County Hospital District Auxiliary

503

Art Director: Tom Schifanella
Creative Director: Robin Shepherd
Copywriter: Amanda Townsend
Studio: Robin Shepherd Studios

504

Art Director: Kit Hinrichs
Designer: Susie Leversee
Copywriter: Jeff Atlas
Studio: Pentagram
Client: Aspen Skiing Co.

505
Art Director: Andrea Kelley
Creative Director: Paul Pruneau
Designer: Andrea Kelley
Photographer: Bill Gallery
Copywriter: Brad Londy
Agency: Apple Communications Design
Client: Apple Computer Inc.

506
Art Director: Terry Koppel
Creative Director: Terry Koppel
Designer: Terry Koppel
Illustrator: Various
Copywriter: Peter Hauck
Studio: Koppel & Scher
Client: Queens Group

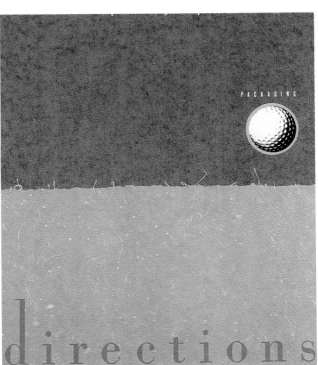

507
Art Director: Emil Micha
Designer: Elliot Schneider
Illustrator: Roy Weiman
Copywriter: Charles Decker

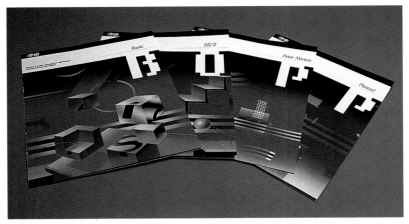

508
Art Director: Amy Watt
            Ann Dakis
            Margaret McGovern
Creative Director: Paul Silverman
Photographer: John Holt
                Eric Meola
Copywriter: Peter Pappas
Agency: Mullen
Client: Timberland Co.

509

Art Director: David Edelstein
Lanny French
Rick Jost
Photographer: Nick Vacarro
Copywriter: David N. Meyer II
Agency: Edelstein Associates
Client: Generra Sportswear

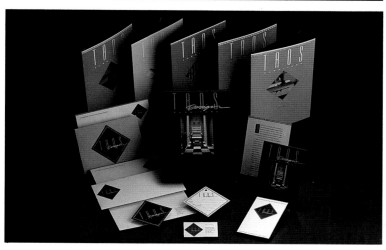

510

Art Director: Rick Vaughn
Creative Director: Rick Vaughn
Designer: Rick Vaughn
Photographer: Robert Reck
Copywriter: Richard Kuhn
Studio: Vaughn/Wedeen Creative
Client: Taos Furniture

511

Art Director: David Edelstein
Lanny French
Rick Jost
Eric Haggard
Photographer: Veronica Simm
Copywriter: David N. Meyer II
Agency: Edelstein Associates
Client: Generra Sportswear

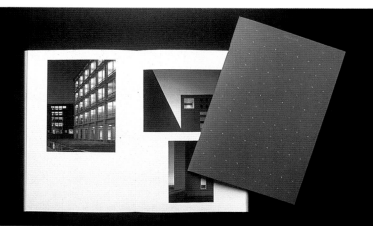

512

Art Director: Lowell Williams
Creative Director: Lowell Williams
Designer: Lana Rigsby
Illustrator: Andy Dearwater
Photographer: Nick Merrick
Copywriter: JoAnn Stone
Studio: Lowell Williams Design Inc.
Client: Maguire Thomas Partners

513
Art Director: Scott Mires
Designer: Scott Mires
Illustrator: Gerry Bustamante
Copywriter: Barry Boyt
Agency: Mires Design
Client: First Capital Life

514
Art Director: Vic Cevoli
Creative Director: Vic Cevoli
Designer: John Avery
Photographer: Clint Clemens
Copywriter: Neill Ray
Agency: Hill, Holliday
Client: Nissan Infiniti

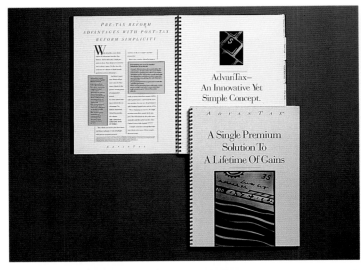

515
Art Director: Doreen Caldera
Designer: Doreen Caldera
  Bart Welch
  Paul Caldera
  Dave Kottler
Copywriter: Leslie Johnson
Photographer: Rodney Rascona
  Dugald Bremner

516
Art Director: James Sebastian
  John Plunkett
Designer: John Plunkett
  Thomas Schneider
  David Reiss
Photographer: Neil Selkirk
  Jody Dole
Client: The L•S Collection

517
Art Director: Bob Dennard
Creative Director: Bob Dennard
Designer: Chuck Johnson
           Art Garcia
           Brad Wines
Illustrator: Various
Photographer: Various
Agency: Dennard Creative, Inc.
Client: Herring Marathon Group

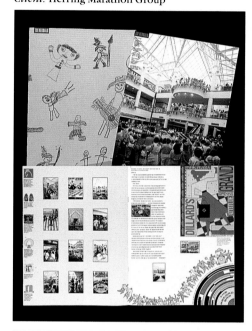
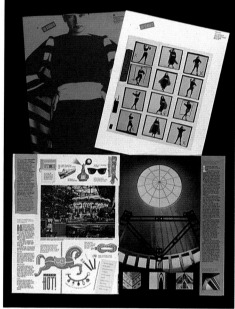

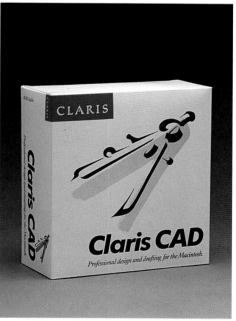

518
Art Director: John Warwicker
Studio: Vivid ID
Client: CBS Records

519
Art Director: Faye H. Eng
              Anthony T. Yee
Designer: Faye H. Eng
           Anthony T. Yee
Photographer: Schecter Lee
Studio: Eng & Yee Designs, Inc.
Client: Museum of American Folk Art

520
Art Director: Marty Neumeier
Designer: Marty Neumeier
           Chris Chu
Illustrator: Chris Chu
             Curtis Wong
Copywriter: Marty Neumeier
             Desiree LaGrone
Studio: Neumeier Design Team
Client: Claris Corp.

521
Art Director: Jennifer Morla
Designer: Jennifer Morla
    Marianne Mitten
Illustrator: Jennifer Morla
    Marianne Mitten
Client: Spectrum Foods

522
Art Director: Charles S. Anderson
    Dan Olson
Designer: Charles S. Anderson
    Dan Olson
Illustrator: Charles S. Anderson
    Dan Olson
Photographer: James Williams
Studio: Charles S. Anderson Design
Client: Aravis Distilleries

523
Art Director: Charles S. Anderson
    Dan Olson
Designer: Charles S. Anderson
    Dan Olson
Illustrator: Charles S. Anderson
    Dan Olson
Photographer: James Williams
Studio: Charles S. Anderson Design
Client: Aravis Distilleries

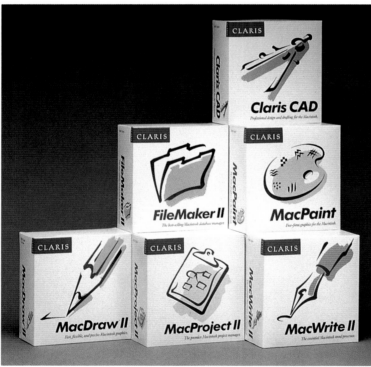

524
Art Director: Marty Neumeier
Designer: Marty Neumeier
    Chris Chu
Illustrator: Chris Chu
    Curtis Wong
Copywriter: Marty Neumeier
    Desiree LaGrone
Studio: Neumeier Design Team
Client: Claris Corp.

525
Art Director: Charles S. Anderson
    Dan Olson
Designer: Charles S. Anderson
    Dan Olson
Illustrator: Charles S. Anderson
    Dan Olson
Photographer: James Williams
Studio: Charles S. Anderson Design
Client: Aravis Distilleries

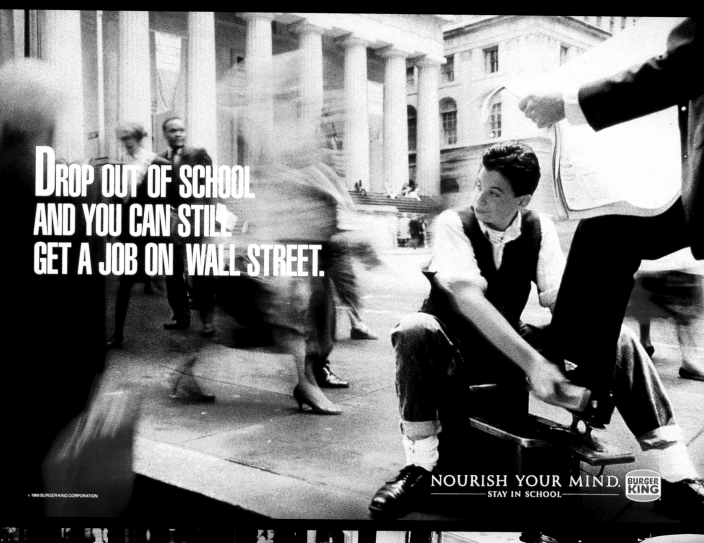

558 Silver
Art Director: David Meador
David Leinwohl
Creative Director: David Hale
Copywriter: Alison Grant
Agency: D'Arcy Masius Benton & Bowles

SO WHAT. DID SHE EVER WIN A HOMBURG?

ANNOUNCING THE 9TH ANNUAL HOMBURG AWARDS — SPONSORED BY THE ADVERTISING CLUB OF SAN DIEGO

YEAH. BUT DID HE EVER WIN A HOMBURG?

ANNOUNCING THE 9TH ANNUAL HOMBURG AWARDS — SPONSORED BY THE ADVERTISING CLUB OF SAN DIEGO

IMPRESSIVE. BUT DID SHE EVER WIN A HOMBURG?

ANNOUNCING THE 9TH ANNUAL HOMBURG AWARDS — SPONSORED BY THE ADVERTISING CLUB OF SAN DIEGO

559 Silver
Art Director: Wade Koniakowsky
Mike Hall
Creative Director: Jim Winters
Copywriter: Bob Kerstetter
Bryan Behar
Agency: Franklin & Associates

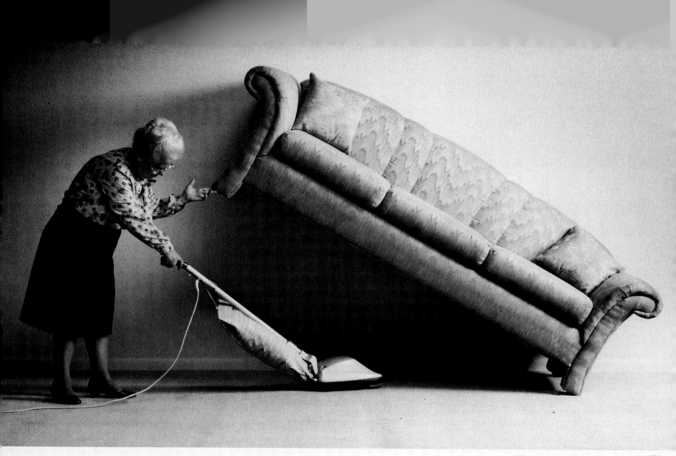

Handy packets of spirulina and natural energizers. For when you need a lift.

Handy packets of spirulina and natural energizers. For those demanding sports.

Handy packets of Spirulina and natural energizers. Stamina for the big event.

561 Distinctive Merit
Art Director: Mark Johnson
Photographer: Jeff Zwart
Copywriter: Tom McElligott
Agency: Fallon McElligott
Client: Porsche

Unclogs major arteries.

Porsche 911 Carrera

(Dealer Name)

Some women will never talk to anyone about being abused.

L.A. BATTERING HOTLINE (213) 392-8381

565 Distinctive Merit

Art Director: Jon Lee
Marty Weiss
Creative Director: Bill Hamilton
Photographer: Mark Weiss
Copywriter: Paula Dombrow
Robin Raj
Agency: Chiat/Day/Mojo Advertising Inc.
Client: NYNEX Information Resources

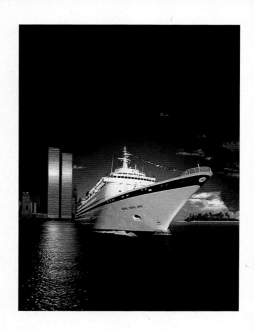

566 Distinctive Merit

Art Director: Rich Silverstein
Creative Director: Jeffrey Goodby
Rich Silverstein
Designer: Betsy Zimmermann
Photographer: Jay Maisel
Copywriter: David Fowler
Agency: Goodby, Berlin & Silverstein
Client: Royal Viking Line

567 Distinctive Merit
Art Director: Jon Lee
Marty Weiss
Creative Director: Bill Hamilton
Photographer: Mark Weiss
Copywriter: Paula Dombrow
Robin Raj
Agency: Chiat/Day/Mojo Advertising Inc.
Client: NYNEX Information Resources

568 Distinctiv
Art Director: Nic
Copywriter: Ty N
Agency: Chiat/Day/Mojc
Client: Pointed Sti

BRECHT'S "DRUMS IN THE NIGHT"
OHIO THEATRE 66 WOOSTER STREET SOHO NYC
NOV 23 - DEC 3 TUESDAY - SUNDAY AT 8.00 PM
$10 (STUDENTS & SENIORS $6) RES: (212) 924 0413
THANKSGIVING PERFORMANCE AND FEAST $30 ($15)
CHAMPAGNE BENEFIT PERFORMANCE (THURSDAY NOV 30) $25
TEXT TRANSLATION BY WILLIAM E SMITH AND RALPH MANHEIM
TINY MYTHIC THEATRE COMPANY   AN EQUITY APPROVED SHOWCASE

TINY MYTHIC THEATRE COMPANY
KRISTIN AMES   FRANCINE ZERFAS   KRISTIN MARTING
TIM MANER   WITH   DAVID BEACH*   BRIAN BEDLIN   LOREN KIDD
DANIEL BLACKMAN   CALVIN CHURCHMAN   MARTY FINKELSTEIN
CINDY DORREL   GEORGE FEASTER*   DAVID MAIER   JOHN MILLER
JAMES FERGUSON   ABIGAIL GAMPEL   RICHARD MORTIMER*
NOAH GARDINER   STEVEN CHESLIK-DEMEYER   JENI STERNBERG
*APPEARS COURTESY OF THE ACTORS' EQUITY ASSOCIATION

A GERMAN COMEDY

WORKS IN PROGRESS 🐧 THE SCIENCE MUSEUM OF MINNESOTA

570 Distinctive Merit
Art Director: McRay Magleby
Creative Director: McRay Magleby
Designer: McRay Magleby
Copywriter: Norman Darais
Studio: BYU Graphics

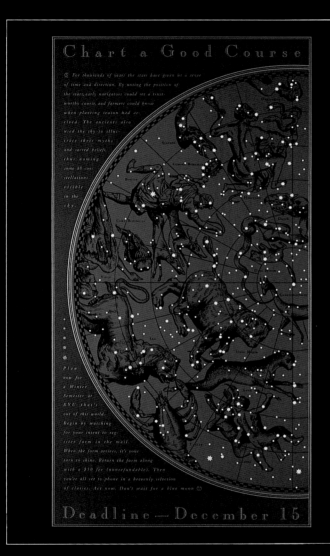

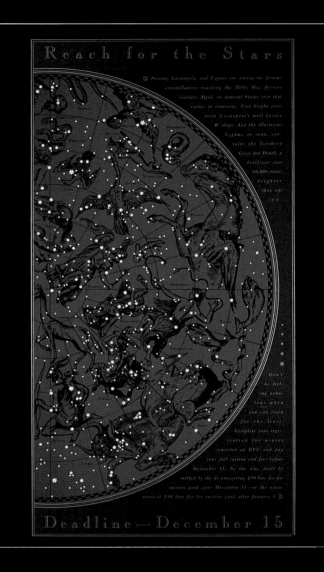

571
Art Director: Mike Martin
Creative Director: Jim Armstrong
Photographer: Shawn Harper
Copywriter: Jim Armstrong
Agency: Armstrong Creative
Client: Madison Advertising Federation

572
Art Director: David Meador
Creative Director: David Hale
Copywriter: Alison Grant

573
Art Director: Mark Johnson
Photographer: Jeff Zwart
Copywriter: Tom McElligott
Agency: Fallon McElligott
Client: Porsche

574
Art Director: Jeff Weekley
Creative Director: John Armistead
Illustrator: Stan Watts
Copywriter: Pieter Dreiband
Agency: DMB&B

575
Art Director: Vickery Eckhoff
Creative Director: Vickery Eckhoff
Copywriter: Vickery Eckhoff
Client: Friends of Animals

576
Art Director: Mike Martin
Creative Director: Jim Armstrong
Photographer: Shawn Harper
Copywriter: Jim Armstrong
Agency: Armstrong Creative
Client: Madison Advertising Federation

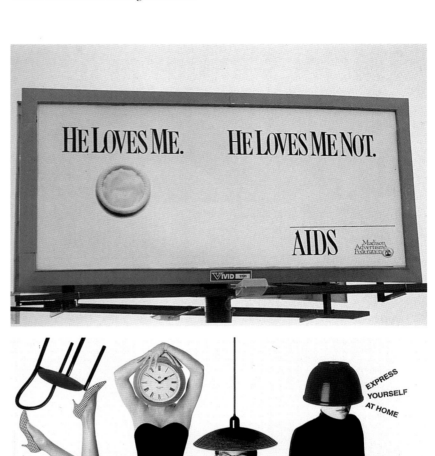

577
Art Director: Gretchen van der Grinten
                Janet Boye
Photographer: Davies & Starr
Copywriter: Sarah Person
Agency: Conran's Habitat

578
Art Director: Mark Johnson
Creative Director: Tom McElligott
Photographer: Jeff Zwart
Copywriter: Tom McElligott
Agency: Fallon McElligott
Client: Porsche

579
Art Director: Silas H. Rhodes
Creative Director: Silas H. Rhodes
Designer: Tony Palladino
Illustrator: Tony Palladino
Copywriter: Dee Ito
Studio: School of Visual Arts Press
Client: School of Visual Arts

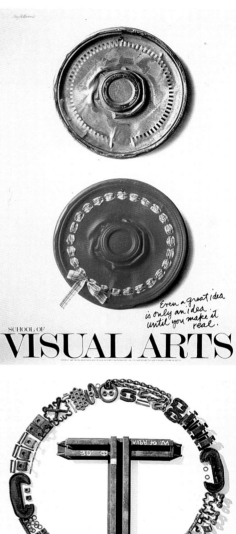

580
Art Director: Peter Favat
Designer: Don Pogany
Peter Favat
Photographer: Dwight Olmsted
Copywriter: Don Pogany
Agency: Ingalls, Quinn & Johnson
Client: Institute of Contemporary Art

581
Art Director: Raul Pina
Creative Director: Jamie Seltzer
Photographer: Jim Galante
Copywriter: David Bernstein
Client: New York Mets

582
Art Director: Joe DelVecchio
Creative Director: John Morrison
Sharon Vanderslice
Copywriter: Sharon Vanderslice
Agency: Della Femina, McNamee WCRS
Client: Pan Am

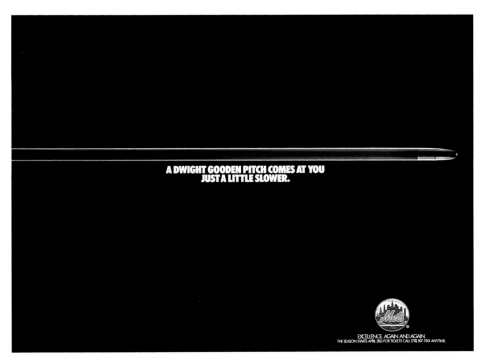

583
Art Director: Raul Pina
Creative Director: Jamie Seltzer
Copywriter: David Bernstein
Agency: Della Femina, McNamee WCRS
Client: New York Mets

584
Art Director: Steve Sweitzer
Designer: Steve Sweitzer
Photographer: Ben Saltzman
Copywriter: Jarl Olsen
Agency: Fallon McElligott
Client: Ben Saltzman

585
Art Director: David Fox
Creative Director: Jac Coverdale
Designer: David Fox
Photographer: Mark LaFavor
Copywriter: Joe Alexander
Agency: Clarity, Coverdale, Rueff
Client: City of Minneapolis Recycling

586
Art Director: David Fox
Creative Director: Jac Coverdale
Designer: David Fox
Photographer: Mark LaFavor
Copywriter: Joe Alexander
Agency: Clarity, Coverdale, Rueff
Client: City of Minneapolis Recycling

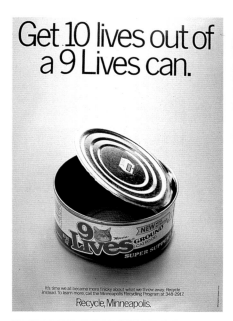

588
Art Director: Jon Lee
　　　　　　Marty Weiss
Creative Director: Bill Hamilton
Photographer: Mark Weiss
Copywriter: Paula Dombrow
　　　　　　Robin Raj
Agency: Chiat/Day/Mojo Advertising Inc.
Client: NYNEX Information Resources

587
Art Director: David Fox
Creative Director: Jac Coverdale
Designer: David Fox
Photographer: Mark LaFavor
Copywriter: Joe Alexander
Agency: Clarity, Coverdale, Rueff
Client: City of Minneapolis Recycling

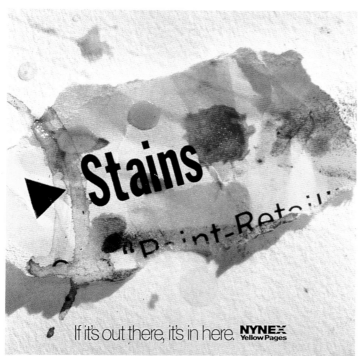

589

Art Director: Jon Lee
　　　　　Marty Weiss
Creative Director: Bill Hamilton
Photographer: Mark Weiss
Copywriter: Paula Dombrow
　　　　　Robin Raj
Agency: Chiat/Day/Mojo Advertising Inc.
Client: NYNEX Information Resources

590

Art Director: Jon Lee
　　　　　Marty Weiss
Creative Director: Bill Hamilton
Photographer: Mark Weiss
Copywriter: Paula Dombrow
　　　　　Robin Raj
Agency: Chiat/Day/Mojo Advertising Inc.
Client: NYNEX Information Resources

591

Art Director: Jon Lee
　　　　　Marty Weiss
Creative Director: Bill Hamilton
Photographer: Mark Weiss
Copywriter: Paula Dombrow
　　　　　Robin Raj
Agency: Chiat/Day/Mojo Advertising Inc.
Client: NYNEX Information Resources

592

Art Director: Chris Graves
Creative Director: Roy Grace
　　　　　　　　Diane Rothschild
Copywriter: David Corr
Client: Paddington

593
Art Director: Richard Ostroff
Creative Director: Allan Beaver
　　　　　　　　Lee Garfinkel
Photographer: Cailor/Resnick
Copywriter: Amy Borkowsky
Agency: Levine, Huntley, Schmidt & Beaver
Client: Ad Council

594
Art Director: Leslie Sweet
　　　　　　　Ernest Neira
Creative Director: Tony DeGregorio
Designer: Leslie Sweet
　　　　　　Ernest Neira
Photographer: Mike Newler
Copywriter: Nat Russo
Agency: Levine, Huntley, Schmidt & Beaver
Client: Dreyfus

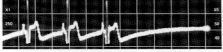

595
Art Director: Jon Lee
　　　　　　Marty Weiss
Creative Director: Bill Hamilton
Photographer: Mark Weiss
Copywriter: Paula Dombrow
　　　　　　Robin Raj
Agency: Chiat/Day/Mojo Advertising Inc.
Client: NYNEX Information Resources

607
Art Director: Nick Cohen
Copywriter: Graham Turner
Agency: Chiat/Day/Mojo Advertising Inc.
Client: Pointed Stick Theater

608
Art Director: Kevin Lory Mote
Creative Director: Jim Anderson
Copywriter: Kevin Lory Mote
Diana Hickerson
Agency: GSD&M Advertising
Client: The *Wall Street Journal*

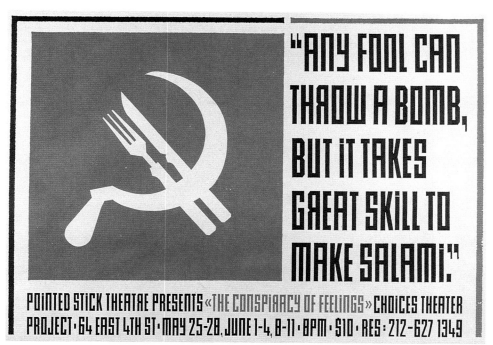

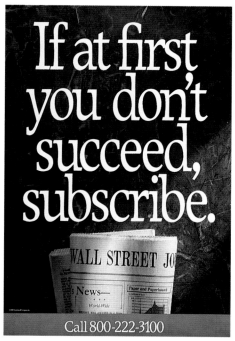

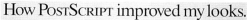

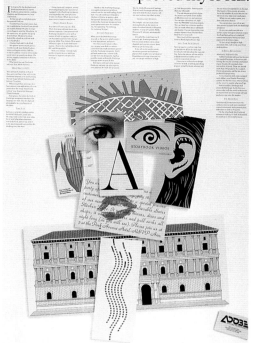

609
Art Director: Marty Neumeier
Designer: Marty Neumeier
Chris Chu
Illustrator: Chris Chu
Les Chibana
Copywriter: Marty Neumeier
Studio: Neumeier Design Team
Client: Adobe Systems Inc.

610
Art Director: Michael Schwab
Designer: Michael Schwab
Illustrator: Michael Schwab
Studio: Michael Schwab Design
Client: Bella Blue

611
Art Director: Mark Geer
Designer: Mark Geer
        Morgan Bomar
Copywriter: Pat Byers
Agency: Boswell Byers
Client: Decorative Center Houston

612
Art Director: Jerry McDaniel
Creative Director: Nina Krammer
Designer: Jerry McDaniel
Illustrator: Jerry McDaniel
Agency: Nike Communications
Client: Mouton-Cadet

613
Art Director: Alyn Carlson-Webster
Creative Director: Jason Grant
Photographer: Photocoloratura
        Stock
Copywriter: Marc Braunstein
Agency: Jason Grant Associates
Client: Gant

614
Art Director: Olga Kaljakin
Creative Director: Tony Seiniger
        Mike Kaiser
Photographer: Merrick Morton
Agency: Seiniger Advertising
Client: Tri-Star/Columbia Pictures

615
Art Director: Michael Prieve
Creative Director: Dan Wieden
David Kennedy
Copywriter: Jim Riswold
Agency: Wieden & Kennedy
Client: Nike

616
Art Director: Bob Brihn
Creative Director: Pat Burnham
Designer: Bob Brihn
Photographer: Rick Dublin
Copywriter: Jarl Olsen
Agency: Fallon McElligott
Client: Power Pac

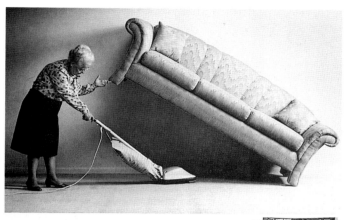

617
Art Director: Pam Cunningham
Creative Director: Lee Clow
Agency: Chiat/Day/Mojo
Client: Nissan

618
Art Director: Warren Eakins
Creative Director: Dan Wieden
David Kennedy
Agency: Wieden & Kennedy
Client: Nike

619

Art Director: Matt Canzano
Creative Director: Joe Sciarrotta
　　　　　　　　Tenney Fairchild
Illustrator: Douglas Fraser
Copywriter: Dave Merhar
Agency: J. Walter Thompson
Client: Miller Brewing Co.

620

Art Director: Paul Davis
Illustrator: Paul Davis
Client: New York Shakespeare Festival

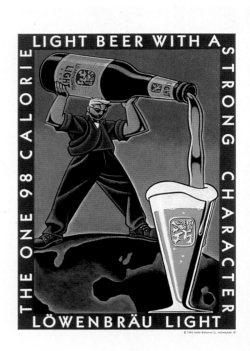

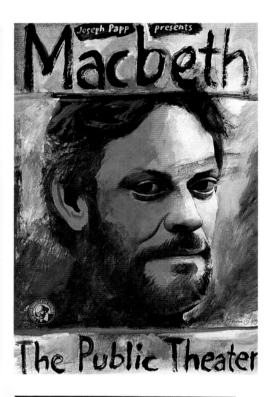

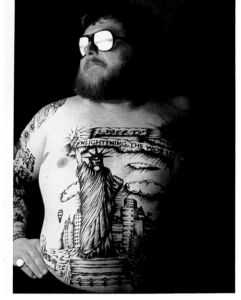

621

Art Director: Rob Biro
Creative Director: Cindy L. Hauser
Designer: Rob Biro
Photographer: Ron Derhacopian
Agency: B.D. Fox & Friends, Inc.
Client: Twentieth Century Fox TV

622

Art Director: Tim Fisher
　　　　　　　Chris Robb
Photographer: Lee Crum
Copywriter: Tim Fisher
　　　　　　　Chris Robb
Agency: Carmichael Lynch

623
Art Director: Lowell Williams
Creative Director: Lowell Williams
Designer: Lowell Williams
          Andy Dearwater
Illustrator: Andy Dearwater
Copywriter: JoAnn Stone
Studio: Lowell Williams Design Inc.
Client: Hedrich Blessing

624
Art Director: Milton Glaser
Designer: Milton Glaser
Agency: Milton Glaser, Inc.
Client: The Society of Newspaper Design

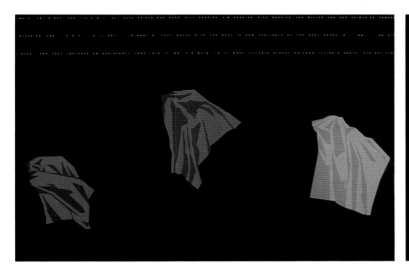

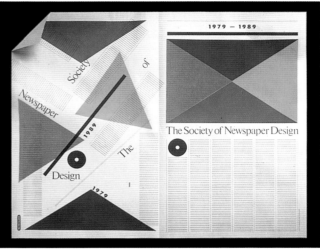

625
Art Director: Onofrio Paccione
Creative Director: Onofrio Paccione
Designer: Onofrio Paccione
Photographer: Onofrio Paccione
Studio: Paccione Photography
Client: Type Directors Club

626
Art Director: Charles S. Anderson
          Dan Olson
Designer: Charles S. Anderson
          Dan Olson
Illustrator: Charles S. Anderson
          Randy Dahlk
Studio: Charles S. Anderson Design
Client: French Paper Co.

627
Art Director: Charles S. Anderson
Designer: Charles S. Anderson
Illustrator: Japanese Menko Cards
Studio: Charles S. Anderson Design
Client: Ginza Graphic Gallery

628
Art Director: Charles S. Anderson
Designer: Charles S. Anderson
Dan Olson
Illustrator: Charles S. Anderson
Randy Dahlk
Copywriter: Lisa Pemrick
Studio: Charles S. Anderson Design
Client: Charles S. Anderson Design

629
Art Director: Charles S. Anderson
Dan Olson
Designer: Charles S. Anderson
Dan Olson
Studio: Charles S. Anderson Design
Client: Minneapolis College of Art & Design

630
Art Director: McRay Magleby
Creative Director: McRay Magleby
Designer: McRay Magleby
Copywriter: Norman Darais
Studio: BYU Graphics

631

Art Director: Don Sibley
Designer: Don Sibley
Illustrator: Don Sibley
Agency: Dancie Ware, Houston
Studio: Sibley/Peteet Design
Client: Galveston Park Board of Trustees

632

Art Director: Jane Kasstrin
　　　　　　David Sterling
Creative Director: Jane Kasstrin
　　　　　　　　David Sterling
Designer: Jane Kasstrin
　　　　　　David Sterling
Photographer: Geoff Spear
Studio: Doublespace
Client: American Express Publishing Corp.

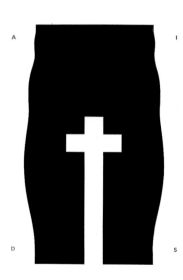

633

Art Director: Neal Posener
Designer: Neal Posener
Illustrator: John Jinks
Agency: Russek Advertising
Client: Playwright Horizons

634

Art Director: McRay Magleby
Creative Director: McRay Magleby
Designer: McRay Magleby
Copywriter: Norman Darais
Agency: BYU Graphics

635

Art Director: Rex Peteet
Designer: Rex Peteet
Illustrator: John Evans
Studio: Sibley/Peteet Design
Client: Sibley/Peteet Design

636
Art Director: Fred Woodward
Designer: Fred Woodward
　　　　　Gail Anderson

637
Art Director: Linda Sullivan
Designer: Linda Sullivan
Studio: BYU Graphics
Client: BYU

638
Art Director: Charles S. Anderson
Designer: Charles S. Anderson
Illustrator: Charles S. Anderson
　　　　　Lynn Schulte
Studio: The Duffy Group
Client: STA Chicago

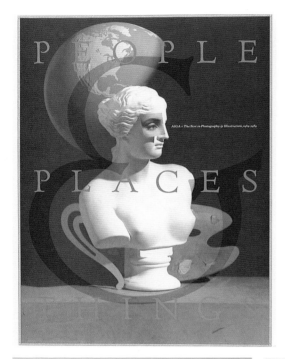

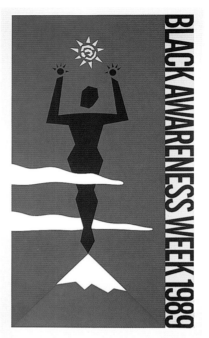

639
Art Director: Don Weller
Creative Director: Don Weller
Designer: Don Weller
Illustrator: Don Weller
Copywriter: Don Weller
Studio: The Weller Institute
Client: TDCTJHTBIPC

640
Art Director: McRay Magleby
Creative Director: McRay Magleby
Designer: McRay Magleby
Copywriter: Norman Darais
Studio: BYU Graphics

641

Art Director: Charles S. Anderson
Designer: Charles S. Anderson
Illustrator: Charles S. Anderson
　　　　　　 Lynn Schulte
Studio: The Duffy Group
Client: French Paper Co.

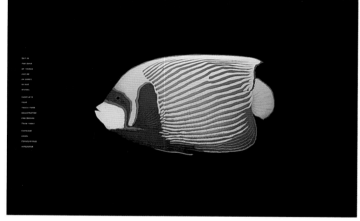

642

Art Director: McRay Magleby
Creative Director: McRay Magleby
Designer: McRay Magleby
Copywriter: Norman Darais
Studio: BYU Graphics

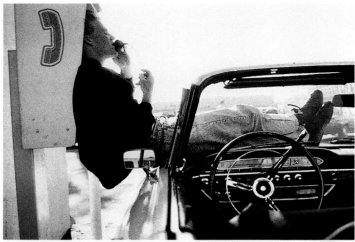

Public phone. Private moment. Lee jeans.

643
Art Director: Mark Johnson
Creative Director: Pat Burnham
Photographer: Kurt Markus
Copywriter: Bill Miller
Agency: Fallon McElligott
Client: Lee Jeans

Four day weekend. Fifth day. Lee jeans.

9 O'clock date. 8:55. Lee jeans.

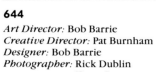

You always come back to the basics.

You always come back to the basics.

You always come back to the basics.

644
Art Director: Bob Barrie
Creative Director: Pat Burnham
Designer: Bob Barrie
Photographer: Rick Dublin
　　　　　　Kerry Peterson
Copywriter: Jarl Olsen
Agency: Fallon McElligott
Client: Jim Beam

BOOKS & JACKETS

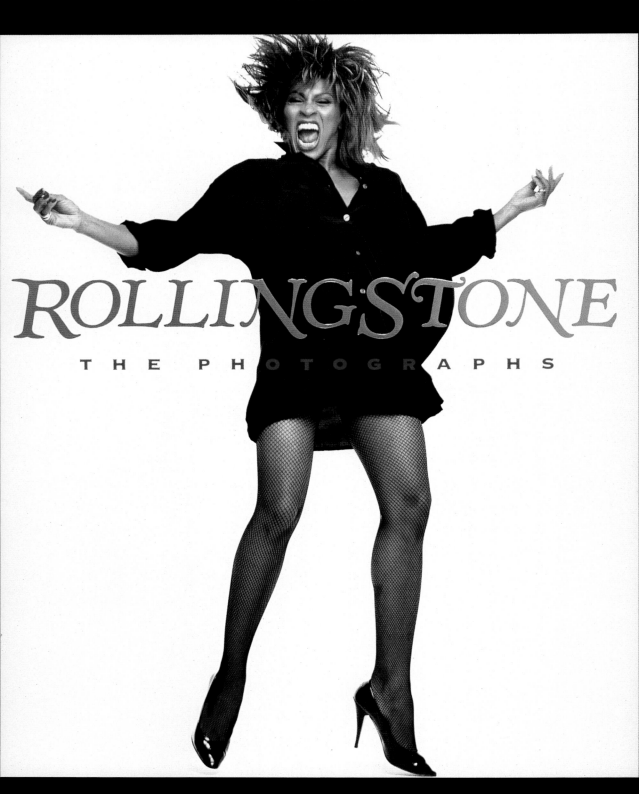

645 Silver

Art Director: Fred Woodward
Designer: Fred Woodward
Photographer: Various
Publication: Simon and Schuster

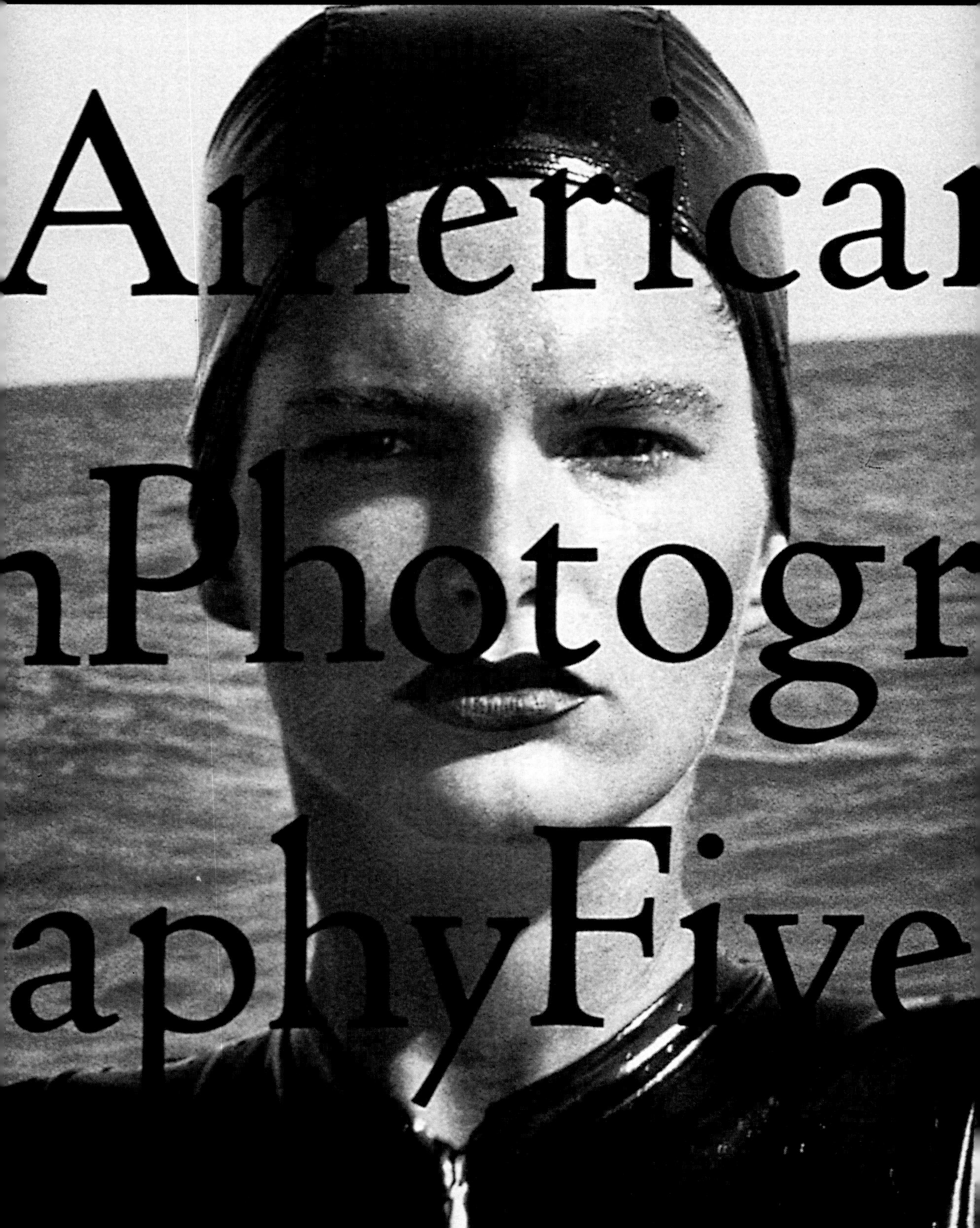

American
Photogr
aphyFive

646 Silver

Art Director: Rosemarie Turk
Creative Director: Stephen Doyle
Agency: Drenttel Doyle Partners
Client: American Photography

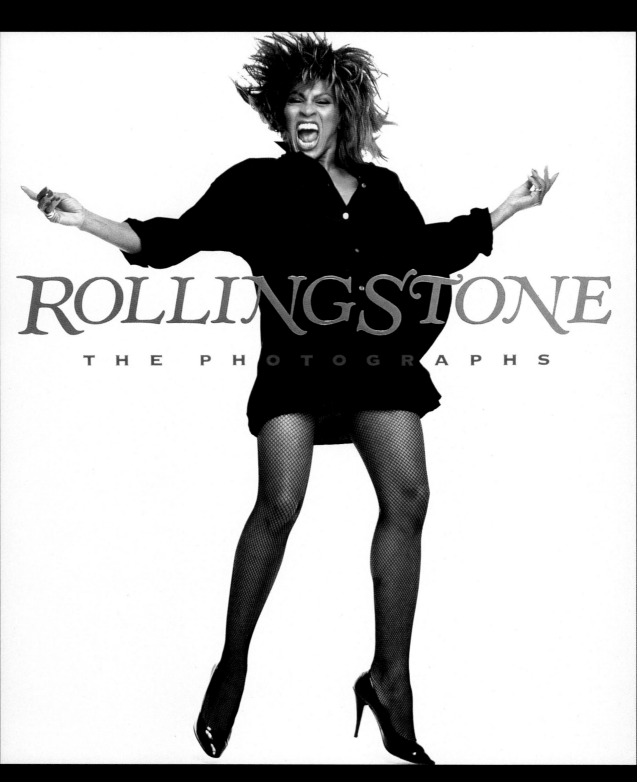

647 Distinctive Merit

Art Director: Fred Woodward
Designer: Fred Woodward
Photographer: Steven Meisel
Publication: Simon and Schuster

648
Art Director: Richard Eckersley
Studio: Nebraska University Press
Client: Nebraska University Press

649
Art Director: Samuel Antupit
Designer: Ray Konai

BRODOVITCH

was the model of the modern art director. The essence of contemporary magazine design—the 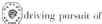 driving pursuit of new ways to present visual material—can be traced to the example he set. While at *Harper's* *Bazaar* from 1934 to 1958, he created a design look whose energy, elegance, and simplicity captured the spirit of American fashion. Magnetic and controversial, he inspired the designers 1 2 3 4 5 6 7 8 9 0 and photographers who attended his famous Design Laboratory with his constant admonition, "Astonish me!"

ANDY GRUNDBERG | MASTERS OF AMERICAN DESIGN

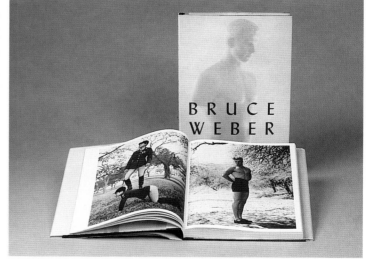

650
Art Director: Woody Pirtle
Illustrator: Jack Unruh
Studio: Pentagram Design
Client: American Illustration

651
Art Director: John Cheim
Designer: John Cheim

652

Art Director: Greg Samata
⠀⠀⠀⠀⠀⠀⠀⠀⠀Pat Samata
Designer: Greg Samata
⠀⠀⠀⠀⠀⠀⠀⠀⠀Pat Samata
Illustrator: Paul Thompson
Copywriter: Steve Huggins
Client: Samata Associates

653

Art Director: Diane Jaroch
Designer: Diane Jaroch
Illustrator: Various
Copywriter: Roger Remington
⠀⠀⠀⠀⠀⠀⠀⠀⠀⠀Barbara Hodik
Studio: The MIT Press Design Department
Client: The MIT Press

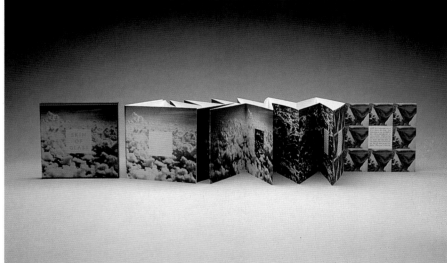

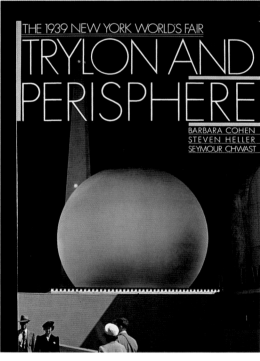

654

Art Director: Nancy Garruba
Designer: Nancy Garruba
Client: Blue House Press

655

Art Director: Samuel Antupit
Creative Director: Seymour Chwast
Designer: Seymour Chwast
⠀⠀⠀⠀⠀⠀⠀⠀⠀Roxanne Slimak
Photographer: Reven Wurman
Studio: The Pushpin Group
Client: Harry N. Abrams, Inc.

656
Art Director: Jennifer Barry
Designer: Jennifer Barry
Charles Tyrone
Photographer: Various
Copywriter: David DeVoss
Client: Collins Publishers

657
Art Director: Don McQuiston
Creative Director: Don McQuiston
Designer: Don McQuiston
Photographer: John Oldenkamp
Cynthia Sabransky
Agency: McQuiston & Partners
Publication: Chronicle Books

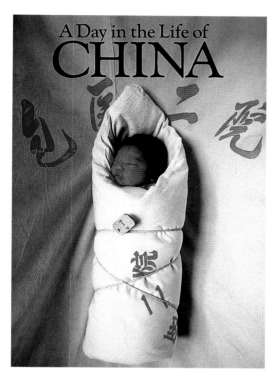

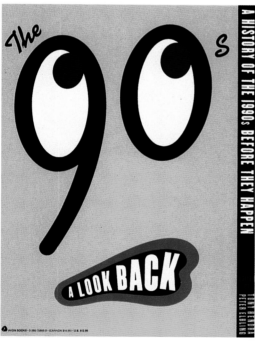

658
Art Director: Paula Scher
Creative Director: Paula Scher
Designer: Paula Scher
Illustrator: Various
Photographer: Various
Studio: Koppel & Scher
Client: Avon Books

659
Art Director: James Wageman
Designer: James Wageman
Publication: Abbeville Press, Inc.

660
Art Director: Jackie Merri Meyer
Creative Director: Jackie Merri Meyer
Designer: Charles S. Anderson
Client: Warner Books

661
Art Director: Neil Stuart
Designer: Neil Stuart
Illustrator: Chris Gall
Client: Viking Penguin

662
Art Director: Neil Stuart
Designer: Neil Stuart
Illustrator: Raphael & Bolognese
Client: Viking Penguin

663
Art Director: Louise Fili
Designer: Louise Fili
Illustrator: Robert Goldstrom
Client: Pantheon Books

664
Art Director: Susan Mitchell
Designer: Marc J. Cohen
Photographer: Edward S. Ross

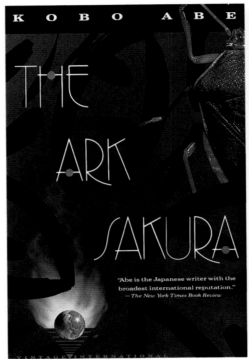

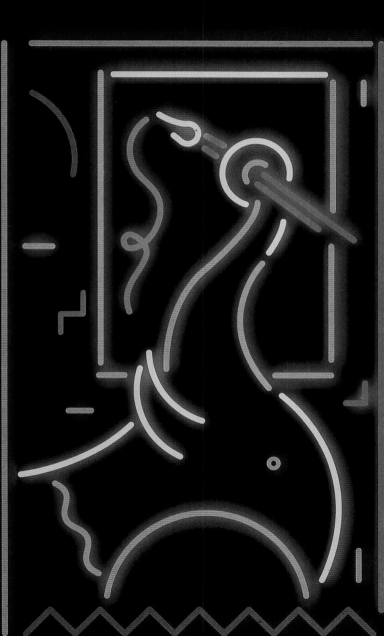

THE MANY RECENT sightings of Elvis Presley have led to a new and illuminating line of inquiry: If Elvis is able to make appearances after his death, shouldn't he have been able to ∿ He is, after all, the King. ∿ Ex-covered a wealth of evidence previ-who were distracted by events of eptics may choose to pooh-pooh rvings – visible only by aircraft ear. They may dismiss as coinci-oriests of the period wore chains

Launaus, France (left): The birth of rock. Not by any means the last time the King will be criticized by Neanderthals. Carvings tell of a benevolent stranger who came out of nowhere, defeated the clan's enemies with martial arts and gave everybody a free horse. Easter Island (right): The audi-ence at the National Geographic Society began to cough and wheeze uncomfortably when forced to confront this picture. Some members of the Memphis Mafia have commented on Elvis's big bust.

ARCH of
TORIC
LVIS

EN·ILLUSTRATIONS BY ANITA KUNZ

around their necks. ∿ The open-minded Elviologist (as opposed to the Presliquarian, with his amateur faddism) can only sigh with tolerance. ∿ Naysayers cannot so easily abrogate the Rouen tapes-try that depicts the martyrdom of Saint Joan of Arc. The figure in the background was assumed to be a Burgundian bishop, chiefly be-cause of his high-collared, gold-sequined robe and the fact that he seems to be sneering at Saint Joan. Embroidered along the bottom: *Je veux un morceau d'amour brûlant.* Loose translation: "I want a hunk, a hunk of burning love." ∿ Compelling evidence of Elvisitation may be seen in any of a thousand Asian jungles, from Cambodia to Ja-pan. There it is commonplace to find great, ornate decaying temples. Should it surprise anyone that, for untold millenniums, these were sites where thousands of worshipers swooned before the imposing centerpiece: a giant statue of a man weighing over 300 pounds? ∿ And is it mere happenstance that these are the same cultures in which originated the art of painting on black velvet? ∿ Why hasn't this proof come to light sooner? A deliberate conspiracy to suppress it? The motive? Scientific ego, unwilling to give credit to the mumifi-cent contributions of the preternatural Presley. The most blatant ex-ample? The 1900 diaries of Walter Reed, the so-called father of the

cure for yellow fever. He describes his first patient: "Hands: shak-ing. Knees: weak. Can't seem to stand on own two feet. Lips: hot (like volcano). Patient delirious. Acts wildly, as if he were a hug. Question: Why is he all shook up?" ∿ Is it not curious that, weeks lat-er, Reed should "dis-cover" the cause of yellow fever to be a mos-quito? And how peculiar that he should find it in Cuba, a land renowned for its "fuzzy trees." ∿ Only Elvis's characteristic modesty prevent-ed him from taking credit for his many cross-cultural contributions, and even doubters agree it's a good thing Colonel Parker never contem-plated the T-shirt rights. ∿ Should you em-brace my theory, prepare to suffer the indigni-ties inflicted on all who hold unpopular beliefs; for truly, the unwashed masses have yet to learn the golden rule: Don't be cruel. In fact, this au-thor has been hounded into virtual seclusion, not unlike the post-Vegas Presley. ∿ Never-theless, I have followed my dream and discov-ered a promising new course of study. Any-body's grandmother can claim to have seen Elvis necking down a grape Slurpy at the local Bob's Big Boy years after his "death." Few, however, have bothered to look for the very real appearances of Elvis in inappropriate places while he was still alive. ∿ Just who was that shadowy pompadoured figure lurking on the Grassy Knoll? ∿ I'll never tell.

Should you em-brace my theory, pre-pare to suffer the indignities inflicted on all who hold unpopular beliefs; for the reason there yet to learn the golden rule: Don't be cruel.

666 Silver
Art Director: Fred Woodward
Designer: Fred Woodward
Illustrator: Anita Kunz
Publication: Rolling Stone

The inner voice which warns us
that someone may be looking.

H. L. Mencken

PAINTING BY BRAD HOLLAND · 1989, DESIGN BY JIM McGUNE, COLOR SEPARATION BY COLOR IMAGE, PRINTING BY LOMBARDI PRESS, PAPER · IRONSIDE'S GLOSS 80 LB. BOOK

B R A D H o l l A N D S L A M

669 Distinctive Merit
Art Director: Dugald Stermer
Illustrator: Dugald Stermer

GARLIC

Garlic plants average 24" to 36" in height.

References to garlic date back thousands of years. Homer mentions it in the Odyssey & poets & writers through the ages have discussed its curative power.

Individual cloves are used as seed for new crop plantings.

Bulbs range in size from 1¼" to 3" in diameter.

BASIC EARLY GARLIC
LE 4050

PART TWO: LIVING WITHOUT ENEMIES

Gorbachev wasn't just revolutionizing his own society; he was transforming ours as well. Since Stalin's day, the Soviets had played the perfect enemy. The evil Russian bear defined our national purpose and gave us a global mission. But here was Gorbachev declaring peace. Could we look at him and still see the face of the enemy? And what posed the greater threat, having an enemy or not having one? BY LAWRENCE WRIGHT

PEACE

54 · Rolling Stone, September 7th, 1989

ILLUSTRATIONS BY BRIAN CRONIN

670 Distinctive Merit
Art Director: Fred Woodward
Illustrator: Brian Cronin
Publication: Rolling Stone

BY TERRI MINSKY

THE 8000-HOUR JOKE

HBO honchos are plotting America's first nonstop comedy channel. MTV hopes to outwit them with HA! TV. But can they keep the laughs coming?

VERYBODY THINKS IT'S A REALLY GREAT JOKE, maybe the best one they've come up with so far. The only trouble is that the joke takes two months to set up.

Here's the idea: When HBO's Comedy Channel – the first all-day, all-night, all-the-time cable comedy station – begins broadcasting November 1st, it would have an official mascot: Happy the Duck. He'd show up in all the advertising and promotion, he'd be part of the logo (THE COMEDY CHANNEL – HONK!), he'd be personified on air as a guy dressed up in a duck suit. He'd be cute.

Too cute.

Actually, he'd be your worst nightmare, the kind of comedy cliché you might fear from such a twenty-four-hour station – only one step up from beetle-browed, big-nosed Groucho glasses.

So: All of the Comedy Channel hosts would hate Happy the Duck. They'd get annoyed whenever he turned up on their shows. Over time it would become clear that the official mascot was not working out. The guy in the duck suit would skulk around in the background, not even bothering to put on his duck head. He'd have audible telephone arguments about his contract with his agent. He'd be Happy the Disaffected Duck. Then one day he'd just be gone, another victim of show business.

As of eighty-six days before the station's launch – a countdown has begun in the office – the Comedy Channel staff hasn't definitively decided whether or not to go with Happy the Duck. Well, Eddie Gorodetsky, the beefy, affable thirty-two-year-old head writer, is

Illustration by Lane Smith

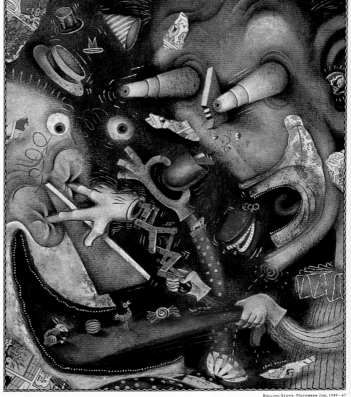

GOLDEN DELICIOUS

PENTHOUSE LETTERS
ART COLLECTOR'S
SPECIAL EDITION

ILLUSTRATIONS BY BLAIR DRAWSON

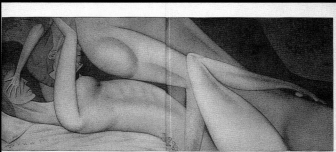

• YOU AND ME •

• THE CANDY APPLE •

• HEAVY BREATHING •

• OPERA NIGHT •

ORIGIN OF THE SPECIES

Carbon-dating comedy does not reveal when the first funny lady emerged from the dark sea of Victorian morality, but it was no later than 1926—the year Mae West waded ashore with her Broadway play *Sex*. A brick-house Venus, West was busty, lusty, and hilarious. Her jokes, timed with a roll of hip and eye, crashed like breakers on a stick-in-the-mud society. Roiling the waters could be dangerous; West's career almost sank when Hollywood's Hays office censored her films in the mid-'30s. But West survived; she knew the ropes, if not the limits. All the early female comics did. As these pioneers in a man's world knew, street smarts had to be masked with buffoonery.

ROBERT RISKO

SPECIAL REPORT

SURVIVAL OF THE FUNNIEST

Lucy Ricardo may have been the national nitwit in the 1950s, but her creator, Lucille Ball, was nobody's fool. As Empress of Comedy, her reign was long (it spanned more than two decades) and fruitful (with husband Desi Arnaz, she built the profitable Desilu Inc.). Her kingdom tottered in the 1970s when it became clear that humor based on an ad-dlepated hausfrau no longer worked—perhaps because most of the audience did; why go after "Ba-Ba-Lu" when the boardroom beckoned? Ball's last TV series, launched in 1986, vanished in eight weeks. Last April, death robbed her of the chance to make a comeback. Yet her legacy of 30-minute sitcoms, now rerun around the planet, ensures that in the gag-eat-gag humor biz, Ball still triumphs.

ROBERT RISKO

SPECIAL REPORT

O nce consigned to the freak show, funny ladies now play the big top. They host talk shows: Oprah Winfrey finds humor in the angst of cellulite and broken hearts. They endorse products: belligerent ac-cordionist Judy Tenuta uses her put-down "Pigs!" to plug Dr Pepper. Now women outside the entertainment industry are expressing their wit. Even den-mother-to-the-nation Barbara Bush gets into the act. "I mean, look at me," she exclaimed to *The New York Times* in all her sensi-bly shod frumpiness. The gales of laughter that greet her are those of solidarity. For as the world becomes a woman's, so does the right to poke fun at it.

ROBERT RISKO

SPECIAL REPORT

47

673 Distinctive Merit

Art Director: Doug Renfro
Creative Director: Jim Darilek
Designer: Doug Renfro

674
Art Director: Dan Larocca
Creative Director: Gordon Hochhalter
Illustrator: Braldt Bralds
Agency: O'Grady
Client: R.R. Donnelley & Sons

675
Art Director: David Bartels
Illustrator: Braldt Bralds
Agency: Bartels & Carstens
Client: St. Louis Zoo

676
Art Director: Pedro Tabernero
Illustrator: Brad Holland
Studio: Pandora
Client: Expo-92

677
Art Director: Don Weller
Creative Director: Don Weller
Designer: Don Weller
Illustrator: Don Weller
Copywriter: Don Weller
Studio: The Weller Institute
Client: Graphic Comm. Society in Oklahoma

678
Art Director: Christopher Johnson
Creative Director: Stephen Doyle
Illustrator: Etienne Delessert
Agency: Drenttel Doyle Partners
Client: Olympia & York/World Financial Center

679
Art Director: Abby Merrill
Designer: Gerard Huerta
Illustrator: Roger Huyssen
Studio: 2H Studio
Client: Society of Illustrators

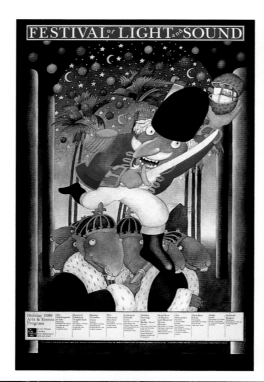

680
Art Director: Chris North
Creative Director: Chris North
              Braldt Bralds
Illustrator: Braldt Bralds
Copywriter: Christopher Robin
Studio: River City Studio
Client: Kansas Art Directors Club

681
Art Director: Peter Galperin
Creative Director: Peter Galperin
Illustrator: Chris Gall
Agency: Middleberg & Associates
Client: Royce Carlin Hotel

682
Art Director: Mike Scricco
Designer: Mike Scricco
Illustrator: Brad Holland
Client: Art Directors Club of Connecticut

683
Art Director: Dugald Stermer
Designer: Dugald Stermer
Illustrator: Dugald Stermer
Client: Perry's

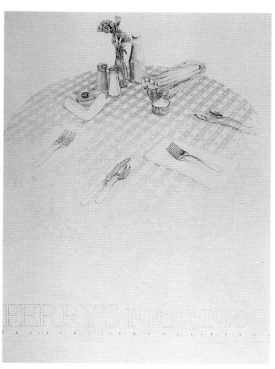

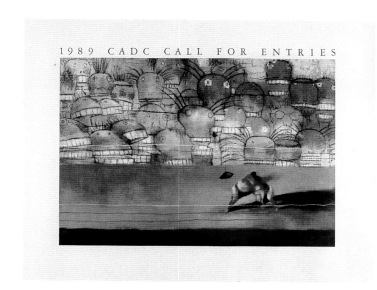

A FAIR OF THE HEART

MAHAFFEY THEATER

684
Art Director: George Halvorson
Creative Director: George Halvorson
Illustrator: Dan Craig
Agency: CME
Client: United Way

685
Art Director: Susan T. Baldassare
Creative Director: Valerie K. Newton
Designer: Susan T. Baldassare
Illustrator: Susan T. Baldassare
Copywriter: Valerie K. Newton
Client: Bay Area Civic Opera

It's Getting Awfully Crowded In There.

686
Art Director: Helen Lindberg
Creative Director: Art Broughton
Illustrator: Nicholas Wilton
Copywriter: Bob Dorfman
Brad Londy
Agency: TFB/BBDO
Client: Businessland

Decisions, Decisions, Decisions.

Need A Hand?

687
Art Director: Bill Freeland
Designer: Seymour Chwast
James McMullan
Milton Glaser
Illustrator: Seymour Chwast
James McMullan
Milton Glaser
Copywriter: Bill Freeland

688
Art Director: Janet Froelich
Designer: Janet Froelich
Illustrator: Matt Mahurin
Publication: The *New York Times*

689
Art Director: Mary Workman
Designer: Timothy W. Brown
Illustrator: Gwyn Stramler
Copywriter: David Hunter
Publication: Tennessee Illustrated

WILLIE HORTON AND ME

HARD-WON MIDDLE-CLASS CREDENTIALS DON'T COUNT, THE AUTHOR FINDS. WHAT COUNTS, STILL, IS HIS FACE, AND IT'S BLACK.

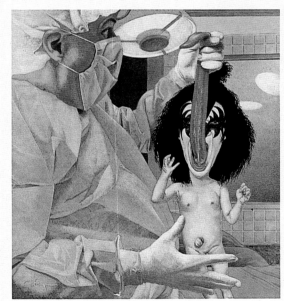

THE HISTORY OF ROCK & ROLL

Kiss the Baby: The Birth of Gene Simmons
BY C.F. PAYNE

690
Art Director: Fred Woodward
Illustrator: C. F. Payne
Publication: Rolling Stone

691
Art Director: Fred Woodward
Illustrator: Matt Mahurin
Publication: Rolling Stone

692
Art Director: Fred Woodward
Designer: Jolene Cuyler
Illustrator: Sue Coe
Publication: Rolling Stone

693
Art Director: Mary Workman
Designer: Timothy W. Brown
Illustrator: Alan Cober
Copywriter: Madison Smartt Bell
Publication: Tennessee Illustrated

694
Art Director: Mary Workman
Designer: Timothy W. Brown
Illustrator: Paul Cox
Copywriter: Carolyn Gray
Publication: Tennessee Illustrated

695
Art Director: Richard Bleiweiss
Creative Director: Frank DeVino
Designer: Richard Bleiweiss
Illustrator: Gottfried Helnwein

PHOTOGRAPHY

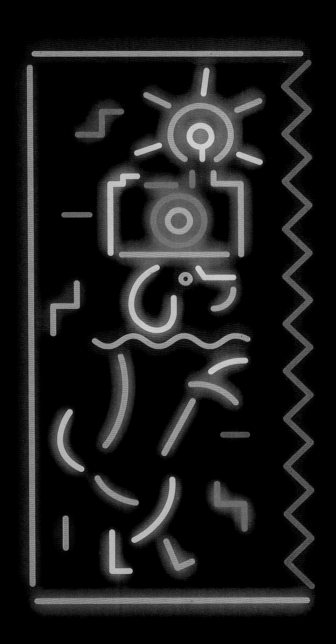

LIVING LEGENDS

BY ANTHONY DeCURTIS

The fingers of guitarist Buddy Guy

It would be nearly impossible to overestimate the importance of the blues in the formation of rock & roll, but the legendary figures of that seminal music still rarely get the opportunity to step out of the shadows of the artists they have influenced and stand alone on their own formidable terms. In this photo gallery, seven major forces in the blues come forward.

Guitarists B.B. King and Albert King – the first a player of breathtaking sweetness and delicacy, the second a blazing virtuoso – and their musical heir Buddy Guy shaped the music of an entire generation of players, including Eric Clapton, Stevie Ray Vaughan and the late Mike Bloomfield. One of the most significant songwriters in the history of the blues, Willie Dixon penned a cache of classic tunes – among them, "You Shook Me," "Back Door Man," "I Can't Quit You Baby," "(I'm Your) Hoochie Coochie Man" and "I Just Want to Make Love to You" – that provided crucial early material for Jeff Beck, Led Zeppelin, the Rolling Stones and the Doors.

John Lee Hooker's insidious, sexually charged boogie – epitomized in songs like "Boogie Chillun," "Boom Boom," "Dimples" and "I'm in the Mood" – fired up everyone from the Animals and Van Morrison to Bruce Springsteen and Bonnie Raitt.

Bo Diddley's propulsive, staccato beat drove songs like "I'm a Man," "Mona" and "Who Do You Love?" and provided a central link between the blues and rock & roll. Junior Wells, the wailing harmonica man best known for his insouciant version of "Messin' With the Kid," was a staple on the Chess Records studio scene, in Chicago. For more than two decades, Wells, as part of a one-two punch with Buddy Guy, has led one of the most active touring blues bands in the country.

Along with the music they created, however, these bluesmen are the product of a world and of a time that has all but disappeared. The photographs that appear on these pages are meant to honor that heritage as well.

"I had two things to choose from," says the seventy-two-year-old John Lee Hooker, whose father was a sharecropper. "One was to stay there with the horses and cows and pigs and work on the farm and go to school and *not* be a musician. I felt from a kid up that wasn't my bag. I was gonna be a musician. I was different from any of the rest of the kids. I was *completely* different."

As a young black person deep in the segregated South in the early [*Cont. on 99*]

PHOTOGRAPHS BY ALBERT WATSON

717 Gold
Art Director: Fred Woodward
Photo Editor: Laurie Kratochvil
Photographer: Albert Watson
Publication: Rolling Stone

718 Silver

Art Director: David Page
Creative Director: Rich Silverstein
Jeffrey Goodby
Designer: David Page
Photographer: Harvey Lloyd
Copywriter: David O'Hare

Timberland. Where the elements of design are the elements themselves.

We Timberland people have never built a shoe unless we could build it better than any and all competitors. Which tells you something about the elements that make up our new women's collec-tion. Glove-soft chamois and full-grain leathers, all of a quality virtually unseen in women's foot-wear. Genuine Timberland handsewn moccasin construction. And a panorama of colors inspired by the environments in which these shoes come alive. The bluffs of Antigua, the coves of the Mediterranean, the valleys of Italy.

A palette of wind, water, earth and sky.

Boots, shoes, clothing, wind, water, earth and sky.

719 Silver

Art Director: John Doyle
Designer: John Doyle
Photographer: Clint Clemens
Copywriter: Paul Silverman
Agency: Mullen

Sporting Hush Puppies.

us to point out our new look. Soft leather men's casuals and women's Body Shoes—with the Comfort Curve® sole to flex where your foot flexes. In a flush of spring cold

721 Distinctive Merit

Art Director: John Butler
Mike Shine
Photographer: Joe Baraban
Copywriter: Tom DeCerchio
Agency: Chiat/Day/Mojo
Client: National Car Rental

Remember when there was more grease in your hair than under the hood?

≋ **National** Car Rental. *Florida Funwheels.*

One ride and you'll understand why most rocket scientists are German.

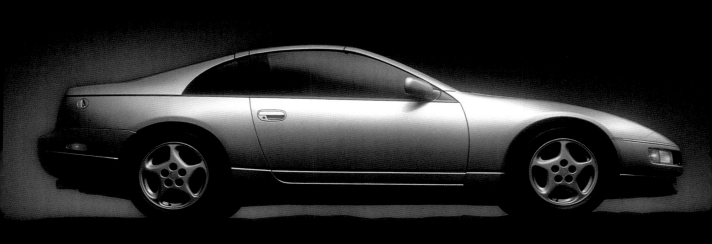

723 Distinctive Merit
Art Director: Lynne Lee Court

OKTOBER

MO	DI	MI	DO	FR	SA	SO	MO	DI	MI	DO	FR	SA	SO	MO	DI	MI	DO	FR	SA	SO	MO	DI
1	2	3	4	5	6	7	8	9	10	11	12	13	14	15	16	17	18	19	20	21	22	23	24	25	26	27	28	29	30	31

JUNI

| 1 | 2 | 3 | 4 | 5 | 6 | 7 | 8 | 9 | 10 | 11 | 12 | 13 | 14 | 15 | 16 | 17 | 18 | 19 | 20 | 21 | 22 | 23 | 24 | 25 | 26 | 27 | 28 | 29 | 30 |

JANUAR

| 1 | 2 | 3 | 4 | 5 | 6 | 7 | 8 | 9 | 10 | 11 | 12 | 13 | 14 | 15 | 16 | 17 | 18 | 19 | 20 | 21 | 22 | 23 | 24 | 25 | 26 | 27 | 28 | 29 | 30 | 31 |

Compromise is for politicians.

One ride and you'll understand why most rocket scientists are German.

In Germany, it doesn't compete with cars. It competes with airplanes.

725 Distinctive Merit

Art Director: Mark Johnson
Photographer: Jeff Zwart
Copywriter: Tom McElligott
Agency: Fallon McElligott
Client: Porsche

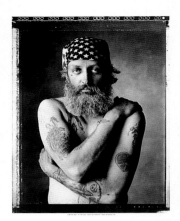

MARC HAUSER

MARC HAUSER

MARC HAUSER

726 Distinctive Merit

Art Director: Marc Hauser
Designer: Steve Liska
Photographer: Marc Hauser
Agency: Liska & Associates

727 Distinctive Merit
Art Director: Fred Woodward
Photo Editor: Laurie Kratochvil
Photographer: Albert Watson
Publication: Rolling Stone

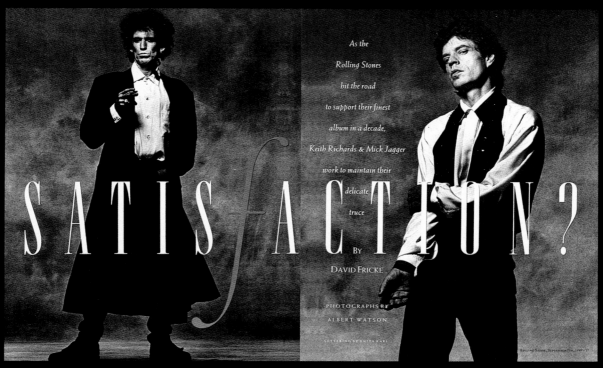

As the
Rolling Stones
hit the road
to support their finest
album in a decade,
Keith Richards & Mick Jagger
work to maintain their
delicate
truce

SATIS*f*ACTION?

BY
DAVID FRICKE

PHOTOGRAPHS BY
ALBERT WATSON

LETTERING BY ANITA KARL

GREENWICH, CONN.

PHOTOGRAPH BY CHIP SIMONS

The New York Times Magazine · MAY 28, 1989

WHY MOW?

THE CASE AGAINST LAWNS

BY MICHAEL POLLAN

Anyone new to the experience of owning a lawn, as I am, soon figures out that there is more at stake here than a patch of grass. A lawn immediately establishes a certain relationship with one's neighbors and, by extension, the larger American landscape. Mowing the lawn, I realized the first time I gazed into my neighbor's yard and imagined him gazing back into mine, is a civic responsibility.

For no lawn is an island, at least in America. Starting at my front stoop, this scruffy green carpet tumbles down a hill and leaps across a one-lane road into my neighbor's yard. From there it skips over some wooded patches and stone walls before finding its way across a dozen other unfenced properties that lead down into the Housatonic Valley, there to begin its march south to the metropolitan area. Once below Danbury, the lawn — now

Michael Pollan, executive editor of Harper's Magazine, is at work on a book about gardening for Atlantic Monthly Press.

728 Distinctive Merit
Art Director: Janet Froelich
Photo Editor: Kathy Ryan
Designer: Justine Strasberg
Photographer: Chip Simons
*Publication: The New York Times
Magazine*

RIVER BLINDNESS

CONQUERING AN ANCIENT SCOURGE

By Erik Eckholm

729 Distinctive Merit

Art Director: Janet Froelich
Photo Editor: Kathy Ryan
Designer: Janet Froelich
Justine Strasberg
Photographer: Eugene Richards
Publication: The *New York Times*
Magazine

742

Art Director: Mark Johnson
Creative Director: Pat Burnham
Photographer: Kurt Markus
Copywriter: Bill Miller
Agency: Fallon McElligott
Client: Lee Jeans

743

Art Director: Mark Johnson
Creative Director: Pat Burnham
Photographer: Kurt Markus
Copywriter: Bill Miller
Agency: Fallon McElligott
Client: Lee Jeans

21 years. 3 months. 6 days. Lee jeans.

Public phone. Private moment. Lee jeans.

744

Art Director: Andre Nel
Creative Director: Dave Henke
Photographer: Jeff Schewe
Copywriter: Dave Henke
Agency: DMB&B St. Louis
Client: Anheuser-Busch

745
Art Director: Jeff Jones
Creative Director: Kevin Lynch
Photographer: Marvy!
Copywriter: Kevin Lynch
Agency: Lynch, Jarvis, Jones
Client: Catholic Education Marketing Initiative

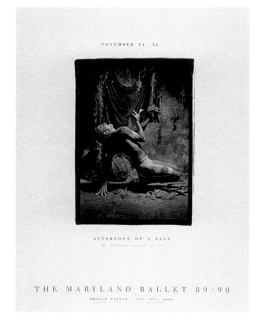

746
Art Director: Jim Mochnsky
Creative Director: James Dale
Designer: Jim Mochnsky
Photographer: Stephen John Phillips
Agency: W.B. Doner
Client: The Maryland Ballet

747
Art Director: Sharon White
Bob Packert
Photographer: Sharon White
Bob Packert

DECISIONS

WHICH ROUTE LEADS TO
YOUR OPTIMUM
INVESTMENT POLICY?

Issue

Number

Four

Kidder, Peabody

748
Art Director: Miles Abernethy
Creative Director: Barry Shepard
Photographer: Rick Rusing
Agency: SHR Communications
Client: Kidder, Peabody

749
Art Director: Art Lahr
Creative Director: Art Lahr
Photographer: Taran Z
Client: Marriott Corp.

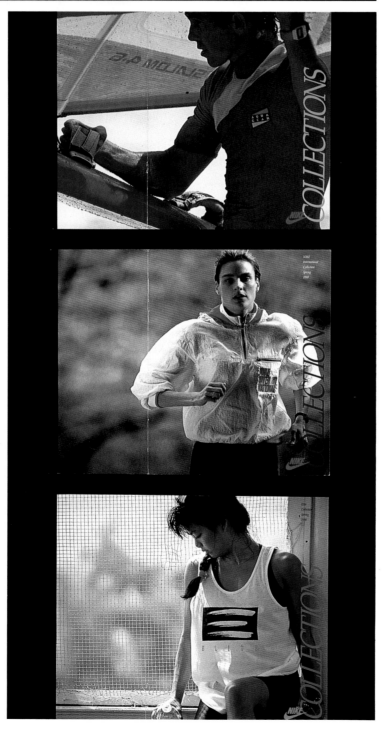

750
Art Director: Ann Schwiebinger
Photographer: Stephen Wilkes
Studio: Nike Design
Client: Nike

751

Art Director: Steve Moscowitz
Nick Vedros
John Muller
Photographer: Nick Vedros
Agency: Hutchins/Young & Rubicam
Muller & Co.
Studio: Vedros & Associates
Client: Vedros & Associates

Four day weekend. Fifth day. Lee jeans.

Public phone. Private moment. Lee jeans.

9 O'clock date. 8:55. Lee jeans.

752

Art Director: Mark Johnson
Creative Director: Pat Burnham
Photographer: Kurt Markus
Copywriter: Bill Miller
Agency: Fallon McElligott
Client: Lee Jeans

753

Art Director: Houman Pirdavari
Creative Director: Pat Burnham
Photographer: Dave Jordano
Copywriter: Bruce Bildsten
Agency: Fallon McElligott
Client: Timex

Suitable for dinner. The Timex Carriage Collection.

Grace under pressure. The Timex Carriage Collection.

Just wash and wear. The Timex Carriage Collection.

754

Art Director: Tom Lichtenheld
Creative Director: Pat Burnham
Designer: Tom Lichtenheld
Photographer: Laurie Rubin
        Kerry Peterson
Copywriter: Jamie Barrett
Agency: Fallon McElligott

755
Art Director: John Butler
　　　　　　　Mike Shine
Photographer: Joe Baraban
Copywriter: Mike Shine
　　　　　　　John Butler
Agency: Chiat/Day/Mojo
Client: NYNEX Boaters Directory

756
Art Director: Bill Heuglin
Creative Director: Bill Heuglin
Photographer: Rick Rusing
Copywriter: Laura Kennedy
Agency: Stone & Adler
Client: Navistar International Transportation

▶ **Pizza Delivery**

Can't get away for a bite to eat? With a complete yellow pages section, the NYNEX Boaters Directory is the perfect guide to help you make the most of your time at sea.

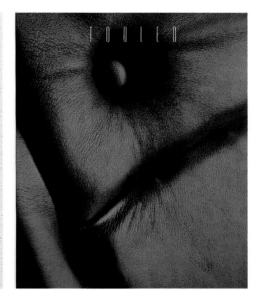

▶ **Cameras**

With everything from boating tips to a complete marine yellow pages, the NYNEX Boaters Directory can prepare you for nearly anything that pops up on a day at sea.

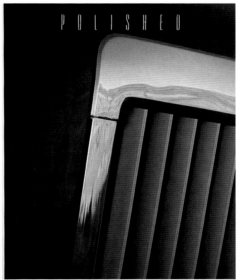

▶ **Boat Cleaning**

With a complete assortment of boating goods and services, the NYNEX Boaters Directory is the only guide you'll need for keeping your poop deck shipshape.

757

Art Director: Mark Danzig
Designer: Mark Danzig
Photographer: Brigitte LaCombe
Publication: The *Washington Post Magazine*

758

Art Director: Mary K. Baumann
Designer: Mary K. Baumann
Photographer: Dennis Marsico
Client: American Express Publishing Corp.
Publication: Favorite Places

759

Art Director: Janet Froelich
Photo Editor: Kathy Ryan
Designer: Janet Froelich
Justine Strasberg
Photographer: Eugene Richards
Publication: The *New York Times Magazine*

760

Art Director: Michael B. Marcum
Creative Director: Jim Darilek
Designer: Victoria Vaccarello
Photographer: Brian Smale
Agency: Whittle Communications
Publication: Special Report: On Sports

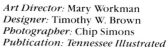

761
Art Director: Mary Workman
Designer: Timothy W. Brown
Photographer: Chip Simons
Publication: Tennessee Illustrated

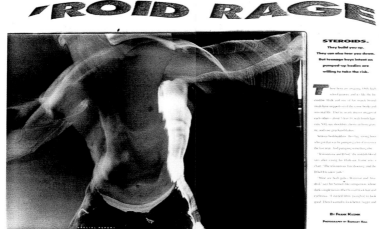

762
Art Director: Michael B. Marcum
Creative Director: Jim Darilek
Designer: James K. Bixby
Photographer: Barnaby Hall
Publication: Special Report: Health

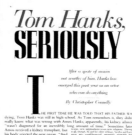

763
Art Director: Robert Best
　　　　　　David Walters
Designer: Robert Best
　　　　　David Walters
　　　　　Mary Ann Salvato
Photographer: Mark Hanauer
Copywriter: Chris Connely
Publication: Premiere

764
Art Director: Mark Danzig
Designer: Mark Danzig
Photographer: Tom Wolff
Publication: The *Washington Post Magazine*

JESSE JACKSON
Entered race October 10, 1987 • Campaign ended July 22, 1988 (with formal nomination of Michael Dukakis)

April 23, 1987   Austin, Texas

In the years between his first campaign and his second, his role in the politics of America had dramatically changed. Once a rank outsider, he had moved rather smoothly to a place inside his party, largely accepted if not always warmly welcomed by its hierarchs. Moreover, where he had once been largely dependent on the support of black Americans to sustain his pursuit, he had managed to construct a genuine rainbow coalition. It was a remarkable transition that, from time to time, seemed to surprise even him. There was very little change, if any at all, in the marvelous electricity of his public performances—and they always had that—inspired, perhaps, but practiced as well. He seemed less frivolous in 1988 than in his previous incarnation, less inclined to deal casually with serious matters, more willing to consider the long-term impact of what he was doing or doing. Yet, there was still an improvisational magic to his presence, a chemical charisma in the connection he made with his audiences—the sparkle in his eyes with or without the television lights, the earnest eagerness in his voice, the overwhelming inner dignity of one man spreading outward, lending that dignity to others.

April 22, 1987   Austin, Texas

October 26, 1988   Sioux Falls, South Dakota

October 25, 1988   Columbus, Ohio

CHOOSE ME
PORTRAITS OF A PRESIDENTIAL RACE

ARTHUR GRACE

FOREWORD BY SAM DONALDSON   ■   TEXT BY JIM WOOTEN

765
Art Director: Pam Castaldi
Photographer: Arthur Grace
Agency: Carol Judy Leslie
Client: New England University Press

766
Art Director: Suez Kehl
Designer: Cinda Rose
       Glover S. Johns III
Publication: NGS Traveler

767
Art Director: Mary Workman
Designer: Timothy W. Brown
Photographer: Russell Monk
Publication: Tennessee Illustrated

TRUE BELIEVERS

BY GEORGE KALOGERAKIS

SUSAN PICKEL-HEDRICK

Every artist, save perhaps the Knack, has devoted supporters. But what distinguishes the average fan from the excessively, even alarmingly, devoted fan – the true believer? Lots of people, after all, buy the albums and stand in line for tickets. But some go much further.

True believers make their devotion the highest priority. Tours take precedence over vacations, gigs over dinner plans, reasonably priced life-size cutouts of Ozzy over delinquent phone bills.

True believers are often collectors. They say "mint" and "alternate take" and "non-LP B side" even more than sixteen-year-olds say, "I was, like . . ." They think nothing of spending next month's rent on a Madonna Japanese tour jacket, and they know, deep down, that no drug can equal the giddy high of finding the Hib-Tone "Radio Free Europe" single for roughly the price of *Crossroads* on CD.

True believers don't worry about boring their friends. If a discussion of toxic-waste disposal systems can't accommodate a slight digression into, say, unusual Dutch picture sleeves, well, they feel, then the art of conversation is truly dead.

True believers remain fiercely loyal. The release of a *Down in the Groove* or a *Pretenders II* brings out their philosophical, defensive best.

True believers, let it be said, don't kill their idols. If they must do something illegal, they make clandestine low-fi audience recordings of concert performances; if they must do something hurtful, they force their friends to listen to these tapes.

Finally, true believers try to understand what it means to be a star and have platoons of true believers. As one fan acknowledges, "I'm sure it's a tough life. It's tough just following them around in a car."

The true believers photographed on these pages are not necessarily the biggest fans. (The biggest fans are already composing sharp notes to the editors of this magazine.) But they are real fans with, incidentally, real jobs, friends and families. In any case, if there are much bigger fans than these, we're not so sure we'd want to meet them.

PHOTOGRAPHS BY MARK SELIGER

DOMENIC PRIORE

768
Art Director: Fred Woodward
Photo Editor: Laurie Kratochvil
Photographer: Mark Seliger
Publication: *Rolling Stone*

PAUL KAHN

EARL SCOTT

CAROL WALSKE AND FERN MARDER

He hasn't CAN *had a big hit album in years. The other Beatles are suing him.* PAUL *But with 'Flowers in the Dirt,' his strong new record,* McCARTNEY *and plans for his first world tour in more than a decade, the* GET *ex-Beatle is doing his best to toughen up his image and climb back* BACK? *to the top.*

BY JAMES HENKE

Help!

ENGLAND IS IN MOURNING. Just three days ago, ninety-five soccer fans, nearly all of them from Liverpool, were killed in a chaotic crush during the early minutes of a match at Hillsborough Stadium, in Sheffield. The incident is the main topic of conversation everywhere. TV news shows cover the tragedy almost exclusively. Newspapers are filled with page after page of articles on the disaster. But on this sunny, slightly chilly spring morning, one of the country's ever-inventive tabloids has finally found some good news to report: The Beatles are back!

According to the *Daily Star*, Liverpool's most famous sons – Ringo Starr, George Harrison and Paul McCartney – were so moved by the events at Hillsborough that they've agreed to get back together to record a single, the

Tug of War

Band on the Run

PHOTOGRAPHS BY HERB RITTS

769
Art Director: Fred Woodward
Photo Editor: Laurie Kratochvil
Photographer: Herb Ritts
Publication: *Rolling Stone*

Victories of the Spirit

IN ST. LOUIS, 3,500 ATHLETES OVER 55 GO FOR THE GOLD.

770

Art Director: Janet Froelich
Photo Editor: Kathy Ryan
Designer: JoDee Stringham
Photographer: Mary Ellen Mark
Publication: The *New York Times Magazine*

EAST BERLIN DIARY

BY CHRISTOPH HEIN

'THIS IS OUR ONE CHANCE
— OUR FIRST AND LAST' THE AUTHOR SAYS.
'IF WE FAIL, WE WILL BE DEVOURED
BY McDONALD'S.'

RIGHT
NOW,
NOTHING
IS FINAL;
GUESSES
ARE
FUTILE;
EVENTS
ARE
MOVING
TOO
FAST.

771

Art Director: Janet Froelich
Photo Editor: Kathy Ryan
Designer: Kandy Uttreil
Photographer: James Nachtwey
Publication: The *New York Times*

772

Art Director: Ken Newbaker
Designer: Ken Newbaker
Photographer: Nelson Bakerman
Publication: *Philadelphia* Magazine

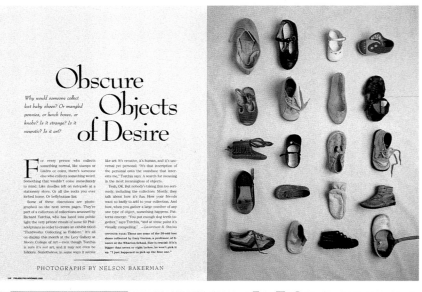

Obscure Objects of Desire

Why would someone collect lost baby shoes? Or mangled pennies, or lunch boxes, or knobs? Is it strange? Is it neurotic? Is it art?

For every person who collects something normal, like stamps or Lladro or coins, there's someone else who collects something weird. Something that wouldn't come immediately to mind. Like doodles left on notepads at a stationery store. Or all the rocks you ever kicked home. Or bellybutton lint.

Some of these obsessions are photographed on the next seven pages. They're part of a collection of collections amassed by Richard Torchia, who has lured into public light the very private rituals of some 60 Philadelphians in order to create an exhibit titled "Fieldworks: Collecting as Folklore." It's all on display this month at the Levy Gallery at Moore College of Art—even though Torchia is sure it's not art, and it may not even be folklore. Nonetheless, in some ways it seems

like art: It's creative, it's human, and it's universal yet personal. "It's that inscription of the personal onto the mundane that interests me," Torchia says. A search for meaning in the most meaningless of objects.

Yeah, OK. But nobody's taking this too seriously, including the collectors. Mostly, they talk about how it's fun. How your friends want so badly to add to your collection. And how, when you gather a large number of any one type of object, something happens. Patterns emerge. "You put enough dog teeth together," says Torchia, "and at some point it's visually compelling." —*Laurence K. Stains*

OPPOSITE PAGE: These are some of the 50-odd lost shoes collected by Gary Gorton, a professor of finance at the Wharton School. Size is crucial: If it's bigger than seven or eight inches, he won't pick it up. "I just happened to pick up the first one."

PHOTOGRAPHS BY NELSON BAKERMAN

ABOVE: Architect Charles Evers has a collection of about 75 miniatures of international monuments. Most were given to him by friends. His favorite is a tiny St. Peter's Basilica, including the piazza, shrunk into all of two inches. "It's vicarious. These are places I've never been, buildings I'll never design."

BELOW: Alan J. Klawans collects old steamship postcards. "It's a nostalgic look at a bygone era," he says. These ships were the Love Boats of their time, taking people on a daylong excursion for 70 cents and giving them a seafood dinner for 30 cents more. "I must have a couple of hundred postcards by now"—and each one takes him far away from his modern life in Willow Grove.

BELOW: Even though they started including asymmetrical objects years ago, Eric and Allison Olds still call it their "Symmetrical Black Rubber Object Collection" because it's so much fun to say. It's also fun to jump out of your car and snap up one of these things by the roadside while other drivers wonder what the hell is so important. They have close to 400 of these things now, mainly because everyone, including Eric's grandparents, keeps coming up with more.

"There was always some sort of character about a glove lying in the street that would make me want to look at it."

A couple of years ago, Kurt Madison picked up his first lost glove. Now he has about 200. And he doesn't pick up every one he sees: "There has to be some sort of gesture to it."

ROYAL VIKING LINE TO BERMUDA
EVERY SATURDAY NIGHT

Bahamian Registry

SATURDAY NIGHT
30 seconds
SFX: Music
ANNCR: Every Saturday night in the city of New York, you can experience many things that are the best of their kind in all the world. Now one of them is a cruise line.
Royal Viking to Bermuda.

773 Gold

Art Director: Rich Silverstein
Steve Diamant
Creative Director: Andy Berlin
Photographer: Michael Duff
Copywriter: Andy Berlin
Jeffrey Goodby
Producer: Elizabeth O'Toole
Director: Stan Schofield
Studio: Sandbank & Partners

ART GALLERY
60 seconds
SFX: Music
VO: You have to drive it to believe it. The new Accord.

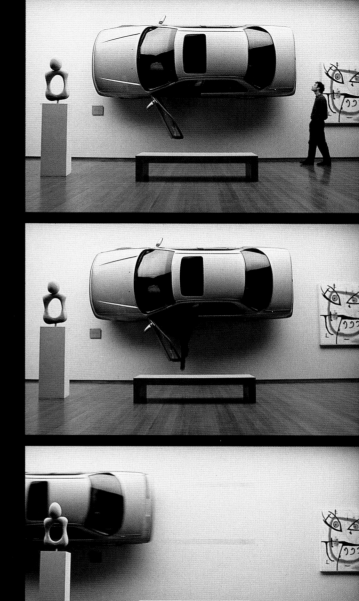

774 Gold
Art Director: Gary Yoshida
Creative Director: Larry Postaer
Copywriter: Bob Coburn
Producer: Gary Paticoff
Director: Henry Sandbank
Agency: Rubin Postaer & Associates
Client: American Honda Motor Corp.

MISSING LINK

60 seconds

STUDENT: O.K. Earl, let's call it a night. Thank you. You're welcome.

STUDENT VO: Despite being wonderful companions over the past semester...my subject group scored below average in all responses. They showed poor communications skills...no understanding of tools and their uses...a complete lack of organization and no decision making abilities. In conclusion... if I can't find some missing link that will unlock the barrier between us...this project...will be cancelled.

STUDENT: Thank you!

STUDENT & CHIMP (sign language): You're welcome.

BIKE MESSENGER
30 seconds
SFX: Jazz music
BIKE MESSENGER: You think Bo Jackson's the only guy who can do this stuff?

776 Gold

Art Director: David Jenkins
Warren Eakins
Creative Director: Dan Wieden
David Kennedy
Copywriter: Steve Sandoz
Jim Riswold
Agency: Wieden & Kennedy
Client: Nike

LITTLE THINGS

30 seconds

VO: Ever get the feeling that some airlines aren't too concerned about the little things? Before you get on an Alaska Airlines plane, we make sure...everything is ship-shape, inside and out.

777 Gold

Art Director: Tim Delaney
Creative Director: Jim Copacino
Producer: Cindy Henderson
Director: Joe Sedelmaier
Agency: Livingston & Co.
Client: Alaska Airlines

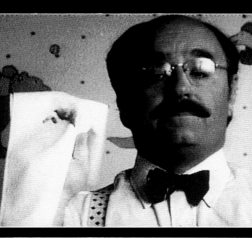

778 Gold

Art Director: Burint Ramany
Creative Director: Gerry Miller
Copywriter: Burint Ramany
Producer: Glant Cohen
Director: Leroy Koetz
Agency: Leo Burnett Co.
Client: Proctor & Gamble

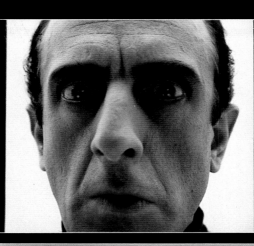

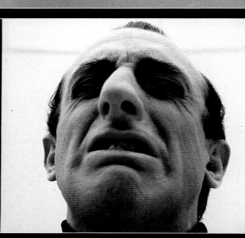

779 Silver
Art Director: Houman Pirdavari
Creative Director: Pat Burnham
Copywriter: Bruce Bildsten
Producer: Char Loving
Director: Roger Woodburn
Agency: Fallon McElligott
Client: Timex

BO DIDDLEY

60 seconds
SFX: Bo Diddley music
GIBSON: Bo knows baseball.
EVERETT: Bo knows football.
SFX: Music continues
JORDAN: Bo knows basketball, too.
SFX: Music continues
MCENROE: Bo knows tennis?
BENOIT: Bo knows running.
GRETZKY: No.
7-11 TEAM: Bo knows cycling.
WEIGHTLIFTERS: Bo knows weights.
SFX: Music continues
DIDDLEY: Bo, you don't know diddley.

780 Silver
Art Director: David Jenkins
Creative Director: Dan Wieden
David Kennedy
Copywriter: Jim Riswold
Agency: Wieden & Kennedy
Client: Nike

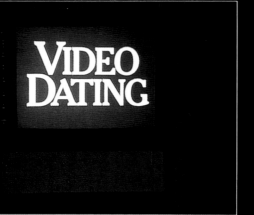

GREGOR

LEONARD

VIDEO DATING

60 seconds

GREGOR: I want a woman who likes to hunt…what do I mean by a woman who likes to hunt…

SFX: Zap

LEONARD: Hi girls my name is Lenny Tepper and I'm looking for a nice girl…

GREGOR: A woman who likes to hunt in the mountains…hunt in the plains…

SFX: Zap

JONATHAN: I am successful, I'm rich and I'm good looking… rich, good looking and successful.

SFX: Zap

GREGOR: Hunt in the mountains with a gun…

SFX: Zap

MAN: I don't do drugs…Ummm Ok I take Lithium.

LEONARD: I want a woman that is hot--Wow…Whooo…

ANNCR: When life is rough, laugh it off with the new Comedy Channel. 24 hours a day, we're there when you need us.

LEONARD: Hi girls it's me Lenny Tepper again…

781 Silver

Art Director: Donna Weinheim
John Colquhoun
Creative Director: Donna Weinheim
Copywriter: Jeff Alphin
Jane King
Rick LeMoine
Cliff Freeman
Agency: Cliff Freeman & Partners
Client: Home Box Office/Comedy Channel

CHANGE OF HEART

60 seconds
MOM: How are things at work, dear?
ABBY: OK. They want me to use a computer.
DAD: A computer? You?
ABBY: I mean, what do I need a computer for? I'm not an accountant....I figure, what? I've been in this business 11 years, right? Why do I need one now? I've done fine without one....Can you imagine me working on a computer?
FRIEND: They figure if you can use one, then anybody can use one.
VO: Macintosh has the power to change your mind about computers. The power to be your best.
ABBY: So, I was wrong.

782 Silver
Art Director: Susan Westre
Creative Director: Steve Hayden
Copywriter: Chris Wall
Producer: Bob Belton
Pat Walsh
Director: Joe Pytka
Studio: Pytka Productions

GLASNOST

60 seconds
(Spoken in Russian)
SFX: Music
FATHER: Noise! Noise! You call that music?
FRIEND: Hey, Dude! Totally awesome day!
VO: (in English) Not very long ago, America introduced Pepsi to the Soviet Union.
LADY: Look! What's this craziness?
FATHER: Look at you! Do you have to dress like that?
VO: (in English) …And while it may be just a coincidence…a lot of refreshing changes have taken place ever since.
FRIEND: Yo! Mickey!
FATHER: Don't you have any normal friends? Kids!
VO: (in English) Pepsi. A generation ahead.
WIFE: Yuri…come on, lighten up.

783 Silver
Art Director: Richard Sabean
Rich Martel
Creative Director: Al Merrin
Copywriter: Michael Patti
Director: Rick Levine
Leslie Dektor
Studio: Rick Levine Productions
Petermann-Dektor

TAXI DRIVER

60 seconds

ANNCR: To understand Asia, you have to understand its customs, its mysteries, its people. You have to know what makes a good impression, and what offends. For over 40 years we've been learning about Asia. So in addition to nearly 90 nonstops weekly, with service from over 200 US cities, and Worldperks, the best frequent flyer program in the sky, we can give you something no other US airline can.

The knowledge, information and insight that comes after 40 years of helping people do business in Asia.

In Seoul you don't have to tip taxi drivers.

784 Silver
Art Director: Doris Cassar
Pat Peduto
Creative Director: Pat Peduto
Copywriter: Paige St. John
Producer: Christine Cacace
Director: Michael Werk
Agency: Saatchi & Saatchi
Client: Northwest Airlines

PLEASE STAND BY
15 seconds
SFX: Office sounds; muffled voices

Please stand by.

We wanted to show you the NYNEX
Business to Business Yellow Pages.

We are looking for a copy
not in use at his time.

785 Silver

Art Director: Gary Goldsmith
Creative Director: Gary Goldsmith
Copywriter: Dean Hacohen
Producer: Trisha Caruso

786 Silver
Art Director: Grant Parrish
Creative Director: Tom Rost
Copywriter: Jan Prager
Producer: Nancy Perez
Director: Leslie Dektor
Agency: Ogilvy & Mather

787 Silver
Art Director: Wendy Hansen
Creative Director: Lyle Wedemeyer
Copywriter: Lyle Wedemeyer
Director: Rick Dublin
Agency: Martin/Williams
Client: Minnesota Department of Health

788 Distinctive Merit

Art Director: Bob Barrie
Creative Director: Pat Burnham
Copywriter: Jarl Olsen
Producer: Char Loving
Director: Rick Dublin
Agency: Fallon McElligott
Client: Hush Puppies

CORPORATE HUSH PUPPIES
15 seconds
SFX: Foot tapping

789 Distinctive Merit

Art Director: Bob Barrie
Creative Director: Pat Burnham
Copywriter: Jarl Olsen
Producer: Char Loving
Director: Rick Dublin
Agency: Fallon McElligott
Client: Hush Puppies

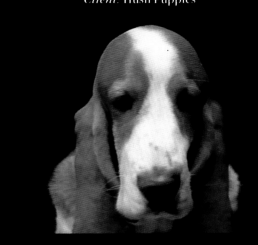

CASUAL HUSH PUPPIES
15 seconds
MUSIC: Lullaby
SFX: Thump; dog snoring

790 Distinctive Merit

Art Director: Jeff York
Creative Director: Tenney Fairchild
Joe Sciarrotta
Copywriter: Ann O'Phelan
Producer: Carol Faron
Director: Victor Haboush
Agency: J. Walter Thompson
Client: Quaker Oats Co.

SARGE

30 seconds
SFX: Drums
SARGE: What's the meal I hate to miss?
TROOPS: Kibbles 'N Bits 'N Bits 'N Bits!
SARGE: Variety--I can't resist.
TROOPS: Kibbles 'N Bits 'N Bits 'N Bits!
SARGE: Crunchy, chewy--I insist.
TROOPS: Kibbles 'N Bits 'N Bits 'N Bits!
SARGE: My dog food goes like this!
TROOPS: Kibbles 'N Bits 'N Bits 'N Bits!
SARGE: Crunchy!
TROOPS: Chewy!
SARGE: Fall in!
TROOPS: Chow down!
SFX: Music
SARGE: For variety, you should enlist!
TROOPS: Kibbles 'N Bits 'N Bits 'N Bits!

791 Distinctive Merit

Art Director: Susan Wood
Creative Director: Al Merrin
Glenn Miller
Copywriter: Glenn Miller
Producer: Barbara Mullins
Lisa Steinman
Director: Joe Pytka
Studio: Pytka Productions
Client: GE Corporate

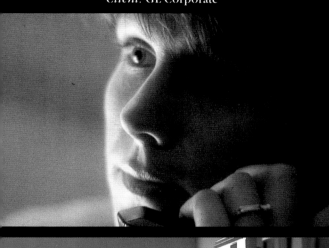

792 Distinctive Merit
Art Director: Michael Prieve
Creative Director: Dan Wieden
David Kennedy
Copywriter: Jim Riswold
Producer: Patti Greaney
Bill Davenport
Director: Bob Giraldi
Agency: Wieden & Kennedy
Client: Nike

795 Distinctive Merit

Art Director: Burint Ramany
Creative Director: Gerry Miller
Copywriter: Burint Ramany
Producer: Glant Cohen
Director: Leroy Koetz
Agency: Leo Burnett Co.
Client: Proctor & Gamble

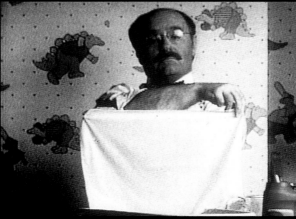

796 Distinctive Merit
Art Director: John Scott MacDaniels
Creative Director: John Scott MacDaniels
Copywriter: Walt Kramer
Producer: Deborah Newman-Cooke
Director: Haskell Wexler
Hobby Morrison
Agency: MacDaniels, Henry & Sproul
Client: Caltrans/Amtrak

Amtrak San Joaquin
It Beats Driving!

Art Director: Gary Goldsmith
Creative Director: Gary Goldsmith
Copywriter: Tom Churm
Gary Goldsmith
Producer: Trisha Caruso
Valerie Edwards
Client: Everlast Activewear

STOPWATCH
15 seconds
SFX: Stopwatch ticking
VO: In the United States, every 10 seconds, another piece of
designer clothing goes out of style.
SFX: Woman screams

798 Distinctive Merit

Art Director: Susan Westre
Creative Director: Steve Hayden
Copywriter: Chris Wall
Producer: Bob Belton
Pat Walsh
Director: Joe Pytka
Studio: Pytka Productions
Client: Apple Computer Inc.

TESTING 1-2-3

60 seconds
WOMAN 1: Can I get on there soon?
WOMAN 2: After me.
KEN: Do you think I can get on here soon?
MAN 1: Yeah, give me a minute, man.
ED: You've been staring out there all day. What are you doing?
JOHN: Testing.
ED: Testing what?
JOHN: Computers. I'm trying to figure out which computer is the most powerful.
ED: Well, that's easy. The one with the most memory...megahertz...MIPS...you know.
JOHN: No, I don't think so. I think the most powerful computer is the one that people actually use.
GIRL: Hi, Ken.
KEN: Hey.
VO: Macintosh has the power to change the way you look at computers. The power to be your best.
ED: That's not really a fair comparison. People like using the Mac.

799 Distinctive Merit
Art Director: Matt Smith
Creative Director: Ross Van Dusen
Copywriter: David O'Hare
Producer: Harvey Greenberg
Jan Ushijima
Director: Gary Weis
Agency: Chiat/Day/Mojo
Client: Rainier Dry Beer

REAL PEOPLE & BEER

30 seconds
GUY 1: Okay, real people and beer.
GUY 2: Yeah, real people are cool.
GUY 1: All right, I love this. Nice couple.
GUY 2: Aw, that's nice....Looks like that girl that dumped
you...
GUY 1: Thanks for the memory. Whoa! stereo. Hello, boys.
GUY 2: Hey, get the guy on the bike.
GUY 1: Okay, I got him. I got him.
GUY 2: Wait a minute. He's coming back.
GUY 1: Who?
GUY 2: The guy on the bike. See him? Can you get him?
Oh, oh...
GUY 1: Let's go.
GUY 2: No, let's get him.
GUY 1: Come on, get out of here.
GUY 2: Did you get the beer in the shot?
GUY 1: Yeah, yeah, yeah, give me the beer.
GUY 2: Come on, he's gaining on us.
GUY 1: Give me the beer.
GUY 2: Pretty cool, huh?

800 Distinctive Merit

Art Director: Susan Westre
Creative Director: Steve Hayden
Copywriter: Chris Wall
Producer: Bob Belton
Pat Walsh
Director: Joe Pytka
Studio: Pytka Productions
Client: Apple Computer Inc.

THE NEW TEACHER

60 seconds
PRINCIPAL: Looks like we got a new teacher. Miss Kassman?
SECRETARY: Miss Kassman.
BROTHER: Amy, I hear your new teacher's real mean.
MISS KASSMAN: Good morning, everybody.
CLASS: Good morning!
DOUG: New teachers have to be tough so you're scared of 'em
MISS KASSMAN: Did you bring your pictures?
CLASS: Yes!
MISS KASSMAN: Amy, would you come up here and bring you
picture with you, please?
SFX: Commotion among the students
PRINCIPAL: I'd better check on Miss Kassman.
SFX: More commotion
ANNCR: There's a special power that can bring students and
teachers closer together. The power to be your best.
BROTHER: Whoa, that's cool! Hey, how's your new teacher?
AMY: Oh, she's OK.

801

Art Director: Kathy Strall
  Eddie Snyder
Creative Director: Eddie Snyder
Copywriter: Dave Nelson
Producer: Eddie Snyder
Director: Lance Russell
Agency: Group 243
Client: The Athlete's Foot

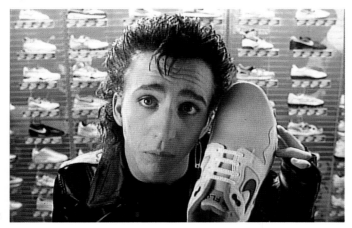

BASIC BLACK

15 seconds
TEEN IN BLACK: Got these Nike's in black? Black? Got 'em in black? Black? Got any blacker?

802

Art Director: Mary Mentzer
Creative Director: Dave Bradley
Copywriter: Joel Mitchell
Director: Jim Beresford
Studio: Bajus Jones
Client: First Minnesota

SENIORS

15 seconds
MAN: I borrowed $200 to take her on a honeymoon to Colorado Springs.
SHE: Borrowed from me.
MAN: From her. Ah…cause I was flat broke.
SHE: You see who's the money manager.
VO: First Minnesota. Taking the family into account.

803

Art Director: Pam Conboy
Creative Director: Lyle Wedemeyer
Copywriter: Emily Scott
Producer: Dain Rodwell
Director: John Kump Zurik
Agency: Martin/Williams
Client: Snyder's Drug Stores

804

Art Director: Gary Goldsmith
Creative Director: Gary Goldsmith
Copywriter: Tom Churm
Gary Goldsmith
Producer: Trisha Caruso
Valerie Edwards

HAIRDO
15 seconds
SFX: '50s music on the radio
SHE: La, la, la…
VO: Out of hair spray? Snyder's has 28 brands of hair spray.
SFX: Deflating sounds

COUNTDOWN
15 seconds
SFX: Bongs
VO: This commercial will last 15 seconds. About as long as most
fashion trends.

805

Art Director: Pam Conboy
Creative Director: Lyle Wedemeyer
Copywriter: Emily Scott
Producer: Dain Rodwell
Director: John Kump Zurik
Agency: Martin/Williams
Client: Snyder's Drug Stores

806

Art Director: Larry Jarvis
Creative Director: Lloyd Wolfe
Copywriter: Rob Rosenthal
Agency: Cole & Weber, Portland
Client: The *Oregonian*

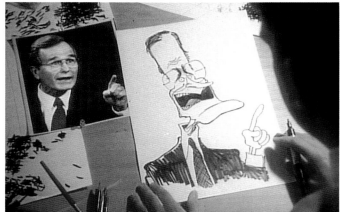

SLAPPING

15 seconds
SFX: Slapping sounds
VO: Out of mosquito repellant? Snyder's has 11 different kinds of protective sprays and lotions.

JACK OHMAN

15 seconds
SFX: Scratching of pen on paper
VO: When a politician steps out of line…
SFX: Scratching stops abruptly
VO: …our man rearranges his face. Jack Ohman. Tomorrow in The *Oregonian*.

807
Art Director: Bob Barrie
Creative Director: Pat Burnham
Copywriter: Jarl Olsen
Producer: Char Loving
Director: Rick Dublin
Agency: Fallon McElligott
Client: Hush Puppies

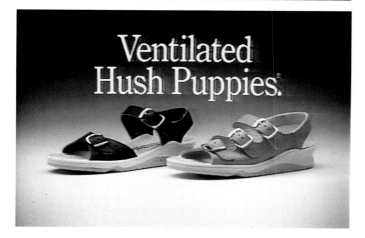

808
Art Director: Bob Barrie
Creative Director: Pat Burnham
Copywriter: Jarl Olsen
Producer: Char Loving
Director: Rick Dublin
Agency: Fallon McElligott
Client: Hush Puppies

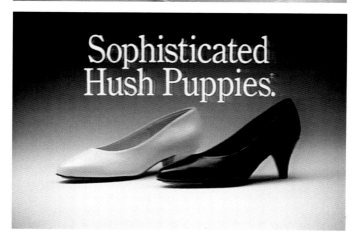

VENTILATED HUSH PUPPIES
15 seconds
SFX: Urban street sounds; rumbling of train

SOPHISTICATED HUSH PUPPIES
15 seconds
SFX: Bottle opening; gurgling sound; dog lapping

809

Art Director: David Fox
Creative Director: Bill Hamilton
Copywriter: Marty Cooke
Producer: Tom Harbeck
           Lee Weiss
Agency: Chiat/Day/Mojo Advertising Inc.
Client: NYNEX Information Resources

SWEEPSTAKES

30 seconds
SFX: Barbecue party sounds
VO 1: Hey, Bob. Nice apron. How ya been?
CHEF: Not bad, not bad. How do you like your steak?
VO 1: Medium, Bob. Medium.
CHEF: Oooops! Hey, Marv. Glad you could make it. How do you like your steak?
VO 2: Well-done, Bob. Burn it.
CHEF: Comin' right up. Ooops!
VO 3: Bob, make mine rare.
CHEF: You got it. Ooooops!
SFX: Sweeping
ANNCR: It's the NYNEX Yellow Pages Sweepstakes. We'll be calling thousands of people to play. So be prepared. The Grand Prize is $25,000.

810

Art Director: Steve Juliusson
Creative Director: Tom McConnaughy
Designer: Steve Juliusson
Copywriter: Jim Schmidt
Producer: Clark Dodsworth
Director: Dennis Manarchy
Agency: McConnaughy, Barocci, Brown
Client: Illinois Department of Tourism

NO COMMERCIALS

30 seconds
SFX: Frogs croaking; owl hooting; geese honking; crickets chirping; loon calling

811

Art Director: Matt Fischer
Creative Director: John Ferrell
Copywriter: Andrew Landorf
Producer: Joy Luettich
Director: Peter Smillie
Agency: Hill, Holliday
Client: Irish Tourist Board

STORYTELLERS

30 seconds
VO: They were called the Seanchai. They spread the legend of
St. Patrick driving out the snakes, of St. Brendan discovering America,
and of Grace O'Malley who beheaded her five husbands…or did she?
So visit Ireland and listen well for there's still a bit of the Seanchai
in all of us.
Ireland. The ancient birthplace of good times.

812

Art Director: John Butler
　　　　　　 Mike Shine
Creative Director: Bill Hamilton
Designer: Graham Clifford
Copywriter: Mike Shine
　　　　　　 John Butler
Producer: Kathi Calef
Agency: Chiat/Day/Mojo Advertising Inc.
Client: Grandy's

ALAN PLATT

30 seconds
VO: Grandy's presents the biggest chickens of all time. In 1956, Alan
Platt broke his wife's crystal vase and blamed it on the dog.
GROUP VO: Chicken!
VO: In 1968, Charlie Bidwell took his date to the drive-in, and actually
watched the movie.
GROUP VO: Chicken!
VO: Now Grandy's is offering their big ten-piece Chicken Family Pack.
With mashed potatoes, vegetable and rolls. We'd like to ask $49.99, but
we'll settle for $9.99.
GROUP VO: Chicken!
VO: Grandy's. The fastest home cooking around.

813

Art Director: Sheri Olmon
Creative Director: Bill Hamilton
Copywriter: Alan Platt
Producer: Andrew Chinich
Agency: Chiat/Day/Mojo Advertising Inc.
Client: American Express Gold Card

814

Art Director: John Butler
　　　　　　　Mike Shine
Creative Director: Bill Hamilton
Designer: Graham Clifford
Copywriter: Mike Shine
　　　　　　John Butler
Producer: Kathi Calef
Agency: Chiat/Day/Mojo Advertising Inc.
Client: Grandy's

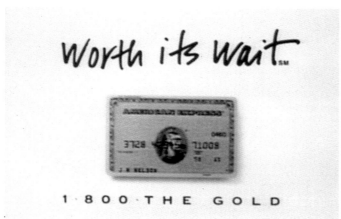

HAT

30 seconds
VO: Bogart. You always told me he was the coolest. Gene Kelly was the smoothest. Sellers was the funniest. Sydney Greenstreet was the meanest. But John Wayne always had the best hat. Happy birthday, Dad. Hope it fits.
The American Express Gold Card.

DAVID WEINER

30 seconds
VO: Grandy's presents the biggest chickens of all time. In 1966, David Weiner was afraid to ask Gwen Lipsky to the prom. She went with his friend Milton instead.
GROUP VO: Chicken!
VO: In 1972, Blake Olson said nothing when his neighbor ran over his petunias with a lawn mower.
GROUP VO: Chicken!
VO: Now Grandy's is offering their big ten-piece Chicken Family Pack. With mashed potatoes, vegetable and rolls. We'd like to ask $49.99, but we'll settle for $9.99.
GROUP VO: Chicken!
VO: Grandy's. The fastest home cooking around.

815

Art Director: Marc Donnenfeld
Creative Director: Andrew Langer
Copywriter: Marc Wolf
Producer: Kathy Tieman
Director: Michael Schrom
Agency: Lowe Marschalk
Client: A-1 Steak Sauce

816

Art Director: Ernie Cox
Copywriter: Jim Doherty
Producer: Bob Carney
Director: Jack Churchill
Agency: NW Ayer
Client: Outboard Marine Corp.

DONE
30 seconds
SFX: Music
VO: A1, it's how steak is done.

CRIB
30 seconds
VO: Studies have shown, it can be determined almost from birth, who's right for an Evinrude outboard motor.
Evinrude owners are born, not made.

817

Art Director: Tony DeGregorio
Creative Director: Tony DeGregorio
Copywriter: Rochelle Klein
Producer: Vera Samama
Director: Paul Giraud
Studio: HSI Productions
Client: Maidenform

818

Art Director: Kristine Pallas
Creative Director: Kristine Pallas
  John Mattingly
Copywriter: John Mattingly
Director: Steve Steigman
Agency: Pallas Advertising
Client: Vipont

BALCONY

30 seconds
VO: It couldn't have happened at a better time. Maidenform. Buy two, get one free.

BEAST

30 seconds
PRESENTER: To demonstrate the new Kick The Habit gradual smoking withdrawal system, we're comparing nicotine to the grasp of a beast. But with the Kick The Habit Level 1 Filter, your nicotine intake is reduced. You'll feel more like this. In a week switch to Level 2. The grasp of nicotine is reduced even more. Week 3? Level 3. Now you're ready to quit. And the monkey's off your back. Kick The Habit. The gradual smoking withdrawal system.

819

Art Director: Phil Triolo
Creative Director: Art Mellor
Robert Greenbaum
Copywriter: Jimmy Siegel
Robert Greenbaum
Producer: Regina Ebel
Director: Rick Levine
Studio: Rick Levine Productions
Client: Federal Express

820

Art Director: Matt Fischer
Creative Director: John Ferrell
Copywriter: Gary Cohen
Producer: Joy Luettich
Director: Peter Smillie
Agency: Hill, Holliday
Client: Irish Tourist Board

MEDITERRANEAN STORM

30 seconds
VO: How to get your package through a Mediterranean storm….Most
Federal Express overseas employees are from overseas. So they not only
know the local customs regulations, they know the local customs…
FEDERAL EXPRESS EMPLOYEE: …Per favore…
VO: …and that helps your package sail right through.
FEDERAL EXPRESS EMPLOYEE: …Grazie!
VO: Because when delivering in Rome, it helps to be a Roman. Federal
Express. The best way to ship it over here is now the best way to ship it
over there.

FRIENDS

30 seconds
VO: It is said in the course of a lifetime you make only one or two true
friends. We know where you just might find a third.
Ireland. The ancient birthplace of good times.

821

Art Director: Gary Goldsmith
Creative Director: Gary Goldsmith
Copywriter: Dean Hacohen
Producer: Trisha Caruso
　　　　　Valerie Edwards
Director: Henry Sandbank

822

Art Director: Michael Prieve
Creative Director: Dan Wieden
　　　　　　　　David Kennedy
Copywriter: Jim Riswold
Producer: Roberta Grubman
　　　　　Bill Davenport
Director: Bob Giraldi
Agency: Wieden & Kennedy
Client: Nike

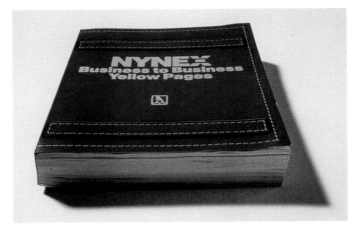

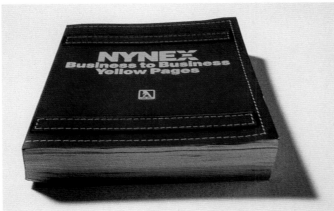

LUNCHTIME
30 seconds
This commercial has no dialogue.

FORCE
30 seconds
SFX: Music

823

Art Director: Andy Dijak
          Mike Mazza
Creative Director: Bob Kuperman
Copywriter: Dick Sittig
Producer: Richard O'Neill

824

Art Director: Andy Dijak
          Mike Mazza
Creative Director: Lee Clow
Copywriter: Brian Belefant
Producer: Michael Paradise
Director: Leslie Dektor

IF I HAD A 240SX

30 seconds
240SX DREAMER: If I had a Nissan 240SX...it would be a red coupe.—Wait! A silver fastback. And I'd go for a spin up Route 7, the twisty part. Just me and Astro...no, Amy. Heck, Christie Brinkley! Wow! Yeah, me and Christie...in my silver—no, red 240SX...driving into the sunset.

WE LEARN FROM RACING

30 seconds
SFX: Music
ANNCR: To Nissan, a truck race is nothing more than a learning experience. It's just another day spent working out the bugs in a new suspension. Tweaking an engine to get more horsepower. Or figuring out which chassis design can withstand the most stress. Oh, sure, we've won a couple hundred races—including the championship at the last Baja 1000. But the fact is, as long as we learn something, we don't really care if we win.
Yeah, right.

825

Art Director: Pam Cunningham
         Andy Dijak
Creative Director: Lee Clow
Copywriter: Steve Bassett
Producer: Richard O'Neill
Director: Michael Werk

ME AND MY SHADOW

30 seconds
SONG: ''Me and My Shadow''
SINGER: Me and my shadow, strolling down the avenue.
  Me and my shadow…
ANNCR: The Nissan 240SX. There's never been a sports car quite like
it. Except for this one. The 240SX Coupe. For a great selection and a
great deal, see your nearest Nissan dealer now.

826

Art Director: Ed Maslow
Creative Director: Charlie Meismer
         Art Mellor
         Ed Maslow
Copywriter: Zoe Heighington
Producer: Barbara Mullins
Director: Fred Petermann
Studio: Fred Petermann
Client: Federal Express

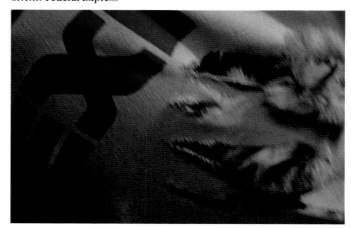

CHANGING ITS STRIPES

30 seconds
VO: In this package is over 40 years of experience in overseas shipping,
and access to more air routes worldwide. Because Flying Tigers has
changed its stripes and merged with Federal Express to form the largest
all-cargo airline in the world.

827
Art Director: Michael Smith
Creative Director: Bob Kuperman
Copywriter: Jerry Fields
Producer: Vicki Blucher
Director: Maxine Tabak

828
Art Director: Pam Cunningham
Creative Director: Bob Kuperman
Copywriter: Steve Bassett
Producer: Richard O'Neill
Director: John St. Clair

RECIPES
30 seconds
SFX: Lighthearted music
VO: No matter what your favorite recipe, it'll always turn out better if you start from scratch. Introducing Dep Everyday Shampoo. Expressly created to gently wash away styling buildup.

Z CLEAN SHEET
30 seconds
SFX: Loud banging
ANNCR: This is where we started—a clean sheet of paper. No boundaries. No rules. No preconceived ideas. Just desire to build the best sports car in the world. A car for one driver in a thousand. The car destined to leave its mark.
SFX: Loud banging
ANNCR: The new Z. From Nissan.

829
Art Director: Michael Smith
Creative Director: Bob Kuperman
Copywriter: Sam Avery
Producer: Vicki Blucher
Director: Mark Coppos

830
Art Director: Angela Dunkle
Creative Director: Bob Kuperman
Copywriter: Dion Hughes

FRAMES
30 seconds
ANNCR: Some people can be very choosy.
WOMAN OC: No. No, no, no.
ANNCR: So to make sure all our customers find what they want…at EyeMasters we carry over 1,500 frames.
WOMAN OC: No. No.
ANNCR: You'll also get…
WOMAN OC: Yes.
ANNCR: Our honest opinion. EyeMasters. We treat you like a person. Not a prescription.

ELVIS
30 seconds
This commercial has no dialogue.

831

Art Director: Rick Boyko
Creative Director: Bob Kuperman
Copywriter: Steve Rabosky
Producer: Brianne Howard
Director: Dennis Manarchy

832

Art Director: Woody Swain
Creative Director: Eric Weber
Copywriter: Andrew Landorf
Producer: Diane Flynn
Director: Jeff Gorman
Agency: Young & Rubicam, Inc.
Client: United States Postal Service

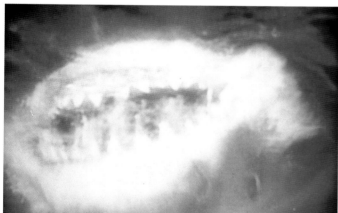

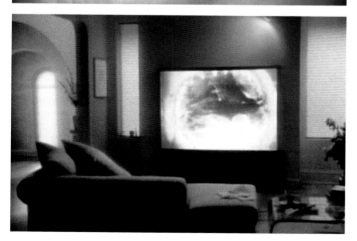

SMALL SCREENS

30 seconds
ANNCR: If you're not watching movies on the Mitsubishi Big Screen television, you're not seeing them the way they were meant to be seen. Introducing the world's first 70 inch TV. At 70 inches, it's not a big television; it's a small theater.

DINOSAURS

30 seconds
MAN: Wait stop! Wait stop! Stop! Stop! Wait stop! Wait wait stop! Don't you know they're coming! Wait stop!
DRIVER: Look out!
MAN: Doesn't anyone…believe me?
POLICE OFFICER: You hear that fellows, dinosaurs are coming to this town.
WOMAN: They're already here.
SFX: Dramatic music
VO: Dinosaur stamps…they're exciting. They're history. They're at your post office now.
MAN: Now do you believe me?

833
Art Director: Dan Weeks
Copywriter: Scott Eirinberg
Producer: Ray Lyle
Director: Jeff Gorman
Studio: Johns & Gorman Films
Client: Sears

834
Art Director: John Cenatiempo
Creative Director: Barry Biederman
Copywriter: Barry Biederman
Producer: Lisa Bifulco
Director: Chris Nolan
Agency: Biederman, Kelly & Shaffer
Client: Tri-State Cadillac Dealers Assoc.

BRANDS
30 seconds
COWBOY #1: Zenith…Braun…Sony…RCA…
SFX: Cattle mooing
VO: At Sears, we've rounded up over 1,000 brands. So now you can get top name brands at great low prices. And we're adding more everyday.
COWBOY #1: …Smith-Corona…
COWBOY #2: Yeah, where is that Smith-Corona, anyhow?
STEER: MOOOOOOOooooooooo…

COMMUTER
30 seconds
COMMUTER: Don't need a lift, Jack…there's my wife in our Lincoln Continental. Ahhh! You're not Doris. And this isn't my car—it's a Taurus. I'm sorry!
VO: It's funny, how much *alike* Ford cars look these days.
COMMUTER: Doris!…Oh, wait…this isn't my car, either--it's a Topaz!!
VO: By contrast, the 1990 Cadillacs are luxuriously, unmistakably Cadillacs.
COMMUTER: Doris…!!Doris…!!Ohhh, not Doris.
VO: See your Cadillac Tri-Statesman…now!

835

Art Director: Raul Pina
Creative Director: Jamie Seltzer
Copywriter: Rich Roth
Producer: Peter Yahr
Director: Carroll Ballard
Agency: Della Femina, McNamee WCRS
Client: Dow

836

Art Director: Mike Mazza
Creative Director: Bob Kuperman
Copywriter: Dick Sittig
Producer: Jack Harrower
Director: John Marles
Agency: Chiat/Day/Mojo
Client: Nissan Motor Corp.

TUNDRA

30 seconds
VO: Today, there's a better way to protect food from the freezing cold. Freezloc, a plastic freezer wrap with special cling strips that seal tighter against freezer burn than any other wrap, to protect your food from the ravages of freezing cold, until the day it's needed. Tough, thick, Freezloc with cling strips for more protection against freezer burn.

4 X 4 DREAMER

30 seconds
4x4 DREAMER: My dream car would be…a truck. A Nissan Hardbody. I'd race in Baja. Whoa, wait a minute, make that the mountains. With nobody around 'cept my girlfriend…and a pizza…and my boss…. Somebody's got to wash the truck.

837
Art Director: Mark Decena
Creative Director: Tom Molitor
Copywriter: David Munroe
Producer: Gale Gortney
Agency: Saatchi & Saatchi DFS/Pacific
Client: U.S. West

838
Art Director: Andy Dijak
　　　　　　　Mike Mazza
Creative Director: Bob Kuperman
Copywriter: Dick Sittig
Producer: Richard O'Neill
Agency: Chiat/Day/Mojo
Client: Nissan Motor Corp.

GUY IN A DINER
30 seconds
SFX: Diner ambiance
VO: 25 million Americans can't read a dinner menu. U S WEST DIRECT volunteers teach literacy classes to show them what they're missing.

IF I HAD A 240SX
30 seconds
240SX DREAMER: If I had a Nissan 240SX…I'd get a red coupe.—No! A silver fastback. And I'd go for a spin up Route 7, the twisty part. Just me and Elvis…maybe Mark. Heck, why not Ken Wahl! Yeah, me and Ken…in my silver--no, red 240SX…driving into the sunset.

839

Art Director: Bob Tabor
Creative Director: Bill Chororos
Copywriter: Roger Feuerman
Producer: Bailey Weiss
Director: Jim Lee
Agency: Backer, Spielvogel, Bates
Client: Best Foods

840

Art Director: Phillip Squier
Creative Director: Scott Montgomery
Ken Sakoda
Designer: Phillip Squier
Copywriter: Michael McKay
Producer: Glenn Miller
Agency: Salvati Montgomery Sakoda
Client: Valley National Bank

UNIVERSITY

30 seconds
STUDENT'S VOICE: None of us will forget that morning. I joined my chums as I too was jolted by the news. Mr. Thomas had moved his bakeshop to America. No more would we have his English muffins, with nooks and crannies and melted butter, to sustain us through our dreary day. University without nooks and crannies?! It was yet another cross for England to bear.
Thomas' English Muffins. For over a hundred years, England's breakfast tradition in America's hands.

PHOENIX SUNS

30 seconds
SFX: Droning noise
VO: To the hearing impaired, watching the news can be a confusing experience. Reading lips and interpreting what they see isn't enough. That's why we at Valley Bank are proud to sponsor channel 12's closed captioned news.
SFX: Droning stops
VO: Because we understand how important it is for everyone to get the whole story.

841
Art Director: Tim Delaney
Creative Director: Roger Livingston
Copywriter: Jim Copacino
Producer: Cindy Henderson
Director: Joe Sedelmaier
Agency: Livingston & Co.
Client: Alaska Airlines

BEEMER

30 seconds
ASSISTANT: That's him, huh, company's top salesman?
CHAUFFEUR: Numero Uno, they say he can sell snow in a snowstorm.
ASSISTANT: A real personality.
CHAUFFEUR: The guy is a dynamo.
VO: Even the most important, dynamic executive can feel downright
unimportant…
EXECUTIVE: Miss, oh, miss…
VO: …on a bad flight.
ASSISTANT: Looks like he's been working non-stop.
CHAUFFEUR: He never lets up, that's why he's making the big bucks.
VO: Next trip fly Alaska Airlines. We try to treat everybody like they're
somebody.

842
Art Director: Earl Cavanah
Creative Director: Sam Scali
Copywriter: Larry Cadman
Producer: Sue Chiafullo
Director: Eli Noyes
Agency: Scali, McCabe, Sloves
Client: Nikon

RED-EYE ROCK

30 seconds
MUSIC: Queen's ''We will rock you''
SFX: Boom…boom…clap. Boom…boom…clap.
CHORUS: Down with, down with Red-eye.
SFX: Boom…boom…clap.
CHORUS: Down with, down with Red-eye.
SFX: Boom…boom…clap. Boom…boom…clap.
CHORUS: Down with, down with Red-eye.
SFX: Boom…boom…clap. Boom…
VO: In response…to popular demand, we proudly introduce the Nikon
Teletouch 300. A totally automatic…dual lens camera…that
significantly reduces…Red-eye.
SFX: Applause

843

Art Director: Simon Bowden
Creative Director: Earl Cavanah
Copywriter: Debbie Kasher
                       Bernie Phillips
Producer: Dane Johnson
Director: Tom Higgins
Agency: Scali, McCabe, Sloves
Client: Volvo

844

Art Director: Bob Tabor
Creative Director: Bill Chororos
Copywriter: Roger Feuerman
Producer: Bailey Weiss
Agency: Backer, Spielvogel, Bates
Client: Best Foods

BUMPER CARS

30 seconds
ANNCR: Every Volvo is equipped with energy-absorbing front and rear crumple zones, rigid steel bars to protect you from side intrusion, and a steel safety cage for all-round protection, which is something you should think about seriously on a ride in the real world.

BRIGADIER

30 seconds
BRIGADIER'S VOICE: It was with great honor that I led a tribute to the town baker, Mr. Thomas. I didn't know the man, but he had been the maker of our marvelous muffins, with nooks and crannies, English to the core. I saluted him now that he had gone off to America. I didn't know the man. But I knew his muffins.
Thomas' English Muffins. For over a hundred years, England's breakfast tradition in American hands.

845

Art Director: Dean Hanson
Creative Director: Pat Burnham
Copywriter: Phil Hanft
Producer: Judy Carter Brink
Director: Henry Sandbank
Agency: Fallon McElligott
Client: Federal Express

846

Art Director: Jim Baldwin
Creative Director: Ray Redding
                      Thomas Hripko
Copywriter: David Longfield
Director: Bob Einstein

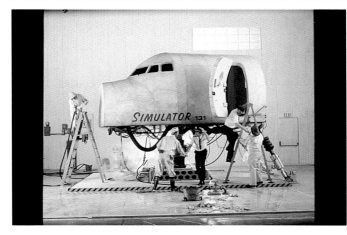

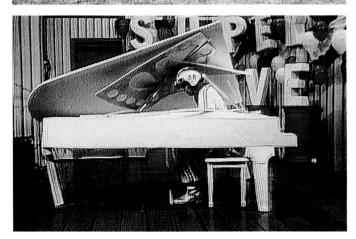

SIMULATOR

30 seconds
PILOT: Tokyo Tower, Tokyo Tower, Flight 101…request permission to land.
VO: Someday…every international air express company will have it all. 24-hour customer service…advanced tracking systems…
CO-PILOT: Whoa.
VO: …and their own fleet of planes flying to Europe, Canada and Japan.
PILOT: Touchdown!
VO: Just like Federal Express.
PILOT: Alright…
VO: But until then the others will just have to pretend.
PILOT: Nice lightning.
VO: Worldwide Service from Federal Express.

SUPER DAVE—HIGHLIGHTS #1

30 seconds
MIKE: PARTNERS Health Plan presents the greatest stunts of Super Dave Osborne.
SFX: Crowd cheers
MIKE: Sensational.
SUPER: Well, thank you, Michael. But, you know, I would not have the confidence to do these stunts without PARTNERS Health Plan.
MIKE: PARTNERS Health Plan.
SUPER: What are you, a parrot? I just said that.
MIKE: Of course you did. PARTNERS Health Plan of Arizona. If it works for Super Dave, it'll work for you.

847

Art Director: Grant Richards
Carl Warner
Creative Director: Stan Richards
Copywriter: David Longfield
Producer: Lisa Dee
Director: Steve Tobin
Client: Pier 1 Imports

YOU NEVER KNOW
30 seconds
MUSIC: ''Hungry Town'' by Australian band Big Pig

848

Art Director: Tom Lichtenheld
Creative Director: Pat Burnham
Copywriter: Phil Hanft
Director: Buck Holzemer
Agency: Fallon McElligott
Client: Amoco

DIPSTICK
30 seconds
VO: Now that Amoco LDO…meets manufacturer's performance
requirements for every car made today…any dipstick can use it.
Amoco LDO. Any dipstick can use it.

849

Art Director: Bill Kreigbaum
Tom Gilmore
Jeff Hopfer
Copywriter: Mike Renfro
Mike Malone
Producer: Lisa Dee
Director: Jeff Bednarz
Studio: Bednarz Films
Client: Metroplex Cadillac Group

850

Art Director: Frank Haggerty
Creative Director: Jack Supple
Copywriter: Kerry Casey
Producer: Jack Steinmann
Director: Tim Francisco
Agency: Carmichael Lynch
Studio: C & H Productions
Client: Rapala

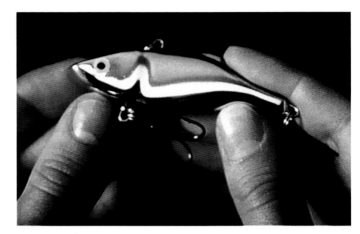

THRILL IS GONE

30 seconds
MUSIC: ''Thrill is gone''
ANNCR: If the thought of yet another expensive European car, with yet another sparkling interior doesn't thrill you, take heart. The 1989 Cadillac Seville STS is here. Take one for a thrilling road test.

DISAPPEAR

30 seconds
SFX: Crickets chirping
ANNCR: Introducing the Rattl'n Rap. With the sound no fish can resist.
SFX: Rattle

851
Art Director: Tom Lichtenheld
Creative Director: Pat Burnham
Copywriter: Bruce Bildsten
Producer: Char Loving
Director: Rick Dublin
Agency: Fallon McElligott
Client: Hyponex

852
Art Director: Pat Burnham
Creative Director: Pat Burnham
Copywriter: Jarl Olsen
Director: Jim Lund
Agency: Fallon McElligott
Client: Knox Kitchen Center

FIRE ANTS
30 seconds
SFX: Thud!
Thud! Thud!
Thud! Thud! Thud!
Thud! Thud! Thud! Thud! Thud! Thud! Thud! Thud! Thud! Thud!
Thud!
VO: The Hyponex Fire Ant Extinguisher.
Guaranteed to kill an entire fire ant mound…in just one step.

KITCHEN
30 seconds
SFX: Crickets; click; man crawling; liquid pouring; click; crickets

853

Art Director: Dean Hanson
Creative Director: Pat Burnham
Copywriter: Bruce Bildsten
Producer: Char Loving
Director: Lol Creme
              Kevin Godley
Agency: Fallon McElligott
Client: First Tennessee Banks

854

Art Director: Bill Oberlander
Creative Director: Ron Arnold
Copywriter: Craig Demeter

HANDSHAKE

30 seconds
VO: It used to be, getting a loan took little more than a firm handshake.
Well, some banks have made it more complicated than that. But at First
Tennessee Bank, with our easy telephone loan applications…we're
making things simple again.

FLIP CARD MAN

30 seconds
MAN: All Mita makes are great copiers. Which may be why nearly 9 out
of 10 people who own them, love them. I know I do. I don't worry
about coming out too dark, too light, crumpled, or not coming out at
all. In fact, I always look 100%. Sometimes even 151%. At Mita, all we
make are great copiers.

855

Art Director: Steve Stone
Creative Director: Jeffrey Goodby
  Rich Silverstein
Photographer: Don Peterman
Copywriter: David Fowler
Producer: Debbie King
Director: Jon Francis
Studio: Jon Francis Films

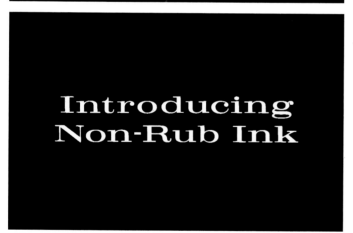

WHAT ELSE

30 seconds
WILL: What else can we do? We've got closing stocks every day…isn't that enough? We've got the Weekend Section on Friday, before the weekend. Wasn't that a big idea? Eh, I guess it wasn't big enough. We've got the Neighborhood Report…what else is there? What?! What more can we do to make this darn paper great?

856

Art Director: Eric David
Creative Director: Peter Cornish
Copywriter: Eric David
  Peter Cornish
Producer: Pat Raftery
Director: Lenny Hirschfield

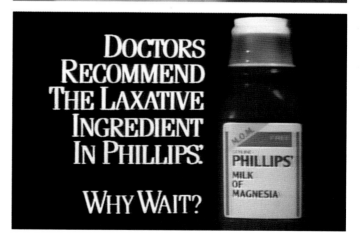

WHY WAIT

30 seconds
SFX: Music builds throughout; musical hits

857

Art Director: Andy Vucinich
Creative Director: Jon Hyde
Copywriter: Paul Cuneo
Producer: Ann Johnston
Director: David Simpson
Agency: J. Walter Thompson, San Francisco
Client: Kaiser Permanente

858

Art Director: Don Schneider
Creative Director: Ted Sann
　　　　　　　Rick Meyer
　　　　　　　Len McCarron
Copywriter: Jonathon Mandell
Producer: Sally Smith
Director: Leslie Dektor
Studio: Petermann-Dektor
Client: Dupont

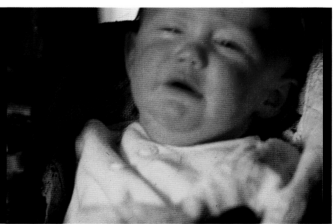

SALUTE

30 seconds
SFX: Piano music
VO: To friends…and families. To those full of history and hard work.
To those who have just arrived and those who have been around a bit
longer. A salute…to the proud people of Baltimore. From Kaiser
Permanente. The people who are proud to be taking care of you.

HOT WORK

30 seconds
SFX: Roar of flames; fireman breathing; sirens
ANNCR: To protect the lives of firefighters, DuPont developed a
remarkable fire-resistant fiber for their clothing called Nomex. But
perhaps even more remarkable is how it protects those who never even
wear it. At DuPont we make things that make a difference.
SFX: Baby crying
ANNCR: Better things for better living.

859

Art Director: Don Easdon
Creative Director: Don Easdon
Bill Heater
Copywriter: Bill Heater
Producer: Mary Ellen Argentieri
Director: Larry Robbins
Agency: Hill, Holliday
Client: Nissan Infiniti

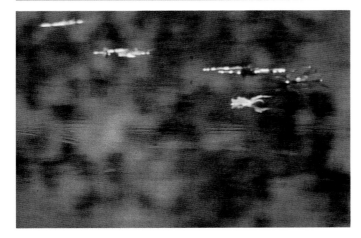

FLOATING LEAVES

30 seconds
VO: From the days of the gilded coach, the concept of luxury in a luxury car has suggested costly indulgence and material abundance. But in Japan centuries ago, and today still where true luxury is a spare, natural idea, and beauty, a close personal experience, there is a different concept of luxury. Infiniti.

860

Art Director: Amy Levitan
Creative Director: Jack Mariucci
Bob Mackall
Copywriter: Deborah Connolly
Producer: Lora Nelson
Director: Peter Cherry
Agency: DDB Needham Worldwide
Client: Colombian Coffee

GALLERY

30 seconds
MAN 1: …classical language.
SFX: People mumbling and talking
MAN 2: …Oh yes, yes.
WOMAN 1: Yes, yes humanist admiration.
HOST: Coffee is served.
MAN 2: …yes, indeed they're rich.
HOST: *Colombian* Coffee.
WOMAN 2: Excuse me.
MAN 2: Excuse me.
WOMAN 1: Excuse me.
ANNCR: 100% Colombian Coffee. Hand-picked by Juan Valdez. The richest coffee in the world.

861

Art Director: Len McCarron
Creative Director: Ted Sann
Copywriter: Rick Meyer
Producer: Linda Horn
Director: Steve Horn
Client: Dupont

862

Art Director: Don Easdon
Creative Director: Don Easdon
Bill Heater
Copywriter: Bill Heater
Producer: Mary Ellen Argentieri
Director: Larry Robbins
Agency: Hill, Holliday
Client: Nissan Infiniti

MARY BRODIE

30 seconds

VO: Mary Brodie won't feel the tiny lump in her breast for another two years. But she'll discover it tomorrow after her first mammogram. Thanks in part to a new x-ray film created by DuPont. That makes it safer to start mammography early. And for Mary early detection means a two year head start on the rest of her life. At DuPont we make the things that make a difference.

WATER ON ROCK

30 seconds

VO: You don't see it, you feel it. You're part of it. You control it. And it is part of you. The Power.
The Q45 luxury sedan from Infiniti.

863

Art Director: Clem McCarthy
Creative Director: Ralph Ammirati
Copywriter: Bill McCullum
Producer: Linda Horn
Director: Steve Horn
Client: B.M.W. of North America

864

Art Director: Don Easdon
Creative Director: Don Easdon
Bill Heater
Copywriter: Bill Heater
Producer: Mary Ellen Argentieri
Director: Larry Robbins
Agency: Hill, Holliday
Client: Nissan Infiniti

RUGBY

30 seconds
PLAYERS: Oh, we had a little party down in Berkeley,
There was very little, very little grace.
Oh, we had a little party down in Berkeley,
and we had to carry Harry from the place.
For the Old Blues,
For the Old Blues, then we start to cry.
We often do or die.
For the Old Blues, For the Old Blues,
For the Old Blues…
VO: The B.M.W. three series is why some enthusiasts are more
enthusiastic than others.
PLAYERS: Yea, Yea.

MISTY TREE

30 seconds
VO: We've paid so much money for so long maybe the time has come
for sanely priced luxury cars and a new set of luxury values, not based
on what you can afford to pay but on what's reasonable to expect in
terms of performance and comfort. That's a new concept in luxury
cars. It's called Infiniti.

865

Art Director: John Sapienza
Creative Director: Bruce Lee
Copywriter: Tom Hansen
Producer: Den Vadies
Director: Klaus Lucka
Agency: Leo Burnett Co.
Client: Allstate

866

Art Director: Bob Brihn
　　　　　　　Mark Johnson
Creative Director: Pat Burnham
Copywriter: George Gier
Agency: Fallon McElligott
Client: Porsche

TRUCK

30 seconds
MAN VO: I should be dead. Last year as I was driving home…I
approached a hill. I saw something more frightening than…anything I
have ever seen. I tried to get out of its way. It was too late. I had a head-
on crash…with a 28,000 pound truck. I'm still alive today…because of
an airbag in my car.
VO: Allstate supports airbags because they save lives and lower
insurance costs.

DRIVING SCHOOL

30 seconds
MUSIC: Alice Cooper's ''School's Out''
VO: What could be more exciting than two days of high performance
racing school? The drive home.

867

Art Director: Houman Pirdavari
Creative Director: Pat Burnham
Copywriter: Bruce Bildsten
Producer: Char Loving
Director: Roger Woodburn
Agency: Fallon McElligott
Client: Timex

868

Art Director: Brent Ladd
Copywriter: Carl Laflamme
Director: Bruce Braden
Client: The *Dallas Morning News*

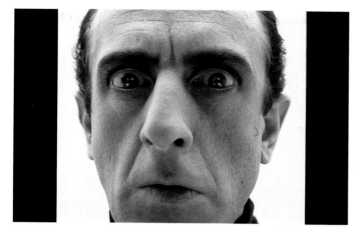

PSYCHIC

30 seconds
SFX: Eerie background music
VO: Timex. It takes a lickin' and keeps on tickin'.

MAGIC TYPEWRITER

30 seconds
SFX: Horses galloping; tennis ball volleying back and forth; basketball dribbling; football players hitting each other; typewriter followed by a buzzer; crowd cheer

869

Art Director: Bryan Buckley
　　　　　　Tom DeCerchio
Copywriter: Tom DeCerchio
　　　　　　Bryan Buckley
Director: Rob Lopes
Agency: Buckley/DeCerchio
Client: Homeplace

870

Art Director: Sal DeVito
Creative Director: Lee Garfinkel
Copywriter: Lee Garfinkel
Producer: Rachel Novak
Director: Carlton Chase
Agency: Levine, Huntley, Schmidt & Beaver
Client: Beneficial

IN THE DARK

30 seconds
SFX: Footsteps, then the sound of a glass table crashing; more footsteps, then shouting; a burst of light and fizzing electronical noises; man yelling, then the crash of a fish tank and water gurgling

QADDAFI

30 seconds
ANNCR: Over the years, U.S. banks have loaned $20 million to people like this. $5.7 billion to people like this. $3 billion to people like this. But for 75 years, we've always believed it was more important to loan money to people like this.
Beneficial. We're not a bank. So we don't have to act like one.

871
Art Director: Bob Meagher
Creative Director: Mike Hughes
Copywriter: Kerry Feuerman
Producer: Morty Baran
Director: Dan Hainey
Agency: The Martin Agency
Client: Residence Inn

872
Art Director: Lisa Bennett
Creative Director: Steve Nubie
Copywriter: Bill Cokas
Producer: Mike Diedrich
Director: Matthew Meshekoff
Agency: Leo Burnett Co.
Client: Heinz

HOUSE TRAILER

30 seconds
SFX: Music
VO: When traveling on business, there are two ways to get a full
kitchen, fireplace and a large, comfortable living room…the other way
is to stay at a Residence Inn.
Residence Inn. People who travel for a living, live here.

MOUTHFUL

30 seconds
VO: We're still trying to make our Heinz Home Style Gravy just like
your own homemade.
JERRY: Mmglbhpb.
ROO: He said, "Nice try."
VO: We made it with real beef and beef juices, so it tastes just like
yours.
JERRY: MMMmmphmbl!
ROO: He feels that while the taste and overall quality are good, there is
still work to be done.
JERRY: MHuh?
VO: And we season and simmer and stir it 'til it's just like homemade.
JERRY: MM-MM…mmglphb!
ROO: He said, "It's close."
VO: Heinz Homestyle Gravy. So close to homemade.

873

Art Director: Marty McDonald
Creative Director: James Dale
Copywriter: John Parlato
James Dale
Jim Lansbury
Director: John Parlato
John Saag
Client: Baltimore Symphony Orchestra

TEAM

30 seconds
MAN 1: I think they're one of the best teams playing today.
WOMAN: I just love their uniforms.
MAN 2: Great stadium, no rain delays.
MUSICIAN: We're feeling good, we're looking good, we're playing good.
FRANK ROBINSON: We could never play like that.
MUSIC: Beethoven's 5th Symphony
ANNCR: The Baltimore Symphony Orchestra. Baltimore's other major league team. For tickets, call 783-8000.
MAN 1: They don't chew tobacco, they don't spit, and they're very polite.

874

Art Director: John Butler
Mike Shine
Creative Director: Bill Hamilton
Copywriter: Mike Shine
John Butler
Producer: Steve Amato
Trish Reeves
Agency: Chiat/Day/Mojo Advertising Inc.
Client: Soho Natural Sodas

NATURAL/ARTIFICIAL 1

30 seconds
SFX: Zydeco music

875

Art Director: Bob Watson
Creative Director: Allen Klein
Copywriter: Tom Johnston
Producer: Glant Cohen
　　　　　　Angelo Antonucci
Director: George Gootsan
　　　　　　Buck Holzemer
Agency: Leo Burnett Co.
Client: Tropicana Twister

876

Art Director: Art Webb
Creative Director: Frank Merriam
Copywriter: Steve Landrum
Director: Mike Caporale
Studio: Caporale
Client: Upper Midwest Marketing

LEERY

30 seconds
MAN VO: Sounds strange to me.
WOMAN VO: Me too.
MAN VO: Us both.
ANNCR: Why are people leery of Tropicana Twister?
MAN VO: It violates the order of nature.
ANNCR: Tropicana Twister. Deliciously tempting flavor combinations
Mother Nature never imagined.
GUY VO: The imagination is a dangerous thing.
ANNCR: Captivating flavors like Orange Passionfruit.
MOM VO: Passionfruit?
ANNCR: Tropicana Twister. Flavors Mother Nature never intended. But
should've.
MAN VO: It's more excitement than decent people need.

BUCKET

30 seconds
SFX: Footsteps
VO: This is the lure that won last year's National Walleye
Championship. A lure so powerful…
SFX: Splash
VO: …it catches fish in places…you'd swear fish don't exist.

877

Art Director: John Butler
　　　　　　　Mike Shine
Creative Director: Bill Hamilton
Copywriter: Mike Shine
　　　　　　　John Butler
Producer: Steve Amato
　　　　　　Trish Reeves
Agency: Chiat/Day/Mojo Advertising Inc.
Client: Soho Natural Sodas

NATURAL/ARTIFICIAL 3
30 seconds
SFX: Zydeco music

878

Art Director: Dave Nathanson
Creative Director: Bill Hamilton
Copywriter: Ken Sandbank
Producer: Steve Amato
Agency: Chiat/Day/Mojo Advertising Inc.
Client: Bissell

VACUUMING EVERYTHING
30 seconds
VO: What if, instead of really cleaning all the things that got dirty, you simply vacuumed them? Absurd? You would never do that, right? Except when it comes to your carpet. Vacuuming may make carpets look clean, but the Bissell steam cleaner gets deep-down dirt that a vacuum never will. The compact, easy-to-use, Bissell steam cleaner. The best way to get the most out of your carpets.

879

Art Director: David Jenkins
Creative Director: Dan Wieden
David Kennedy
Copywriter: Jerry Cronin
Agency: Wieden & Kennedy
Client: Nike

880

Art Director: Steve Fong
Creative Director: Ross Van Dusen
Copywriter: Dave Woodside
Producer: Harvey Greenberg
Jan Ushijima
Director: Jeff Gorman
Agency: Chiat/Day/Mojo
Client: Worlds of Wonder

HIGH PLAINS

30 seconds
SFX: Piano music
WOMAN: There are clubs you can't belong to…neighborhoods
you can't live in…schools you can't get into…but the roads are
always open.

YOU CAN RUN

30 seconds
SFX: Music; beeping
KID VO: Introducing Hide N' Sneak
MOM: Boys!
KID: Ahhh!…Ahhhh!
KID VO: Hide N' Sneak. You can run, but you can't hide!

881
Art Director: Susan Hoffman
Creative Director: Dan Wieden
David Kennedy
Copywriter: Steve Sandoz
Agency: Wieden & Kennedy
Client: Nike

882
Art Director: Sal DeVito
Creative Director: Lee Garfinkel
Copywriter: Lee Garfinkel
Producer: Rachel Novak
Agency: Levine, Huntley, Schmidt & Beaver
Client: Beneficial

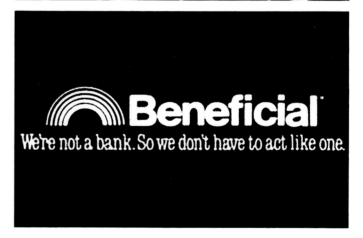

JUST FACE IT/KIDS
30 seconds
SFX: Music
SINGER: Just kick it.
Just bounce it.
SFX: Kids screaming
SINGER: Just zap it.
Just flip it.
Just rock it.
Just face it.

FOUR LEADERS
30 seconds
ANNCR: Banks don't give everyone who applies for a loan a hard time. He got loans for $20 million. They were kind enough to loan him $600 million. And he borrowed $5.7 billion. We think something is wrong when it's easier for someone like him to get a loan than it is for you. Beneficial. We're not a bank, so we don't have to act like one.

883

Art Director: John D'Asto
Creative Director: Jan Zechman
Copywriter: Barton Landsman
Producer: Jan Jolivette
　　　　　 Renee Raab
Director: David Wild
Studio: Highlight Commercials
Client: Mindscape, Inc.

884

Art Director: Len Fink
Creative Director: Bill Hamilton
Copywriter: Peter Levathes
Producer: Steve Amato
Agency: Chiat/Day/Mojo Advertising Inc.
Client: New England Apple Products

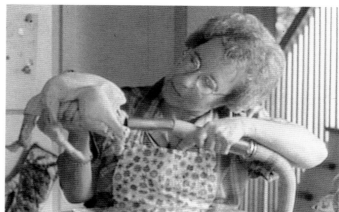

PAPERBOY

30 seconds
VO: Warning: Such behavior is irresponsible, immature and very
foolish. We recommend you try it at home. Paperboy from Mindscape.
For your Nintendo Entertainment System.

THIRST DETECTOR

30 seconds
VO 1: Juice?
VO 2: Veryfine. The Veryfinest.

885

Art Director: Steve Fong
Creative Director: Bill Hamilton
Copywriter: Glenn Porter
Producer: Carey Zeiser
              Lee Weiss
Agency: Chiat/Day/Mojo Advertising Inc.
Client: Reebok International Ltd.

886

Art Director: John D'Asto
Creative Director: Jan Zechman
Copywriter: Jim Carey
Producer: Laurie Berger
Director: Robert Black
Studio: Travisano, Digiacamo
Client: State of Illinois

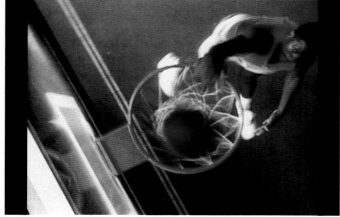

PUMP

30 seconds
ALTERNATING SPEAKERS: This is your Pump.
Push this little thing here…
And you just pump.
Pump.
Pump.
You know how to do that, don't you?
Five or six pumps.
I'd say fifteen pumps.
Twenty to twenty-five times.
Seventy pumps will do it.
You know, I'm also going to use this to intimidate people.
These things in here, I don't know what they're called.
Airbags.
When you want to release, there is a little button back here that you
just push down and you can hear the air…
…leaving the pump.
I think we're on to something.
VO: Pump it up.

MARTIANS

30 seconds
BARBER: Here in Spring Grove we are often visited by Martians.
VO: There are over 1000 festivals in Illinois.
BARBER: They're purple in color, like eggplant, and real nice.
VO: So get out and join the fun.
BARBER: But don't bark at their tentacles. That gets 'em riled. Why Fifi
here (gesturing toward cat), she used to be a dog.
VO: Just watch out for the storytelling contest down in Spring Grove.
BARBER: A German shepherd.

887

Art Director: Brent Ladd
Creative Director: Gary Brahl
Copywriter: Clay Hudson
Producer: Steve Gilbert
Agency: GSD&M Advertising
Client: Coors Brewing Co.

888

Art Director: Lori Brown
Creative Director: Guy Bommarito
Copywriter: David Smith
Producer: Dorothy Taylor
Agency: GSD&M Advertising
Client: Southwest Airlines

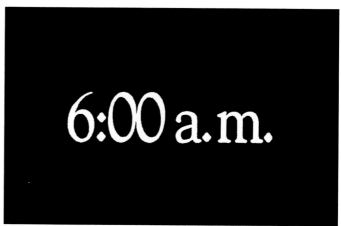

BIRTHDAY

30 seconds
SPOKESMAN: Hey, party timers, I got some special birthday party tips for ya from Extra Gold Draft. First, don't forget the Extra Gold. More beer taste, extra smooth. Ask for an Extra. Another tip—when you make a wish…make it a *wish*—yes, yes—no!
ANNCR: When you want more beer, ask for an Extra.
TOM: Come here—whoaaa…

SKIP

30 seconds
SFX: Scratchy record playing Lefty Frizzell tune
ANNCR: Flying to Los Angeles on business?
SINGER: If you've got the money,
    I've got the time…(record gets stuck)
    I've got the time…
    I've got the time…
    I've got the time…
    I've got the time…
    I've got the time…
SFX: Music fades out
VO: With 18 flights a day to Los Angeles International Airport, flying Southwest Airlines is like having your own company plane.

889

Art Director: Don Fibich
Copywriter: Chuck Withrow
Producer: Ann Russo
Roseanne Lowe
Celeste Sciortino
Director: Kenny Mirman
Agency: Wyse Advertising
Client: Cleveland Zoo

FACES

30 seconds
SFX: Music
VO: One of the most beautiful things about faces like these…is the look they'll bring to a face like this.
The Cleveland Metroparks Zoo. It's wild.

890

Art Director: Richard Crispo
Mark Erwin
Jon Reeder
Copywriter: Brent Bouchez
Hillary Jordan
Rob Siltanen
Producer: Ben Grylewicz
Director: Brent Thomas
Agency: Ketchum, Los Angeles

COMPANY CAR

30 seconds
SHE: Well, what did he say?
HE: He said, Kirkwood…
BOSS: You're smart, you're aggressive, you're…
HE: Brilliant, creative, aggressive, brilliant…
SHE: He said all that, did he?
HE: Well, something to that effect.
SHE: C'mon, c'mon, c'mon, what else?
HE: Stock. Sign-on bonus. Company car. Of course I'm going to turn it down.
SHE: The job?
HE: The car.
VO: The Legend Sedan from Acura. Number one in customer satisfaction three years in a row.

891

Art Director: Warren Eakins
Creative Director: Dan Wieden
David Kennedy
Copywriter: Steve Sandoz
Agency: Wieden & Kennedy
Client: Nike

892

Art Director: Steve Beaumont
Creative Director: Brent Bouchez
Copywriter: Brent Bouchez
Producer: Ben Grylewicz
Director: Caleb Deschanel
Agency: Ketchum, Los Angeles
Client: American Honda Motor Corp.

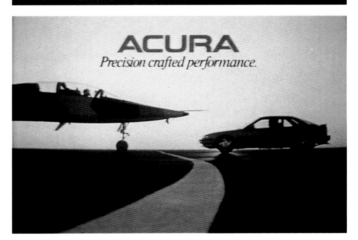

BIKE MESSENGER
30 seconds
SFX: Jazz music
BIKE MESSENGER: You think Bo Jackson's the only guy who can do this stuff?

JET
30 seconds
VO: The anti-lock brakes on the 1990 Acura Integra were inspired by those used to stop jet aircraft. And while you might expect to find such technology on a multi-million dollar airplane, you might not expect to find it on an automobile that costs…considerably less.

893

Art Director: Jac Coverdale
Creative Director: Jac Coverdale
Designer: Jac Coverdale
Copywriter: Jerry Fury
Producer: Kate O'Toole
Agency: Clarity, Coverdale, Rueff
Client: United Recovery Center

894

Art Director: Michael Vitiello
Creative Director: Lee Garfinkel
Copywriter: Lee Garfinkel
Producer: Bob Nelson
Director: Henry Sandbank
Agency: Levine, Huntley, Schmidt & Beaver
Client: Subaru of America

HIT BOTTOM
30 seconds
ANNCR: Most people with a drinking problem have to hit bottom before they'll get help for themselves. To help someone you care about before they hit bottom, call United Recovery Center for a free consultation.

BARN
30 seconds
ANNCR: The old grey Subaru ain't what she used to be. Introducing the larger, more powerful Subaru Legacy.

895

Art Director: Susan Westre
Creative Director: Steve Hayden
Copywriter: Chris Wall
Producer: Bob Belton
                Pat Walsh
Director: Joe Pytka
Studio: Pytka Productions
Client: Apple Computer Inc.

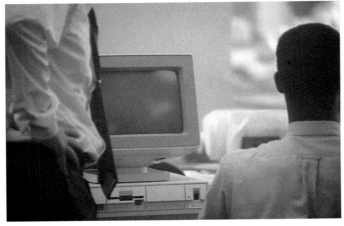

TESTING 1-2-3

60 seconds
WOMAN 1: Can I get on there soon?
WOMAN 2: After me.
KEN: Do you think I can get on here soon?
MAN 1: Yeah, give me a minute, man.
ED: You've been staring out there all day. What are you doing?
JOHN: Testing.
ED: Testing what?
JOHN: Computers. I'm trying to figure out which computer is the most powerful.
ED: Well, that's easy. The one with the most memory…megahertz…MIPS…you know.
JOHN: No, I don't think so. I think the most powerful computer is the one that people actually use.
GIRL: Hi, Ken.
KEN: Hey.
VO: Macintosh has the power to change the way you look at computers. The power to be your best.
ED: That's not really a fair comparison. People like using the Mac.

896

Art Director: Mark Haumersen
Creative Director: Lyle Wedemeyer
Copywriter: Lyle Wedemeyer
Director: Michael McNamara
Agency: Martin/Williams
Client: On Mark Group

WAITING

60 seconds
ANNCR: For all those people who have ever waited for someone…and particularly for those who have ever waited for someone to come home from the hospital…St. Francis Hospital has these words of comfort. Through the advanced technology of our Pittsburgh Laser Center, we've helped thousands of patients recover more quickly and with less complications after surgery…for procedures ranging from opthamology to general surgery. All of which means less waiting for the people doing the waiting. If you or someone you know needs surgery, call the Pittsburgh Laser Center at 1-800-648-8877 for a free brochure or to arrange a consultation.
The Pittsburgh Laser Center at St. Francis. Enlightened medicine that's making the wait a little easier.

897

Art Director: Doug Bartow
Creative Director: Doug Bartow
Designer: Doug Bartow
Producer: Bruce Allen
Director: Claude Mougin
Agency: Grey
Client: Bloomingdale's

VIVE LA FRANCE

60 seconds
(Spoken in French)
SHE: I've heard enough.
HE: It's truly horrible.
SHE: Who cares what you think?
HE: You think it's nice? It's an insult to 18th century architecture.
SHE: No, you don't understand at all.
MOM: Let's go Celeste, hurry up. We're going to the museum, we'll see the Mona Lisa in a great big chateau.
LITTLE GIRL: Yes, I'm coming.
MOM: Come on, what are you doing? Stop dreaming. Hurry…
HE: I would say Egyptian
SHE: Very American
HE: French
SHE: Hollywood, very French
VO: (in English) Vive La France. Bloomingdale's celebration of what's new, what's important, what's very French. It's the legendary chic of Paris' great designers working in pure wool. Vive La France at Bloomingdale's. It's like no other store in the world.

898

Art Director: Susan Westre
Creative Director: Steve Hayden
Copywriter: Chris Wall
Producer: Bob Belton
          Pat Walsh
Director: Joe Pytka
Studio: Pytka Productions
Client: Apple Computer Inc.

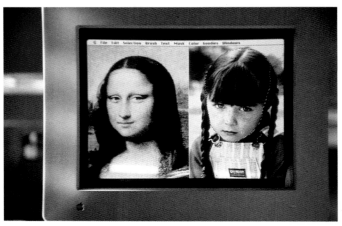

THE NEW TEACHER

60 seconds
PRINCIPAL: Looks like we got a new teacher. Miss Kassman?
SECRETARY: Miss Kassman.
BROTHER: Amy, I hear your new teacher's real mean.
MISS KASSMAN: Good morning, everybody.
CLASS: Good morning!
DOUG: New teachers have to be tough so you're scared of 'em.
MISS KASSMAN: Did you bring your pictures?
CLASS: Yes!
MISS KASSMAN: Amy, would you come up here and bring your picture with you, please?
SFX: Commotion among the students
PRINCIPAL: I'd better check on Miss Kassman.
SFX: More commotion
ANNCR: There's a special power that can bring students and teachers closer together. The power to be your best.
BROTHER: Whoa, that's cool! Hey, how's your new teacher?
AMY: Oh, she's OK.

899
Art Director: Don Easdon
Creative Director: Don Easdon
　　　　　　　　 Bill Heater
Copywriter: Bill Heater
Producer: Mary Ellen Argentieri
Director: Joe Pytka
Agency: Hill, Holliday
Client: Nissan Infiniti

900
Art Director: Mike Mazza
Creative Director: Bob Kuperman
Copywriter: Dick Sittig
Producer: Richard O'Neill
Director: Mike Mazza

RELATIVE IMPORTANCE OF STUFF
60 seconds
WISE OLD MAN: I have a friend…he's not successful and he hasn't accomplished everything he wants to accomplish…but, he's on his way. He's a fisherman, he loves fishing. He does this. What do you call that?
CALLOW YOUTH: Fly fishing?
WISE OLD MAN: That's exactly right. That's his luxury, he's a fly fisherman. He calls it his one luxury. What's your luxury?
CALLOW YOUTH: I don't think of luxury like that. Luxury is a big house, a boat, a luxury car, clothes.
WISE OLD MAN: Luxury is something expensive then? Is that right?
CALLOW YOUTH: Well…that's what they say. I mean…yeah, I think that's luxury. A mink coat is luxury.
WISE OLD MAN: Well, let me ask you this. Which is more of a luxury? Something expensive or something that gives you satisfaction?

TURBO Z DREAMER
60 seconds
TURBO Z DREAMER: So I'm havin' this dream—I'm in a Turbo Z…and these guys are after me…but they can't catch me…so they get a car… but they can't catch me…so they get a plane…just as they're about to catch me--the…twin…turbos…kick…in.
SFX: Jet engine

901

Art Director: Susan Westre
Creative Director: Steve Hayden
Copywriter: Chris Wall
Producer: Bob Belton
Pat Walsh
Director: Joe Pytka
Studio: Pytka Productions
Client: Apple Computer Inc.

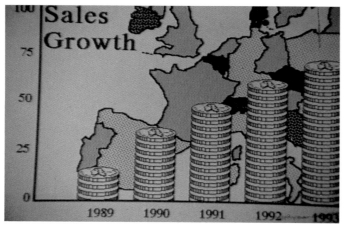

HIT THE ROAD, MAC

60 seconds
SFX: Music; French announcements over airport public address
PHILLIPE MICHEL: Ah, no.
AIDE: (in French) I have the tickets, sir.
PHILLIPE MICHEL: (in Italian) I speak 7 languages, but I can't understand this!
VO: Introducing the first portable computer you already know how to use.
PHILLIPE MICHEL: Excuse me, ah, it's my computer. I seem to be having trouble. I know nothing about computers.
CINDY: I'm sorry. I don't know anything about computers either.

902

Art Director: Rich Silverstein
Steve Diamant
Creative Director: Andy Berlin
Photographer: Michael Duff
Copywriter: Andy Berlin
Jeffrey Goodby
Producer: Elizabeth O'Toole
Director: Stan Schofield
Studio: Sandbank & Partners

SATURDAY NIGHT

60 seconds
SFX: Music
ANNCR: Every Saturday night in the city of New York, you can experience many things that are the best of their kind in all the world. Now one of them is a cruise line.

903

Art Director: Leslie Caldwell
Creative Director: Mike Koelker
Copywriter: Mike Koelker
Producer: Steve Neely
Director: Leslie Dektor
Agency: Foote, Cone & Belding

904

Art Director: Susan Westre
Creative Director: Steve Hayden
Copywriter: Chris Wall
Producer: Bob Belton
    Pat Walsh
Director: Joe Pytka
Studio: Pytka Productions
Client: Apple Computer Inc.

CHICAGO
60 seconds
SFX: Music
VO: The city.
JAZZ MAN: I don't know where it comes from ya know, jus' as long as it keeps coming, right?
YOUNG MUSICIAN: This is my bass note and this is my treble, what am I suppose to do?
JAZZ MAN: How old are you?
KID: 15.
JAZZ MAN: Wow?!

ENTREPRENEUR
60 seconds
EX-BOSS: I told Greg he was crazy to start his own business. He won't have our resources. He won't have our computers…
ANNIE: Good morning, Greg!
GREG: Good morning, Annie.
GUY AT DESK: Sure, it's a lot of space for one guy. He says he's planning to grow.
WORKER: This noise bothering you, pal?
GREG: No problem, thanks.
EX-BOSS: He won't have our, uh, graphics department, he won't…
EX-ASSOCIATE: He won't have our bureaucracy.
TOM: I heard Greg Clancey went independent.
BOB: Wish I had his guts.
EXEC 2: Who are these guys anyway?
EXEC 3: Greg's the creative guy. Clancey's just a bean counter.
VO: Macintosh has the power to make you independent. The power to be your best.
WORKER: How come you got so much space?
GREG: I'm an optimist.

905

Art Director: Richard Sabean
Creative Director: Ted Sann
                Michael Patti
                Richard Sabean
Copywriter: Michael Patti
Producer: Gene Lofaro
Director: Terrence Donovan
Studio: Terrence Donovan Ltd.
Client: Pepsi Cola

SIMPLY IRRESISTIBLE
60 seconds
ROBERT PALMER: How can it be permissible?
    Don't compromise my principle…Yeah Yeah.
    This kind of love is mythical;
    It's anything but typical.
    It's a craze you'd endorse; it's a powerful force.
    You're obliged to conform, 'cause there's no other choice.
    It use to look good to me but now I find it…
    Simply Irresistible…
    Simply Irresistible….She's all mine…
    There's no other way to go…
    Simply Irresistible.

906

Art Director: Rich Martel
Copywriter: Al Merrin
Producer: Tony Frere
Director: Leslie Dektor
Agency: BBD&O

GLASNOST
60 seconds
(Spoken in Russian)
SFX: Music
FATHER: Noise, noise, why all this noise?
KID: Hey Dude! Totally awesome day.
VO: (in English) Not very long ago, America introduced Pepsi to the
Soviet Union…
OLD WOMAN: Look, look, what is this?
FATHER: Look at you! Why do you dress like that?
VO: (in English) …And while it may be quite a coincidence, a lot of
refreshing changes have taken place ever since.
KID: Yo…Misha!
FATHER: Don't you have any normal friends? Kids!
VO: (in English) Pepsi…a generation ahead.
OLD WOMAN: Yuri…come on, lighten up.

907

Art Director: Donna Weinheim
Creative Director: Donna Weinheim
Copywriter: Jeff Alphin
　　　　　　Jane King
Producer: Ann Kurtzman
Director: Tony Kaye
Agency: Cliff Freeman & Partners
Client: Home Box Office/Comedy Channel

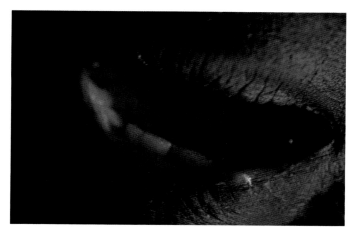

SNORING
60 seconds
SFX: Snoring; grunting
ANNCR: When life is rough, laugh it off with the new Comedy
Channel. 24 hours a day. We're there when you need us.

908

Art Director: John Butler
　　　　　　Mike Shine
Creative Director: Bill Hamilton
Copywriter: Mike Shine
　　　　　　John Butler
Producer: Steve Amato
　　　　　　Trish Reeves
Agency: Chiat/Day/Mojo Advertising Inc.
Client: Soho Natural Sodas

NATURAL/ARTIFICIAL
45 seconds
SFX: Zydeco music

909

Art Director: Burint Ramany
Creative Director: Gerry Miller
Copywriter: Gerry Miller
Producer: Glant Cohen
Director: Leroy Koetz
Agency: Leo Burnett Co.
Client: Proctor & Gamble

910

Art Director: Susan Hoffman
Creative Director: Dan Wieden
                  David Kennedy
Copywriter: Geoff McGann
Agency: Wieden & Kennedy
Client: Nike

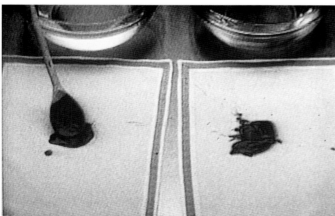

SPAGHETTI

45 seconds
SFX: Music
VO: Nobody's better in cold than All Temperature Cheer.

TENNIS LESSONS

60 seconds
INSTR: Today, we'll talk more about proper tennis procedure....Let's begin with the stroke. Always keeping your eye on the ball and maintaining a steady and bodied position. Keep...
SFX: Loud music
INSTR: ...Never, never try to hit too hard...
SFX: Loud music
INSTR: ...Avoid over-excitement.
SFX: Loud music
INSTR: In tennis, conservative attire is a must. Remember, tennis is a civilized sport, so always obey all court rules and regulations...
SFX: Loud music
INSTR: See...now you're on your way to really having fun.
SFX: Loud music
INSTR: Maybe we should go over this one more time...

911

Art Director: Tom Schwartz
Rory Monaghan
Creative Director: Rory Monaghan
Greg Taubenek
Copywriter: Jeff Sherman
Producer: Ron Nelken
Director: Leslie Dektor
Agency: Leo Burnett Co.
Client: United Airlines

SPEECH

60 seconds

BEN: I got a phone call this morning. From one of our oldest customers. He fired us. After 20 years. He fired us. Said he didn't know us anymore. I think I know why. We used to do business with a handshake—face to face. Now it's a phone call and a fax, and we'll get back to you later. With another fax, probably. Well, folks, something's gotta change. That's why we're going to set out for a little face to face chat with every customer we have.
SENIOR EXECUTIVE: But Ben, that's gotta be over 200 cities.
BEN: I don't care. Edwards…Ryan…(under) Nicholas…
ANNCR: If you're the kind of business that still believes personal service deserves a lot more than lip service…
BEN: (under) Give Joe my best.
ANNCR: …welcome to United. That's the way we've been doing business for over 60 years.
BEN: Willis.
GUY: Ben, where you going?
BEN: To visit that old friend who fired us this morning.
ANNCR: United. Come fly the friendly skies.

912

Art Director: Steve Stone
Creative Director: Jeffrey Goodby
Rich Silverstein
Photographer: Don Peterman
Copywriter: David Fowler
Producer: Debbie King
Director: Jon Francis
Studio: Jon Francis Films

WHAT ELSE

60 seconds

WILL: What? What?
LADY: Dear Will, the Widow's Investment Club of Marin really appreciates those closing stocks in the afternoon paper.
WILL: It's not enough.
LADY: P.S. Will. July Pork Bellies…
OTHER LADY: Dump 'em.
SFX: Motorcycle engine
BIKER: Hey Will! Love that Friday Entertainment Section and its sensitive coverage of the local mime scene.
WILL: We've got to go further.
NUN: Dear William. I love the Neighborhood Section. Who was born, who got married, who got ripped off.
WILL: We've got to do more.
NUN: P.S. I can get you a police scanner. At cost.
BIKER: P.S. Thanks, Will. I'm sending you some steaks, man.
WILL: What? What more can we do to make this darn paper great?!

913

Art Director: John Butler
Mike Shine
Creative Director: Bill Hamilton
Copywriter: Mike Shine
John Butler
Producer: Steve Amato
Trish Reeves
Agency: Chiat/Day/Mojo Advertising Inc.
Client: Soho Natural Sodas

NATURAL/ARTIFICIAL 1
30 seconds
SFX: Zydeco music

914

Art Director: Nick Scordato
Ken Sausville
Copywriter: Jeanne Chinard
Gordon Hasse
Rich Wagman
Walter Burek
Producer: Patti McGuire
Director: David Cornell
Agency: NW Ayer

SMALL TOWN
2 minutes, 30 seconds
WOMAN VO: Oh, good morning congressman. No, that's all right.
We're all up. Here he comes.
MAN VO: When? Friday? You're kidding! Vicki do you speak Russian?
We've got company coming. We've got to get the word out.
LYRICS: How to get it done…
MAN VO: Order me some Russian flags. 1500. No, make it 2500.
LYRICS: How to get it done…
MAN VO: Patty's even quoted here. Says he's coming here to try her
apple pie.
WAITRESS VO: Yeah, they were here…
MAN VO: Oh, that kid wrote him…a letter, right? How's your story
coming? Are we gonna make the deadline?
LYRICS: We're there for you.
MAN VO: First Russian fax I've ever seen. Nice.
LYRICS: There for you. Yeah.
MAN VO: Big Bear's on his way.
WOMAN VO: Here comes the band!
LYRICS: How to get it done.

915

Art Director: Andy Dijak
Creative Director: Bob Kuperman
Copywriter: Dick Sittig
Producer: Vicki Blucher
Karen Smith
Director: Brent Thomas
Agency: Chiat/Day/Mojo
Client: Eveready Battery Co.

916

Art Director: Michael Prieve
Creative Director: Dan Wieden
David Kennedy
Copywriter: Jim Riswold
Producer: Patti Greaney
Bill Davenport
Director: Bob Giraldi
Agency: Wieden & Kennedy
Client: Nike

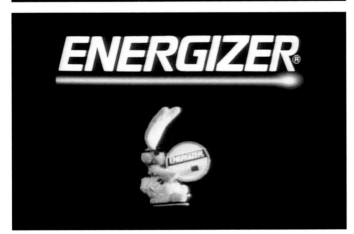

BUNNY/PLAYOFFS

20 seconds
1ST ANNCR: Don't be fooled by commercials where one battery
company's toy outlasts the other's. The fact is, Energizer was never
invited to their playoffs. Because nothing outlasts the Energizer. They
keep going and going…
2ND ANNCR: Stop the bunny, please.
1ST ANNCR: …and going, and going.

FORCE

30 seconds
SFX: Music

917

Art Director: Pam Cunningham
Andy Dijak
Creative Director: Lee Clow
Bob Kuperman
Copywriter: Steve Bassett
Producer: Richard O'Neill
Director: John St. Clair
Michael Werk
Agency: Chiat/Day/Mojo

Z CLEAN SHEET

30 seconds
SFX: Loud banging
ANNCR: This is where we started—a clean sheet of paper. No
boundaries. No rules. No preconceived ideas. Just desire to build the
best sports car in the world. A car for one driver in a thousand. The car
destined to leave its mark.
SFX: Loud banging
ANNCR: The new Z. From Nissan.

918

Art Director: Peter Arnell
Neal Slavin
Creative Director: Peter Arnell
Copywriter: Peter Arnell
Producer: Adrian Lichter
Director: Neal Slavin
Studio: Firebird Productions
Agency: Arnell/Bickford
Client: European American Bank

BLIND SOFTBALL

60 seconds
VO: I think that all of us are blind at one time or another, in the dark, or
at night, or…mentally even sometimes, so this game makes the people
come out of their shell.
SFX: Cheers; softball beeping
VO: People grow by playing this game.
SFX: Cheers; softball beeping
VO: It's like climbing the top of a mountain when you smack that
thing, Bang-o.
SFX: Cheers
VO: One of the wonders of the game is to catch a fly ball. Anything you
think is gonna happen will ultimately happen, right?
SFX: Cheers

919

Art Director: Andy Dijak
Mike Mazza
Creative Director: Bob Kuperman
Copywriter: Dick Sittig
Producer: Helen Erb
Ken Domanski
Director: Richard O'Neill
Agency: Chiat/Day/Mojo
Client: Nissan Motor Corp.

920

Art Director: Gary Yoshida
Copywriter: Bob Coburn
Producer: Gary Paticoff
Tena Montoya
Director: Henry Sandbank
Jeff Zwart
Klaus Lucka
Agency: Rubin Postaer & Associates
Client: American Honda Motor Corp.

IF I HAD A 240SX

30 seconds
240SX DREAMER: If I had a Nissan 240SX…I'd get a red coupe.—No!
A silver fastback. And I'd go for a spin up Route 7, the twisty part. Just
me and Elvis…maybe Mark. Heck, why not Ken Wahl! Yeah, me and
Ken…in my silver—no, red 240SX…driving into the sunset.

ON THE ROAD

30 seconds
SFX: Car engine; music
VO: If you think the new Honda Accord Coupe looks good on
television…you should see it on the road. You have to drive it to
believe it. The new Accord from Honda.

921

Art Director: Jeremy Postaer
Creative Director: Jeffrey Goodby
Photographer: Amir Hamed
Copywriter: Jeffrey Goodby
Ed Crayton
Producer: Debbie King
Director: Gary Johns
Studio: Johns & Gorman Films

FOOTBALL

30 seconds
VO: It's been suggested that you might know more about us at U.C. San Francisco if we had a sports program the way other schools do. Take Dr. Nelson Artiga here….He oversees dental care and education for thousands of underprivileged patients who might not have sought treatment. Now if we had sports teams made up of remarkable people like Dr. Artiga, you'd probably know all about us, right? Yeah, probably not.

922

Art Director: John Colquhoun
Steve Miller
Joe Sedelmaier
Creative Director: Cliff Freeman
Copywriter: Cliff Freeman
Rick LeMoine
Joe Sedelmaier
Agency: Cliff Freeman & Partners
Client: Little Caesars Enterprises

INSURANCE

30 seconds
ANNCR: Some pizza places have a lot of overhead. Trucks, maintenance, drivers…insurance.
SFX: Clomp! Tire screeching
ANNCR: We don't have all that overhead at Little Caesars—that's how we can afford to give you 2 great pan pizzas…
LITTLE CAESAR: Pan! Pan!
ANNCR: For one low price.

923

Art Director: Steve Stone
Creative Director: Jeffrey Goodby
Rich Silverstein
Photographer: Amir Hamed
Copywriter: Jeffrey Goodby
Producer: Cindy Fluitt
Director: Gary Johns
Studio: Johns & Gorman Films

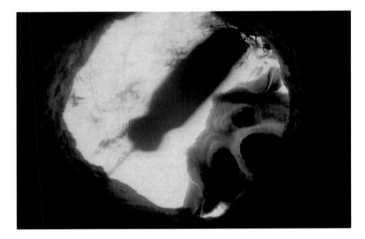

RUSTY'S GOT IT

30 seconds
SFX: Birds chirping; digging
DAD: Hey Honey, where's my red screwdriver?
MOM: Well, where did you leave it? Did you check your tool box?
DAD: No, it's not in my tool box. Hey kids, pardon me, have you seen my red screwdriver anywhere?
KID: Um…no.
DAD: Have you seen it? Have you?
OTHER KID: Uh-uh.
KID: Hey Dad, remember when you lost your glasses and they were just sitting there right on your face?
DAD: Very funny.
SFX: Digging

924

Art Director: Keith Weinman
Creative Director: Larry Postaer
Copywriter: Karen Koritz
Producer: Joel Ziskin
Gary Paticoff
Director: Larry Bridges
Client: Bugle Boy Industries

BEACH

30 seconds
SFX: Music; waves; seagulls
BUGLE BOY MAN: Hey, only a friend is gonna tell you but, you know, hanging out in that suit, well, you're attracting the wrong kind of attention….At a party, you got people offering you deals on kiwi farms instead of plates of hors d'oeuvres. I mean, loosen up. Like, like be yourself. Try changing your clothes for starters. Then, maybe, get a dog. A Bouvier…a Shar-Pei…something…

925

Art Director: Frank Costantini
　　　　　　Phillip Halyard
Creative Director: Hal Friedman
　　　　　　Michael Hart
Copywriter: Brian Sitts
　　　　　　Larry Volpi
　　　　　　Mimi Emilita
Agency: J. Walter Thompson
Client: Eastman Kodak

926

Art Director: Bob Barrie
Creative Director: Pat Burnham
Copywriter: Jarl Olsen
Producer: Char Loving
Director: Rick Dublin
Agency: Fallon McElligott
Client: Hush Puppies

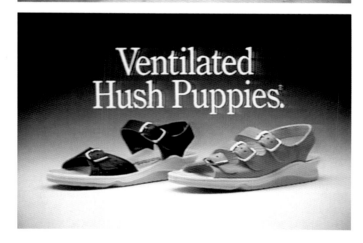

DADDY'S LITTLE GIRL

60 seconds

MAN SINGS: You're the end of the rainbow,
　　My pot of gold,
　　Daddy's little girl,
　　To have and to hold.
　　A precious gem, is what you are,
　　A ray of hope, a shining star.
　　You're as bright as the sunshine,
　　Morning's first light,
　　You warm my day and brighten my night.
　　You're sugar, you're spice, you're everything nice,
　　And you're Daddy's little girl.
VO: Don't the pictures of your lifetime deserve Kodak film?

VENTILATED HUSH PUPPIES

15 seconds

SFX: Urban street sounds; rumbling of train

927

Art Director: Jeff Hopfer
　　　　　　Glenn Dady
Creative Director: Stan Richards
Copywriter: Mike Malone
Producer: Lisa Dee
Director: Leslie Dektor
Agency: Petermann-Dektor

ZION HARMONIZERS
30 seconds
MUSIC: The Zion Harmonizers singing

928

Art Director: Leslie Caldwell
Creative Director: Mike Koelker
Copywriter: Mike Koelker
Producer: Steve Neely
Director: Leslie Dektor
Agency: Foote, Cone & Belding, San Francisco

CHICAGO
60 seconds
SFX: Music
VO: The city.
JAZZ MAN: I don't know where it comes from ya know, jus' as long as it keeps coming, right?
YOUNG MUSICIAN: This is my bass note and this is my treble, what am I suppose to do?
JAZZ MAN: How old are you?
KID: 15.
JAZZ MAN: Wow?!

929

Art Director: Don Fibich
Copywriter: Chuck Withrow
Producer: Ann Russo
　　　　　Roseanne Lowe
　　　　　Celeste Sciortino
Director: Kenny Mirman
Agency: Wyse Advertising
Client: Cleveland Zoo

FACES

30 seconds
SFX: Music
VO: One of the most beautiful things about faces like these…is the look they'll bring to a face like this. The Cleveland Metroparks Zoo. It's wild.

930

Art Director: Don Easdon
　　　　　Dan Ahearn
Creative Director: Don Easdon
　　　　　Bill Heater
Copywriter: Bill Heater
　　　　　Craig Caldwell
Producer: Mary Ellen Argentieri
Director: Larry Robbins
Client: Nissan Infiniti

LIGHT CHANGES IN FOREST

30 seconds
VO: We feel a customer should be able to enter an Infiniti showroom and feel, right away, a different kind of luxury experience. An experience perfectly unlike any showroom experience in the world. Shopping for a luxury car should be as luxurious as owning one. Infiniti.

931

Art Director: Sal DeVito
Creative Director: Lee Garfinkel
Copywriter: Lee Garfinkel
Producer: Rachel Novak
Director: Carlton Chase
Agency: Levine, Huntley, Schmidt & Beaver
Client: Beneficial

932

Art Director: Marv Lefkowitz
Creative Director: Agi Clark
Copywriter: Bob Elgort
Producer: Bob Smith
Director: Claude Mougin
Agency: LGFE
Client: Fasolino

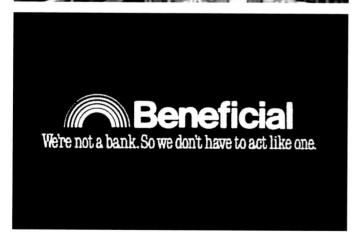

QADDAFI

30 seconds
ANNCR: Over the years, U.S. banks have loaned $20 million to people like this. $5.7 billion to people like this. $3 billion to people like this. But for 75 years, we've always believed it was more important to loan money to people like this.
Beneficial. We're not a bank. So we don't have to act like one.

ANGELINO

30 seconds
SPOKESMAN: Right now you wouldn't know a Fasolino from an Angelino…but Angelino is Italian for angel. And thank goodness they come in all sizes and shapes. And Fasolino is Italian for Pasta…which also comes in all sizes and shapes. Fasolino's. It's Italian for Pasta.

933

Art Director: Steve Montgomery
Earl Cavanah
Simon Bowden
Copywriter: Richard Kelley
Mike Feinberg
Larry Cadman
Agency: Scali, McCabe, Sloves
Client: Volvo

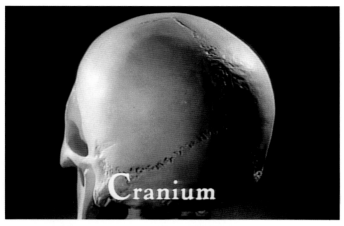

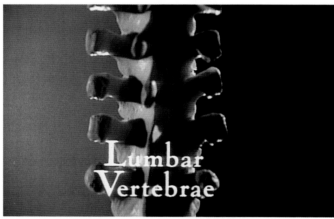

REPLACEMENT PARTS
30 seconds
VO: Drive a Volvo because replacement parts are hard to find.

934

Art Director: Michael Prieve
Creative Director: Dan Wieden
David Kennedy
Copywriter: Jim Riswold
Agency: Wieden & Kennedy
Client: Nike

CAN/CAN'T
30 seconds
SFX: Funk music
MARS: Yo! This is Mars Blackmon. And this is my main man Michael Jordan and this is a pair of hyped Air Jordans from Nike. This is something you can buy.
MARS (VO): And this is a patented vicious high-flying 360 slam dunk.
MARS: This is something you cannot do. Let me repeat myself. This you can buy.
MARS (VO): You cannot do this.
MARS: Can.

935

Art Director: Don Easdon
Creative Director: Don Easdon
Bill Heater
Copywriter: Bill Heater
Producer: Mary Ellen Argentieri
Teri Hechter
Agency: Hill, Holliday
Client: Nissan Infiniti

FLOCK OF GEESE

30 seconds

VO: An automotive designer looks at the shapes of nature, the soft lines. And because he sees things a certain way, those lines suggest an automobile design that is honest and natural. Where the driver is more important than the car itself. And what is discovered just watching nature, is an ancient Japanese notion of what is beautiful. It's called Infiniti.

936

Art Director: Sheri Olmon
Creative Director: Bill Hamilton
Copywriter: Marty Cooke
Alan Platt
Producer: Andrew Chinich
Lee Weiss
Agency: Chiat/Day/Mojo Advertising Inc.
Client: New York Life

SOCCER

30 seconds

TOM: I wanted to live in the Rocky Mountain region. I enjoy the great outdoors. I like to fish, play soccer.
MAN 1: What Tom does…he doesn't care if we make mistakes. He doesn't get down on anybody. He treats everybody fair.
MAN 2: It's all teamwork…no individual players.
ANNCR: A lot of these players depend on Tom Dater for their life insurance. He's been on their team for 10 years. And with New York Life for 18 years.
MAN 3: Why would I buy insurance from a stranger when I can buy it from the worst fullback in Boise?
ANNCR: New York Life. The company you keep.

937

Art Director: Pat Chiono
Bill Shea
Roger Rowe
Creative Director: Sean Fitzpatrick
Copywriter: Robert Woolcott
Rona Oberman
Paul Cappelli
Agency: McCann-Erickson
Client: Coca-Cola USA

CHRISTMAS TREE

60 seconds
KID (BRIAN BONSALL): Are you sure it's gonna work, Grandpa?
GRANDPA (ART CARNEY): Trust me, kid. I got a good feeling about this one.
KID: You mean like the time we took Grandma water skiing?
GRANDPA: (chuckle) Now, silver shovel, thank you, Grandma's fruitcake. And now, Grandpa's magic pine cone. In exactly two weeks, we should see something.
KID: Is it time, Grandpa?
GRANDPA: It's time. Let's go.

938

Art Director: Matt Smith
Creative Director: Ross Van Dusen
Copywriter: Jeff Billig
Producer: Harvey Greenberg
Director: Jeff Gorman
Agency: Chiat/Day/Mojo
Client: Worlds of Wonder

BASKETBALL

15 seconds
BOY #1: (laughs)
BOY #2 OC: C'mon man
BOY #1 OC: Sorry....Sorry....Sorry....Sorry....Nice shot.
BOY #2 OC: Oh oh!
SFX: Sports whistle
ANNCR: Substitution!!
SFX: Arena cheering
ANNCR: Kooky Katcher from Worlds of Wonder.

939

Art Director: Susan Hoffman
Creative Director: Dan Wieden
David Kennedy
Copywriter: Geoff McGann
Agency: Wieden & Kennedy
Client: Nike

940

Art Director: Jerry Torchia
Creative Director: Mike Hughes
Copywriter: Andy Ellis
Producer: Morty Baran
Agency: The Martin Agency
Client: Signet Bank

MEET FELETIA

30 seconds
SFX: Organ music

CRONYN/TANDY

60 seconds
CRONYN: Apollinaire said, ''Come to the edge.'' But they held back
and they said, ''It's dangerous.'' He said, ''Come to the edge.'' And they
said, ''We may fall.'' And he said, ''COME TO THE EDGE.'' So, they
went to the edge and he pushed them…and they flew. Affirmation.
And that's something I think we share, don't we?
TANDY: Who's doing the pushing?
CRONYN: Sometimes you push, sometimes I push. Isn't that right?
TANDY: Right!

941

Art Director: Dick Lemmon
              Mitch Gordon
Creative Director: Jan Zechman
Copywriter: Jan Zechman
Producer: Laurie Berger
Director: Ted Bokhoff
Studio: Cityworks
Client: State of Illinois

942

Art Director: Mike Martin
Creative Director: Jim Armstrong
Copywriter: Jim Armstrong
Producer: ProVideo
Agency: Armstrong Creative
Client: Madison Advertising Federation

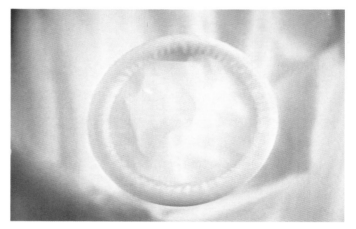

CRANE

30 seconds
SFX: Drum solo
VOICE OF CARL SANDBURG: This is one song of Chicago. Nothing like us ever was.

HE LOVES ME, HE LOVES ME NOT

15 seconds
VO: He loves me....He loves me not.
SFX: Tearing

943

Art Director: George Halvorson
Creative Director: George Halvorson
Copywriter: Tom Evans
Producer: Jim Geib
Director: Charlie Diercks
Agency: CME
Client: Boating Safety

944

Art Director: Brian Nadurak
Creative Director: Stan Richards
Copywriter: Marc Harty
Producer: Greg Lane
Director: Lol Creme
Agency: The Richards Group
Client: Texas Department of Health

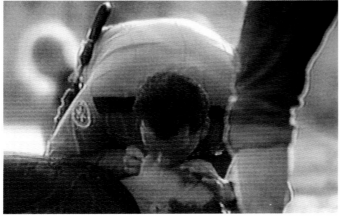
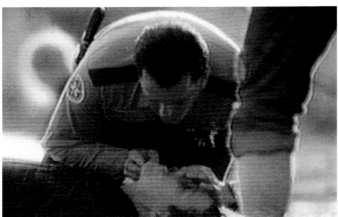

BREATH TEST

30 seconds
ANNCR: Last year, 473 drunk boaters failed to pass this breath test.

CHANGING FACES

30 seconds
WOMAN 1: You may have slept with me…
MAN 1: Or me, because if you've had two sex partners…
WOMAN 2: In the last year, and each of your partners…
MAN 2: Had two other partners the year before…
WOMAN 3: And so on for the last nine years…
MAN 3: It's as if you've slept with 512 people…
WOMAN 4: Any one of them could have given you the virus that causes AIDS…
MAN 4: Find out what to do now…
WOMAN 1: Call the toll-free Texas AIDSLINE. All calls are anonymous.

945

Art Director: John Lointi
Creative Director: Rick DeChant
Copywriter: Tom Woodward
Producer: Rick DeChant
　　　　　　Maura Mooney
Studio: Hi-Tech Productions
Agency: Liggett-Stashower
Client: United States Coast Guard

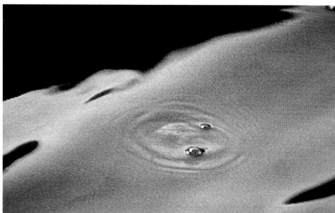

FLOATER

15 seconds
SFX: Steady, ominous tone
ANNCR: If you're wearing your life preserver in a boating accident, you'll be floating on top immediately.
If you're not wearing one, it might take a week or so.

946

Art Director: Charlotte Moore
Creative Director: Stephen Heller
Copywriter: Evelyn Monroe
Producer: Carol Hardin
　　　　　　Patti Greaney
Director: Bob Giraldi
Agency: Ogilvy & Mather
Client: Centers for Disease Control

REMOTE

60 seconds
MOM: When your father and I were married sex was a very different…
GIRL VO: I can tell by looking at her what she's going to say.
MOM: We dated for awhile before he had the nerve to kiss me…
GIRL VO: They went to a soda fountain and shared a straw…
MOM: …sex is a natural thing between two people…
MOM & GIRL VO: …who love each other.
SFX: Fast forward
GIRL VO: Fast forward through pregnancy and nice young men.
MOM: …young men who respect you.
SFX: Fast forward
GIRL VO: And now for the closing remarks.
MOM: …AIDS is one of them.
GIRL VO: Whoa!
SFX: Rewinding
MOM: There are risks in becoming sexually active. AIDS is one of them. Theresa, let's start at the beginning. HIV is the name of the virus that causes AIDS…
ANNCR: We can help you talk about AIDS. Call for a guide.

947
Art Director: Mike Martin
Creative Director: Jim Armstrong
Copywriter: Jim Armstrong
Producer: ProVideo
Agency: Armstrong Creative
Client: Madison Advertising Federation

948
Art Director: Tim Musta
Copywriter: Jan Pettit
Producer: LuAnn Truso
Studio: Northwest Teleproductions
Agency: Miller Meester Advertising
Client: Tom Thumb

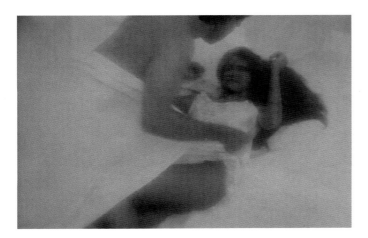

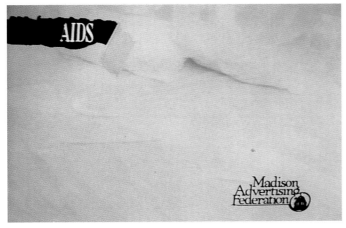

GARY'S ON HIS DEATHBED

15 seconds
VO: Gary is on his deathbed.
SFX: Tearing

NIGHT CALLER

30 seconds
SFX: Phone ringing throughout
VO: As the parent of a teenager, who would you rather hear from in the middle of the night? The police department? The emergency room? The coroner? Or...
SFX: Ringing stops, phone is picked up
TEENAGER VO: Mom? I'm at a party. Could you, uh, come and get me?
VO: When your kids aren't OK to drive, make it OK to call. This message brought to you by Tom Thumb.

949

Art Director: Richard Ostroff
Creative Director: Allan Beaver
              Lee Garfinkel
Copywriter: Amy Borkowsky
Producer: Rachel Novak
Director: Mark Story
Agency: Levine, Huntley, Schmidt & Beaver
Client: Ad Council

FRYING PAN

30 seconds
VO: Last year, 400,000 women killed their husbands with a frying pan. Reduce your intake of high-fat fried foods and reduce your risk of cancer and heart disease.
For a free booklet on low-fat eating, call 1-800-EAT-LEAN.

950

Art Director: Doug Johnson
Creative Director: Gary Dixon
Photographer: Brian Capener
Copywriter: Stan Ferguson
Producer: Jim Rutherford
Director: Stan Ferguson
Agency: Bonneville Media Communications
Client: LDS Church

HARD LESSON

60 seconds
NEW FATHER VO: Dear Mom, thanks for helping Janet and me with the new baby the past two weeks. You were there, as always….But, there was a time when I wasn't sure I wanted your help. Remember when we walked all the way to town and back? And then you discovered the new toy I had.
WOMAN: Um…where did you get that?
NEW FATHER (AS A CHILD): From the store…
WOMAN: I didn't know you had any money…
NEW FATHER VO: I didn't have any money….Taking that toy back was one of the hardest things I ever had to do.
NEW FATHER (AS A CHILD): I took this, and I'm sorry.
OWNER: It takes a big man to face up to a mistake, son. But, bringing it back was the right thing to do.
NEW FATHER VO: Thanks, Mom, for teaching me the hard lessons.
ANNCR: Family values…pass them on. Your children need them now more than ever. From The Church of Jesus Christ of Latter-day Saints.

951

Art Director: Richard Ostroff
Creative Director: Allan Beaver
Lee Garfinkel
Copywriter: Amy Borkowsky
Producer: Rachel Novak
Director: Phil Marco
Agency: Levine, Huntley, Schmidt & Beaver
Client: Ad Council

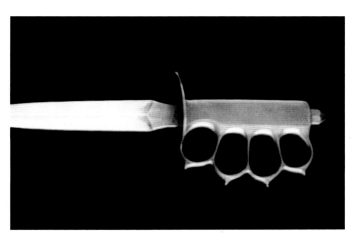

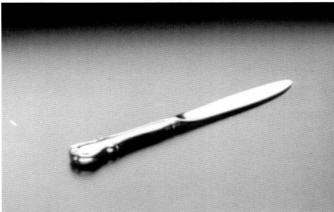

KNIVES

30 seconds
VO: The stiletto. Outlawed in most major cities. The trench knife. It boasts a seven-inch, solid steel blade. The survival knife. Designed to cut through virtually anything. Yet, the most dangerous knife of all may be this one.
For a free booklet on how to reduce your risk of cancer and heart disease through low-fat eating, call 1-800-EAT-LEAN.

952

Art Director: Gary Johnston
Mark Sitley
Creative Director: Robin Raj
Copywriter: Robin Raj
Producer: Mark Sitley
Julie Hampel
Director: Bob Giraldi
Agency: Chiat/Day/Mojo Advertising Inc.
Client: National Coalition for the Homeless

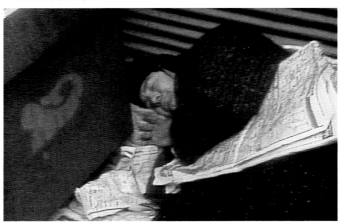

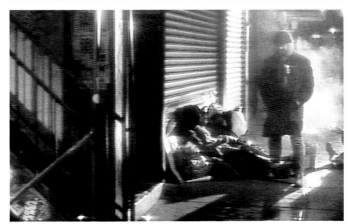

LIFESTYLES OF THE HOMELESS

60 seconds
ROBIN LEACH VO: Say, what's it like to live a life of complete independence? George Rutallo knows. Yes. Every morning he wakes up to a commanding view of Third Avenue. A panoramic vantage he must pay dearly for. It's here he rubs shoulders with the power elite. A perfect location, close to restaurants and shopping. George's digs are nothing if not spacious, and he shares them freely with family, friends, even total strangers. His bedroom sleeps hundreds, and a spectacular dining room caters to literally thousands. Yes, Mr. Rutallo is living like there's no tomorrow. It's a world of scenic make-believe. But for George this is no fairy tale. It's just a little place he calls home. What can you do about the 3 million Americans living in our streets? You can pick up the phone and call Washington.
ANNCR: What can you do about the 3 million men, women and children living in our streets? You can write the National Coalition for the Homeless.

953

Art Director: David Page
Creative Director: Jeffrey Goodby
Photographer: Barney Colangelo
Copywriter: David O'Hare
Producer: Cindy Fluitt
Director: Jeffrey Goodby
Studio: Fleet Street Pictures

954

Art Director: Mary Mentzer
             Tim Musta
Copywriter: Jan Pettit
Producer: LuAnn Truso
Studio: Northwest Teleproductions
Agency: Miller Meester Advertising
Client: Tom Thumb

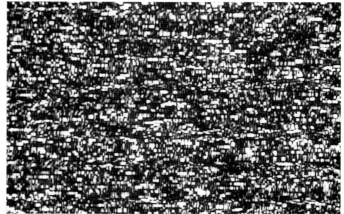

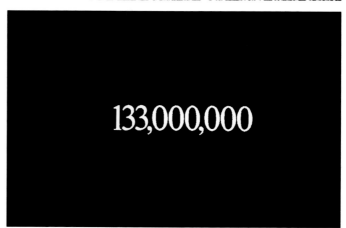

TOBY

30 seconds
MAN: What's wrong?
WOMAN: That was the Fowlers. Gretchen's pregnant; they think Toby's the father.
MAN: How do they know?
WOMAN: He's over there every night. And when he's not, he's out running around.
MAN: He's young.
WOMAN: He's out of control.
MAN: What do you want me to do, chain him up in the backyard?
WOMAN: If that's what it takes to stop this selfishness…wait, it's him.
VO: Will you please get your dog fixed. It's painless, it's cheap, and, well, he's just not going to do it himself.

REASONS FOR PEACE

30 seconds
ANNCR: Between the U.S. and the Soviet Union, we have a combined total of 24,562 nuclear warheads. And, while that's a very powerful reason for disarmament, there's one even more powerful. We also have a combined total of 133 million children.
This message brought to you by Tom Thumb.

955

Art Director: Wendy Hansen
Creative Director: Lyle Wedemeyer
Copywriter: Lyle Wedemeyer
Director: Rick Dublin
         Eric Young
         Kevin Smith
Agency: Martin/Williams
Client: Minnesota Department of Health

956

Art Director: Allen Kay
Creative Director: Lois Korey
Copywriter: Neil Leinwohl
Producer: Milda Misevicius
Director: Henry Sandbank
Studio: Sandbank & Partners
Client: Members Only

ANIMALS

30 seconds
ANNCR: If you think this looks ridiculous, remember…smoking is just as unnatural for you as it is for them.

BADGE

30 seconds
SFX: Police radio transmissions and echoed gunfire
VO: This message has been brought to you by Members Only.

957

Art Director: Ron Fisher
April Norman
Creative Director: Ron Fisher
Photographer: Glenn Bewley
Copywriter: Virgil Shutze
Producer: Dottie Martin
Director: Jimmy Collins
Agency: HutchesonShutze
Client: Atlanta's Table

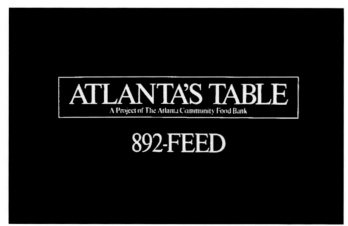

WORK FOR FOOD

30 seconds
NARRATOR: He carried a sign that said, "I'll work for food." Hard times had cinched his belt halfway around again. Pants hung low on his hips. I tried to look away, but couldn't. He didn't seem to mind. He just looked at me for a long minute, then the light changed.
ANNCR: Help drive hunger from the face of Atlanta. Give to Atlanta's Table.

958

Art Director: Robert Valentine
Designer: Robert Valentine
Illustrator: Chesley McLaren
Producer: Kelly Mosley
Nancy Lawrence

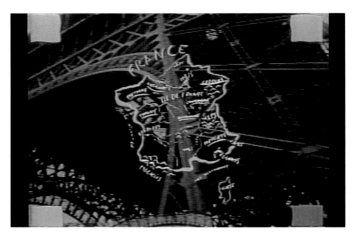

VIVE LA FRANCE

1 minute, 19 seconds
MUSIC: "La Vie En Rose"

959

Art Director: Ron Arnold
Creative Director: Ron Arnold
Copywriter: Patti Goldberg
Producer: Kathryn Speiss
Director: Eli Noyes

960

Art Director: Tony Smith
Creative Director: Tony Smith
Copywriter: Jonathan Young
Producer: Ed Galvez
　　　　　　Kathy Wheelock
Director: Drew Takahashi
Agency: McCann-Erickson
Studio: Colossal Pictures
Client: National Dairy Board

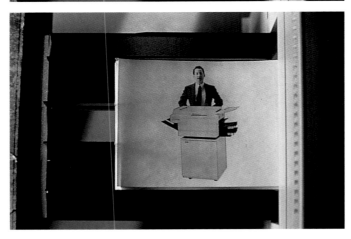

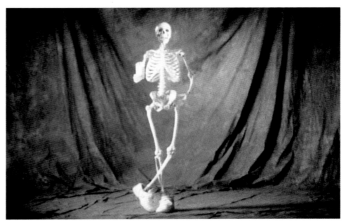

FLIP CARD MAN

30 seconds

MAN: All Mita makes are great copiers. Which may be why nearly 9 out of 10 people who own them, love them. I know I do. I don't worry about coming out too dark, too light, crumpled, or not coming out at all. In fact, I always look 100%. Sometimes even 151%. At Mita, all we make are great copiers.

PRESTON CHANGO

30 seconds

PRESTON CHANGO: I know I should drink milk 'cause it will help me grow up big and strong. Milk's got stuff that's good for my bones and stuff that's good for my muscles. And I guess that's okay, but I'm more interested in having fun! That's what makes milk so neat; you can drink a lot of it and it tastes cool. Milk can be a real pick-me up! Milk, it does a body good.

961

Art Director: Jeffrey Bacon
John O'Brien
Photographer: Bob Graham
Director: Jim Edwards
Agency: Cimarron/Bacon/O'Brien
Client: Bacon/O'Brien Design

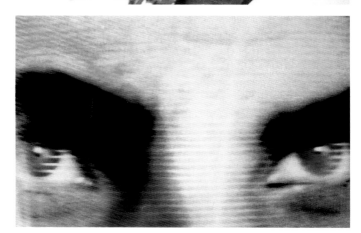

BITS AND PIECES

5 minutes
JOHN: Bits and pieces.
JEFF: Yes, bits and pieces....I think the company was founded on the orange. I lost my roommate, Pete, an ordinary naval orange took Pete's head off. I needed a new roommate, from then on we just hung out.
JOHN: Pete's never been the same.
JEFF: I would wake up at three in the morning and just have to do a painting. It used to drive my parents nuts.
JOHN: I would wake up in the morning and just have to draw underneath the table with crayons.
JEFF: ...The thing that we're good at is making things.
JOHN: It's all about quality. How you see things....The final concept.
JEFF: I don't want to do it if we're not going to do it better than anyone else would do it.
JOHN: It's finished when we feel it.
JEFF: John beaned Pete in the head with an orange and that's what we want to do.
JOHN: Bits and pieces of bits and pieces.
JEFF: We just want to hit the top, that's exactly where we want to be.

962

Art Director: Marty Weiss
Creative Director: Marty Weiss
Nat Whitten
Copywriter: Nat Whitten
Producer: Marty Weiss
Nat Whitten
Director: Andy Parke
Laura Belsey
Agency: Weiss, Whitten Inc.

WEISS, WHITTEN PROMOTIONAL REEL

5 minutes, 35 seconds
MRS. WEISS: I am Helen Weiss.
MR. WEISS: And I am Bernie Weiss. We are the parents of Martin Weiss.
MR. WHITTEN: I'm Benjamin Whitten.
MRS. WHITTEN: And I'm Jane Whitten.
MRS. WEISS: Whitney is a writer and my son is an art director.
INTERVIEWER: Could you tell us what business your son is starting?
MR. WEISS: No, I'm not sure what kind of business he's getting into.
MRS. WEISS: That was Marty Weiss' first print ad. But then I thought to myself, what's he mean, artist? He's gonna grow up a bum...
MR. WEISS: We do have some items he doesn't let us throw out...
INTERVIEWER: What is it?
MR. WEISS: I don't know what it is.
MRS. WHITTEN: Call Weiss, Whitten, they're tops.
MR. WHITTEN: That could be better. More enthusiasm.
MRS. WHITTEN: Call Weiss, Whitten, they're tops.
MR. WHITTEN: No, don't stop on "toopps"...call Weiss, Whitten, they're tops...tops...tops...
MRS. WHITTEN: Stacato...call Weiss, Whitten, they're tops.

963

Art Director: David Hukari
Photographer: Fred Vanderpoel
Copywriter: Frank Priscaro
Producer: Fred Vanderpoel
Director: Fred Vanderpoel
Agency: Priscaro & Hukari
Client: Infoworld

964

Art Director: Robert Barthelmes
Producer: Suzanne Bauman
Director: Suzanne Bauman
Studio: Soulstar Films
Client: *Vogue* Magazine

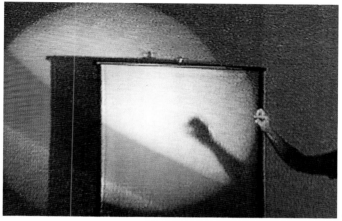

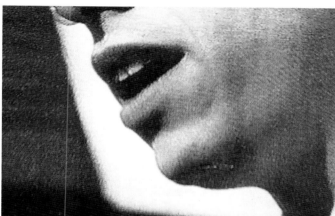

TEST CENTER SPIES

11 minutes, 4 seconds
1ST VO: Swanky-Flueger Investigations presents Case B-701, the InfoWorld Test Center.
2ND VO: We sent our crack crew in disguised as the Industrial Light Pollution Council...
ERNIE: You have a test center downstairs....Why?
SACKS: Well, computer products have become pretty complicated, so we needed a way to test them accurately...
2ND VO: Now, who's...this?
1ST VO: Must be Lauren Black, Director of the Test Center.
ERNIE: How many products do you test...?
BLACK: We test between 700 and 800 a year...
2ND VO: Oh, this is Michael Miller, he's the—
MILLER: I'm Michael Miller, Executive Editor...
2ND VO: Told you.
MILLER: ...in charge of all the reviews here.
1ST VO: In summation...shut that thing off!
2ND VO: Well, I...ah...would...if I...
1ST VO: There! You did it!

IN VOGUE

11 minutes, 34 seconds
ANDRE LEON TALLEY: It's a more relaxed *Vogue,* more relaxed about make-up, hair. Things are not as preconceived. Accidents happen, and most often, accidents are big successes.
ANNA WINTOUR: I don't want that kind of plastic image of the perfect woman anymore. I think that we're all smarter than that...
ALEXANDER LIBERMAN: I think fashion now comes from the youth. It's the youth that dares.
TALLEY: In the '60s when Diana Vreeland was here, fashion only came from one place: her mind, her fantasy, and Paris....Now fashion comes from Paris, Milan, Tokyo...down the street...MTV...Madonna.
WINTOUR: If you look back at *Vogue*'s history, the features have always been very important. And I feel that it's the substance and the tone of the features that has set *Vogue* apart from other magazines.
LIBERMAN: ...As they take 20 shots, photographers don't really see what they take. They hope they're getting something. I think that's how we capture the spirit of the time: by these fleeting instants where a model becomes herself, or it's catching a woman in life as if unobserved. This, for me, is the concept of modern creativity.

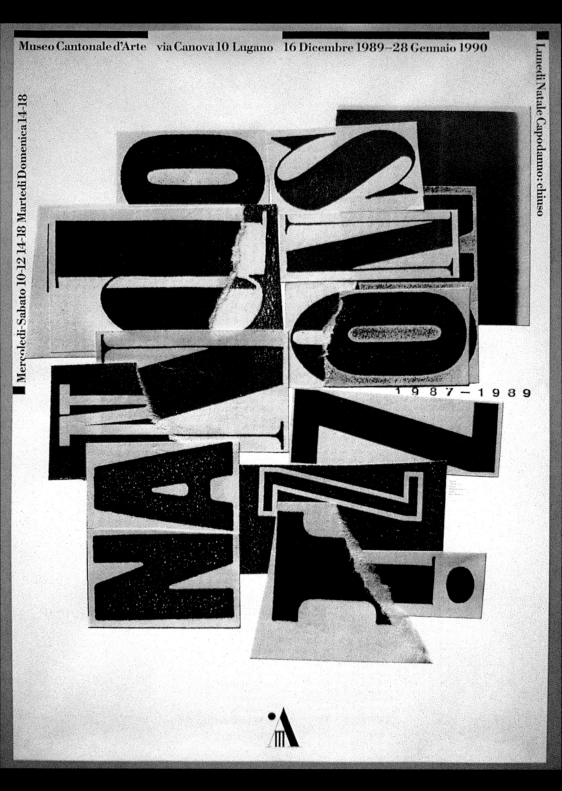

Museo Cantonale d'Arte   via Canova 10 Lugano   16 Dicembre 1989–28 Gennaio 1990

Lunedì Natale Capodanno: chiuso

Mercoledì-Sabato 10-12 14-18 Martedì Domenica 14-18

1987 – 1989

965 Gold
Art Director: Bruno Monguzzi
Designer: Bruno Monguzzi
Studio: Bruno Monguzzi
Client: Museo D'Arte

966 Gold

Art Director: Francesc Petit
Creative Director: Francesc Petit
Paulo Ghirotti
Copywriter: Paulo Ghirotti
Agency: DPZ Propaganda
Client: DPZ/Globo

967 Silver

Art Director: Ursula Ferrara
Designer: Ursula Ferrara
Illustrator: Ursula Ferrara

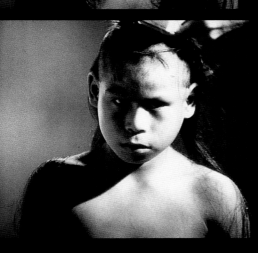

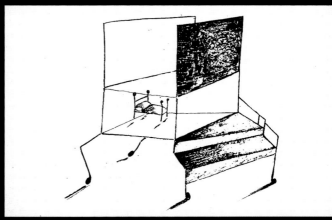
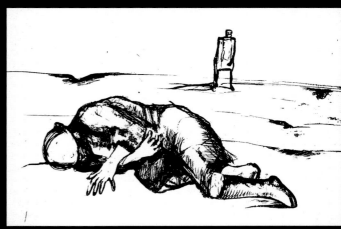

LITTLE INDIAN BOY

45 seconds
SFX. Forest and bird noise, a strong noise from an electric saw.

FUTURE SUBJUNCTIVE

2 minutes, 15 seconds
This piece has no dialogue. The only audio is music.

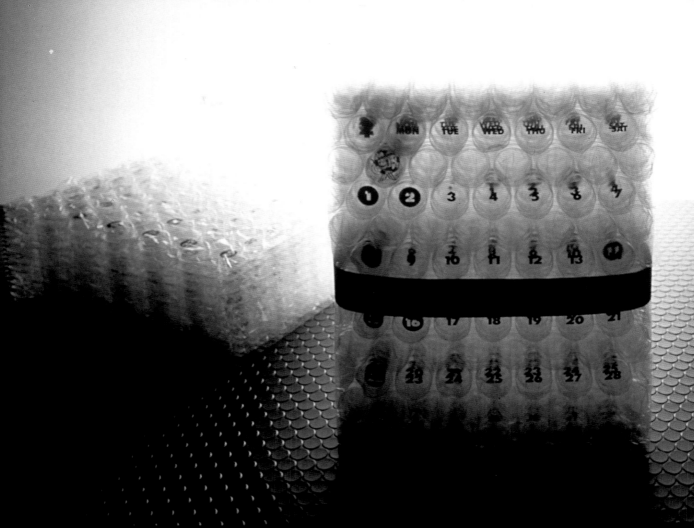

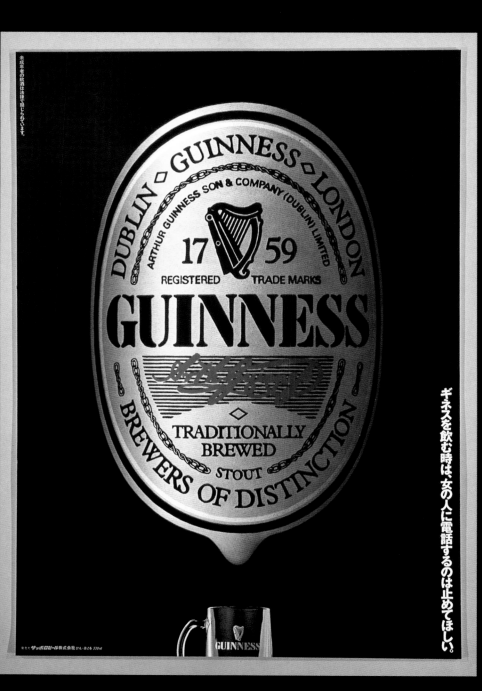

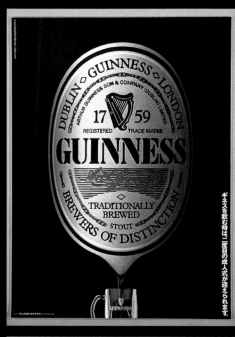

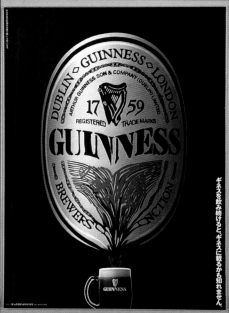

970 Distinctive Merit
Art Director: Atsushi Ebina
Creative Director: Okihiko Okubo
Designer: Atsushi Ebina
Photographer: Shoji Sato
Copywriter: Takao Fujino
Agency: I & S Corp.
Client: Sapporo Breweries Ltd.

971 Distinctive Merit

Art Director: Shotaro Sakaguchi
Katsumi Yutani
Creative Director: Katsumi Yutani
Designer: Keizo Tada
Shotaro Sakaguchi
Photographer: Hatsuhiko Okada
Copywriter: Taketo Suzuki

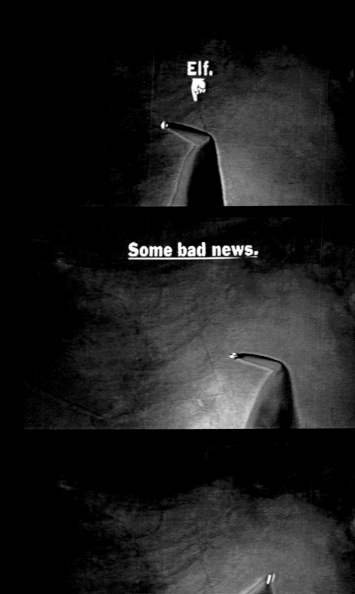

TIEN-AN-MEN

30 seconds

SFX: Gunfire; crowd screaming

VO: A man, alone, can alter history…

SFX: Roar of a tank

VO: He can move mountains. il Sabato pays tribute to that man who is within each of us.

SOME BAD NEWS

60 seconds

ELF: Good evening. I am authorized by my employer, one of S. Claus, to read you the following statement. (clears throat)

''I'm not coming. Every year, I get frozen stiff, sitting behind— *behind,* note—an aging team of incontinent reindeer, one of whom has a drinking problem; I have to figure out ways to get into chimney-less houses without getting done for burglary or being chewed by the family Doberman; I have to give splendid prezzies to undeserving and ungrateful kids, and I'm expected to go 'Ho Ho Ho' at the same time. And what do *I* get? (pause) Exactly. I'm the *only* one who never gets a prezzie. So I'm not coming. Unless I get a Parker. Ideally a Duofold. In blue. So there. Ho, Ho, Ho.''

That is the end of the message. Thank you and goodnight.

ELF OC: How was my make-up?

974
Art Director: Börje Stille
Copywriter: Ingemar Johannesson
Agency: Johannesson & Stille AB
Client: Folksam

975
Art Director: Toshio Iwata
Designer: Yoshihiro Ohkubo
Illustrator: Bungo Saito
Copywriter: Hiromi Tanaka

Tid Time	Destination	Linje Flight	Pir/ Gate
8:00	STÖLD	B313	A6
8:25	SJUKDOM	F791	B1
9:05	RÅN	U481	A7
9:40	RESEAVBROTT	A415	B3
10:10	STÖLD	S101	A8
10:30	SJUKDOM	U413	C1
10:50	RÅN	G891	A3
11:05	RESEAVBROTT	H585	B2
11:35	STÖLD	C432	A1
12:00	SJUKDOM	E932	A5
12:20	RÅN	B493	C3
12:50	RESEAVBROTT	A491	B7
13:10	STÖLD	F381	B5
13:40	SJUKDOM	K418	A2
14:10	RÅN	L301	C4
14:25	RESEAVBROTT	S413	A9
14:50	STÖLD	U793	B4

Åk inte dit.

FOLKSAM

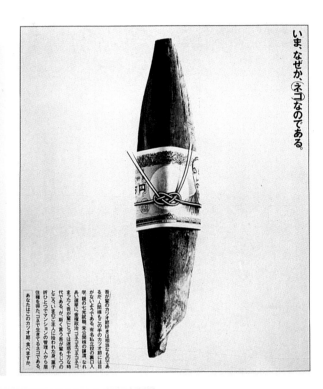

976
Art Director: André Plaisier
Creative Director: G. Van Der Stighelen
Illustrator: Edmond Tang
Copywriter: Eric Debaene

977

Art Director: Martin Spillmann
Creative Director: Hansjörg Zürcher
Copywriter: Gaby Girsberger
Agency: Advico Young & Rubicam
Client: Ringier AG

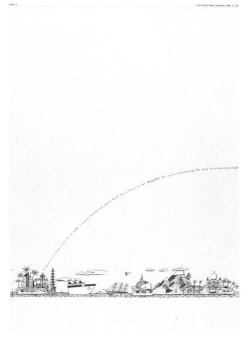

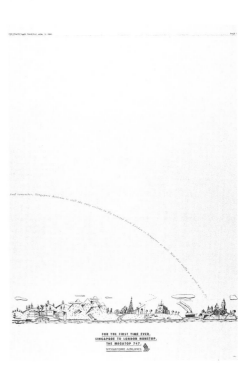

978

Art Director: John Finn
Illustrator: Jeremy Fisher
Agency: Batey Ads
Client: Singapore Airlines

979
Art Director: Clas Engwall
Creative Director: Lasse Collin
Photographer: Bengt Eriksson
Copywriter: Lasse Collin
Agency: Collin Annonsbyrå
Client: Ecco, Sverige

980
Art Director: Doug Bramah
Creative Director: Gary Prouk
Photographer: Vincent Noguchi
Copywriter: Bill Keenan
Agency: Scali, McCabe, Sloves (Canada) Ltd.
Client: Harvey's of Bristol (Export) Ltd.

981
Art Director: Arturo Massari
Creative Director: Andrea Concato
Photographer: Chris Broadbent
Copywriter: Gianluca Nappi
Agency: TBWA Italia SpA
Clieni: Carpene' Malvolti

982
Art Director: Fernando Lion
Creative Director: José Zaragoza
　　　　　　　Helga Miethke
Photographer: Moacyr Lugato
Copywriter: Antonio Paes
　　　　　　Luciana Sales
Agency: DPZ-Propaganda
Client: Deca

983
Art Director: Masamichi Yoshino
Creative Director: Masamichi Yoshino
Designer: Masamichi Yoshino
Photographer: Takayuki Watanabe
Copywriter: Ryoichi Akiba
Agency: Dentsu Inc.
Client: Mitsubishi Pencil Co., Ltd.

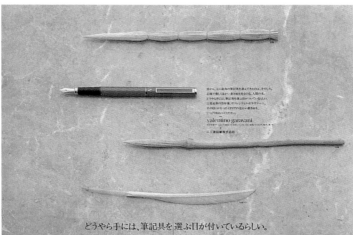

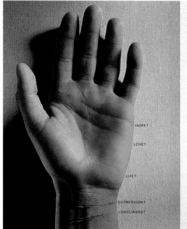

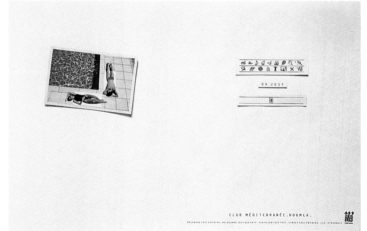

984
Art Director: Paul Shearer
Photographer: Paul Bevitt
Copywriter: Rob Jack
Agency: Butterfield, Day, DeVito, Hockney

985
Art Director: Andrew Lees
Creative Director: Andrew Lees
Copywriter: Chris Cudlipp
Agency: Chiat/Day/Mojo
Client: Club Mediterranee

986
Art Director: Nigel Rose
Creative Director: John O'Donnell
Photographer: Nadav Kander
Agency: Collett Dickenson & Pearce
Client: Benson & Hedges

987
Art Director: Andrew Lees
Creative Director: Andrew Lees
Designer: Andrew Lees
Copywriter: Andrew Lees
Agency: Chiat/Day/Mojo
Client: Club Mediterranee

988
Art Director: Dave Baldwin
Creative Director: Chris Whittaker
　　　　　　　　　John O'Sullivan
Photographer: Duncan Sim
Copywriter: Pete Cass
Agency: KHBB
Client: Gallo Wines

989
Art Director: Stephan Auer
Creative Director: Carlos Obers
Designer: Stephan Auer
Photographer: Dieter Eickelpoth
Copywriter: Rita Obers
Agency: RG Wiesmeier
Client: Elbeo Werke

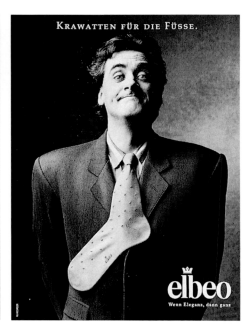

990
Art Director: Koji Mizutani
Designer: Osamu Kitajima
Ichiro Mitani
Photographer: Sachiko Kuru
Agency: Blue International Co. Ltd.

991
Art Director: Haruyuki Aoki
Creative Director: Haruyuki Aoki
Designer: Keiko Nagano
Photographer: Keisuke Minoda
Copywriter: Shinichi Enami
Agency: Dentsu Inc.
Client: Wako

992
Art Director: Peter Heßler
Creative Director: Peter Heßler
　　　　　　　　　 Jochen Beithan
Photographer: Mane Weigand
Copywriter: Cornelia Arnold
　　　　　　　　 Jochen Beithan

993
Art Director: Peter Heßler
Creative Director: Peter Heßler
　　　　　　　　Jochen Beithan
Photographer: Günter Pfannmüller
Copywriter: Jochen Beithan

994
Art Director: Gavino Sanna
Creative Director: Gavino Sanna
Photographer: Leo Torri
Copywriter: Gaspare Giua
Agency: Young & Rubicam Italia SpA
Client: Castelli SpA

995
Art Director: Helga Miethke
Creative Director: José Zaragoza
                      Helga Miethke
Photographer: Manolo Moran
Copywriter: Paulo Leite
Agency: DPZ-Propaganda
Client: Hering

996
Art Director: Roberto Cipolla
Creative Director: Francesc Petit
                      Paulo Ghirotti
Photographer: Luiz Crispino
Copywriter: Ruy Lindenberg
Agency: DPZ-Propaganda
Client: Colorcenter

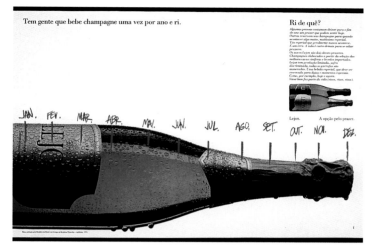

997
Art Director: Marcello Serpa
Creative Director: Francesc Petit
Paulo Ghirotti
Photographer: Andreas Heiniger
Copywriter: Paulo Ghirotti
Luiz Toledo
Agency: DPZ-Propaganda
Client: Heublein

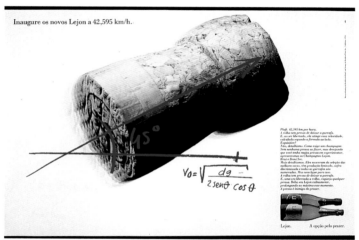

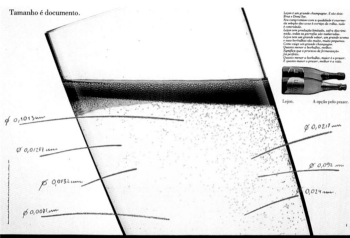

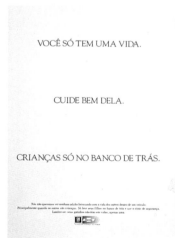

998
Art Director: Roberto Cipolla
Creative Director: Francesc Petit
Paulo Ghirotti
Photographer: Andreas Heiniger
Copywriter: Ruy Lindenberg
Agency: DPZ-Propaganda
Client: General Motors

999
Art Director: José Zaragoza
Creative Director: José Zaragoza
Helga Miethke
Photographer: Moacyr Lugato
Copywriter: Antonio Paes
Agency: DPZ-Propaganda
Client: Artex

A COBERTURA DOS SEUS SONHOS. LENÇÓIS ARTEX.

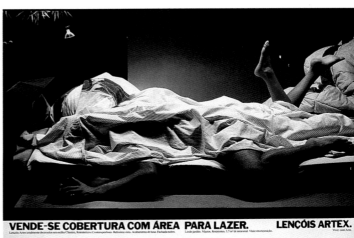

VENDE-SE COBERTURA COM ÁREA PARA LAZER. LENÇÓIS ARTEX.

Extintor de incêndio.

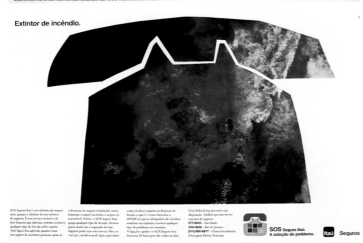

Saída de emergência.

SOS Seguro Itaú. A solução do problema. Itaú Seguros

Pára-choque.

SOS Seguro Itaú. A solução do problema. Itaú Seguros

1000
Art Director: Marcello Serpa
Creative Director: Francesc Petit
Paulo Ghirotti
Copywriter: Luiz Toledo
Agency: DPZ-Propaganda
Client: Itaú seguros

1001
Art Director: Helga Miethke
Creative Director: José Zaragoza
                Helga Miethke
Photographer: Manolo Moran
Copywriter: Paulo Leite
Agency: DPZ-Propaganda
Client: Hering

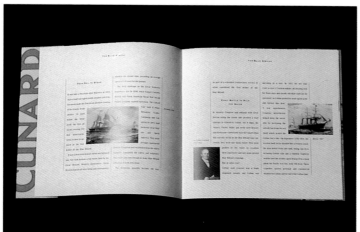

1002
Art Director: David Pocknell
Designer: Mark Welby
         Jonathan Russell

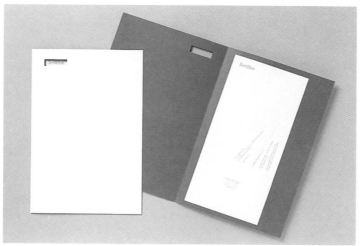

1003
Art Director: Klaus Winterhager
Client: Zanders Feinpapiere AG

1004
Art Director: Planungsteam K. Nengelken
Agency: Planungsteam K. Nengelken
Client: Zanders Feinpapiere AG

1005
Art Director: György Kara
Designer: György Kara
Photographer: Géza Molnár
Client: Artex

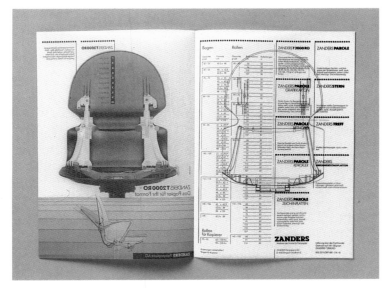

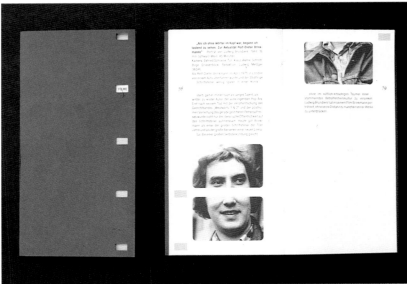

1006
Art Director: Holger Giffhorn
V. Thomas Serres
Creative Director: Holger Giffhorn
V. Thomas Serres
Designer: Holger Giffhorn
V. Thomas Serres
Agency: Giffhorn V. Serres
Client: Kultusministerium des Laudes Nordrheim

1007
Art Director: Peter Horlacher
Creative Director: Peter Horlacher
Designer: Peter Horlacher
Copywriter: H. J. Nieber
P. Wiechmann
R. W. Trowitzsch
Client: Bit-Verlag

1008

Art Director: Richard Henderson
Creative Director: Flett Henderson & Arnold
Designer: Flett Henderson & Arnold
Photographer: Ray Kinnane
Copywriter: Michael Heffernan
      Pat Gringer
Agency: Flett Henderson & Arnold
Client: Flett Henderson & Arnold

1009

Art Director: Michael Johnson
Creative Director: Kit Cooper
Designer: Michael Johnson
Photographer: Derek Seawood
Copywriter: Len Weinreich
Studio: Sedley Place
Client: BWBC & Co.

1010

Art Director: Katsu Asano
Creative Director: Katsu Asano
Designer: Kinue Yonezawa
Photographer: Bungo Saito
Copywriter: Katsu Asano
Agency: ASA 100 Co.
Client: Lunetta BADA

1011

Art Director: Lynn Trickett
      Brian Webb
Designer: Colin Sands
Photographer: Glynn Williams
Agency: Trickett & Webb
Client: Computer Cab

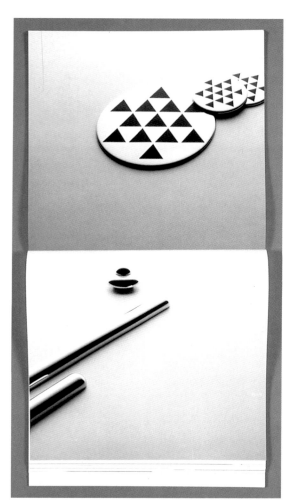

1012
Art Director: Shin Matsunaga
Designer: Shin Matsunaga
Photographer: Noritoyo Nakamoto
Client: Daichi Co., Ltd.

1013
Art Director: Hiroaki Nagai
Creative Director: Taosa Tohgura
                    Satoru Miyata
Photographer: Tsutomu Wakatsuki
Copywriter: Hiroshi Mitsui
Agency: Commons Co. Ltd.
Client: Yokohama Rubber Co., Ltd.

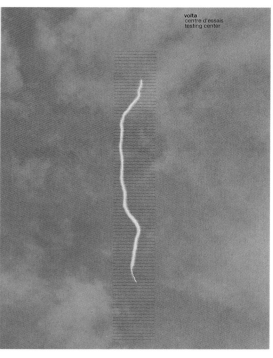

1014
Art Director: Jean-Marc Barrier
Creative Director: Jean-Marc Barrier
Designer: Jean-Marc Barrier
Photographer: Jean-Marc Barrier
Client: Merlin Gerin SA

1015
Art Director: Hisao Sugiura
Creative Director: Yohji Yamamoto
Designer: Hisao Sugiura
            Studio Super Compass Ltd.
Photographer: Loren Hammer
Studio: Studio Super Compass Ltd.
Client: Y's

1016
Art Director: Koji Mizutani
Designer: Hirokazu Kuvelodyashi
Photographer: Yoshihiko Ueda
Copywriter: Kdoru Izima
Client: Melrose Co. Ltd.

1017
Art Director: Gavino Sanna
Creative Director: Gavino Sanna
Photographer: Mario Zappalà
Agency: Young & Rubicam Italia SpA
Client: Castelli SpA

1018
Art Director: Hiromi Inayoshi
Creative Director: Toru Ando
Yukuo Sato
Designer: Hiromi Inayoshi
Illustrator: Jean-Michel Folon
Agency: Dentsu Inc.
Client: Mitsukoshi Ltd.

1019
Art Director: Yoshiaki Bando
Designer: Yoshiaki Bando

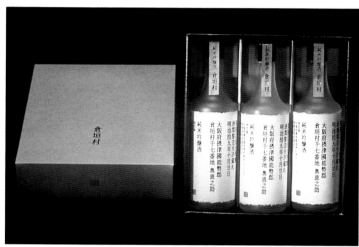

1020
Art Director: Belinda Duggan
Designer: Belinda Duggan
Client: John Harvey & Sons

1021
Art Director: Yoshitomo Ohama
Designer: Kazunori Umezawa

1022
Art Director: Frances Lovell
Creative Director: Duncan D. Bruce
Designer: Frances Lovell
Client: Black's Photo Corp.

1023
Art Director: James Gardiner
Creative Director: Ian Woodyer
Designer: James Gardiner
　　　　　Ian Woodyer
Client: Caledonian Brewery

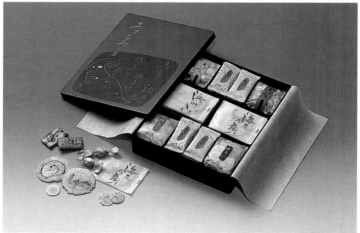

1024
Art Director: John Blackburn
Designer: John Blackburn
Client: Taylor Fladgate

1025
Art Director: Koko Nabatame
Creative Director: Koko Nabatame
Designer: Nabatame Design Office
Client: Nakamuraya Co., Ltd.

1026
Art Director: Akio Okumura
Designer: Akio Okumura
Client: Kazu Jewelry Design Studio

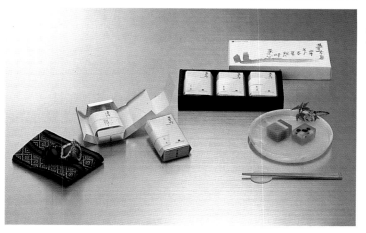

1027
Art Director: Kazuki Maeda
Designer: Seiichi Maeda
               Kenichi Tawaratsumiia

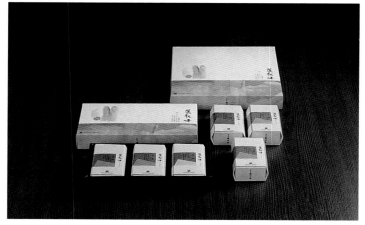

1028
Art Director: Ken Miki
Creative Director: Takuya Kihara
Designer: Ken Miki
               Junji Osaki
Client: Be-In International Inc.

1029
Art Director: John Blackburn
Designer: Belinda Duggan
         Tom Sutherland
Illustrator: Colin Elgie
         Jean-Paul Tibbles
         Jane Thompson
Agency: Blackburn's Ltd.
Client: Berry Bros. & Rudd

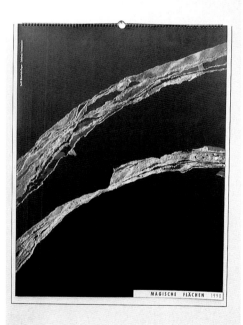

1030
Art Director: Michael Domberger
Designer: Michael Domberger
Illustrator: Peter Anderson
Client: Offizin Scheufele

1031
Art Director: Don Friedrich
Designer: Don Friedrich
Photographer: Franz Wagner
Client: Wagner Siebdruck

1032
Art Director: Manfred Grupp
Creative Director: Manfred Grupp
Designer: Gret Lengerer
Photographer: Claude Bornand
Copywriter: Michael Thevoz
Studio: Papierfabrik Scheufelen GmbH & Co.

1033

Art Director: Holger Nicolai
                Wolfgang Heuwinkel
Designer: Holger Nicolai
                Wolfgang Heuwinkel
Photographer: Hans Hansen
Copywriter: F. Mellinghoff
Agency: Nicolai Werbeugentur, Hamburg
Client: Zanders Feinpapiere AG

1034

Art Director: Thomas Bartsch
Creative Director: Thomas Bartsch
Designer: Thomas Bartsch
Agency: Illuverlag
Client: Illuverlag

1035

Art Director: Gary Martin
Creative Director: Andrew Niccol
Photographer: Andreas Heumann
Copywriter: Mark Goodwin
                Andrew Niccol
Agency: BBDO London
Client: Dormeuil

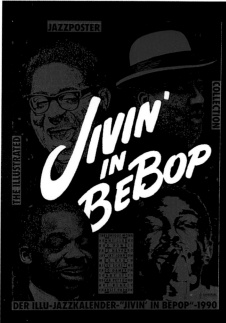

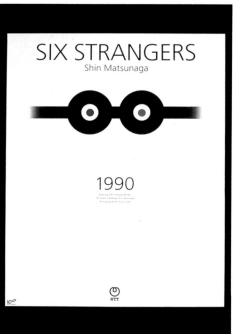

1036

Art Director: Toshihiko Maejima
Designer: Toshihiko Maejima
Photographer: Dominique Issermann
Agency: Dentsu Inc.
Client: Tasaki Shinju

1037

Art Director: Shin Matsunaga
Designer: Shin Matsunaga
Client: Nippon Telephone & Telegram Corp.

1038

Art Director: Shin Matsunaga
Designer: Shin Matsunaga
Client: Nippon Telephone & Telegram Corp.

1039

Art Director: Alan Fletcher
Creative Director: Alan Fletcher
Designer: Alan Fletcher
Illustrator: Alan Fletcher
Client: Pentagram
G & B Arts

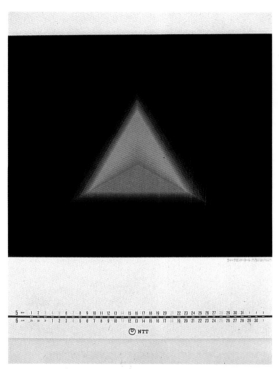

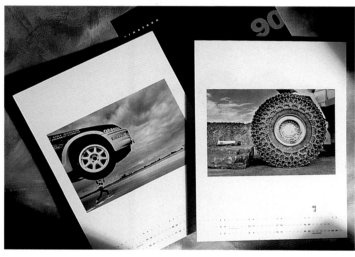

1040

Art Director: Martyn Hey
Photographer: Stuart Redler
Studio: Giant
Client: Kuwait Petroleum

1041

Art Director: Margaret Calvert
Designer: Peter Willberg
Jason Godfrey
Illustrator: Various
Studio: Royal College of Art
Client: IBM Germany

1042
Art Director: Sakutaro Nakagawa
Creative Director: Naotake Bando
Designer: Yutaka Oshiro
       Hitoshi Hirano
Copywriter: Sakutaro Nakagawa
Studio: Word Shop Inc.
Client: Misawa Homes Co., Ltd.

  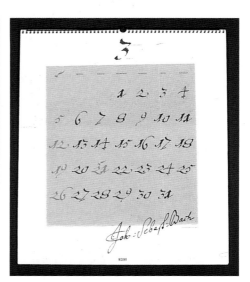

1043
Art Director: Norico Hirai
Designer: Tsutomu Nakazato
Illustrator: Fumihiko Enokido
Studio: Core Produce Ltd.
Client: Bell & Howell Japan

1044
Art Director: Ian Jensen
Creative Director: Noel Harris
Designer: Ian Jensen
Copywriter: Don Blackley
Agency: Chiat/Day/Mojo
Client: Chiat/Day/Mojo

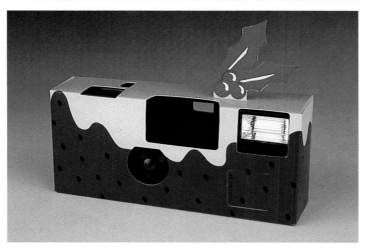

1045
Art Director: Klaus Wuttke
Designer: Eileen Robertson
            Christiane Ella
Illustrator: Eileen Robertson
Agency: Klaus Wuttke & Partners Ltd.
Client: Klaus Wuttke & Partners Ltd.

1046
Art Director: Tom Meenaghan
Creative Director: Tom Meenaghan
Designer: Tom Meenaghan
Illustrator: Mary Murphy
Studio: Designworks
Client: Guinness Corp. Affairs

1047
Art Director: Glenn Tutssel
Creative Director: Glenn Tutssel
Designer: Glenn Tutssel
Illustrator: Harry Willock
Agency: Michael Peters & Partners
Client: Tutssel/Warne

1048
Art Director: Richard Clewes
Designer: Richard Clewes
Agency: 360 Degrees
Client: Peter Hutchings Photography

1049
Art Director: Tom Meenaghan
Creative Director: Joanne Hugo
Designer: Joanne Hugo
Illustrator: Mary Murphy
Copywriter: Mary Murphy
Studio: Designworks
Client: Wiggins Teape

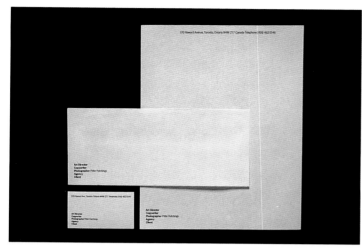

1050
Art Director: Béatrice Mariotti
Creative Director: Béatrice Mariotti
Designer: Béatrice Mariotti
Agency: Carre Noir
Client: Le Bon Marché

1051
Art Director: Catherine Pike
Illustrator: Raffi Anderian
Brett Lodge
Publication: The *Toronto Star*

1052
Art Director: Hans-Georg Pospischil
Designer: Peter Breul
Bernadette Gotthardt
Illustrator: Fernando Botero
Photographer: Abe Frajndlich

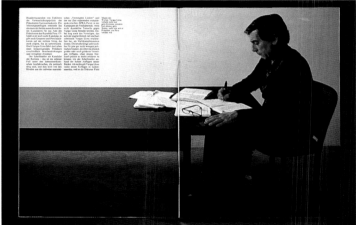

1053
Art Director: Hans-Georg Pospischil
Designer: Peter Breul
            Bernadette Gotthardt
Illustrator: Heinz Edelmann

1054
Art Director: Hans-Georg Pospischil
Creative Director: Seymour Chwast
Designer: Seymour Chwast
Illustrator: Seymour Chwast
Studio: The Pushpin Group
Client: Frankfurter Allgemeine Magazin

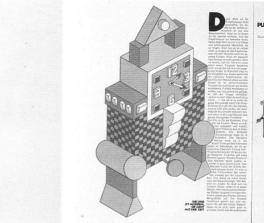

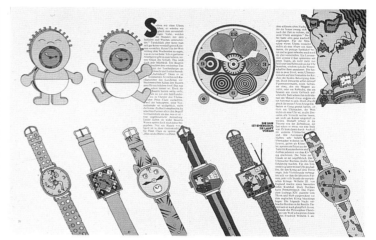

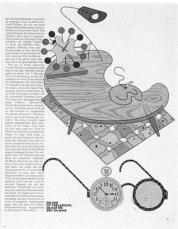

1055
Art Director: Hans-Georg Pospischil
Designer: Peter Breul
          Bernadette Gotthardt
Illustrator: The Pushpin Group

1056
Art Director: Hans-Georg Pospischil
Designer: Peter Breul
          Bernadette Gotthardt
Photographer: Jürgen Röhrscheid

1057
Art Director: Hans-Georg Pospischil
Designer: Peter Breul
          Bernadette Gotthardt
Illustrator: Brad Holland

1058
Art Director: Hans-Georg Pospischil
Creative Director: Seymour Chwast
Designer: Seymour Chwast
Illustrator: Seymour Chwast
Studio: The Pushpin Group
Client: Frankfurter Allgemeine Magazin

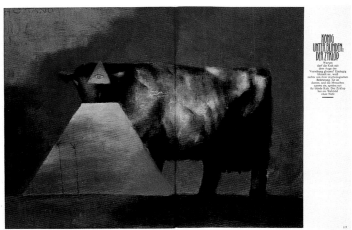

1059
Art Director: Hans-Georg Pospischil
Designer: Peter Breul
          Bernadette Gotthardt
Illustrator: Hans Hillmann

1060
Art Director: Hans-Georg Pospischil
Creative Director: Seymour Chwast
Designer: Seymour Chwast
Illustrator: Seymour Chwast
Agency: The Pushpin Group
Client: Frankfurter Allgemeine Magazin

1061
Art Director: Hans-Georg Pospischil
Designer: Peter Breul
Bernadette Gotthardt
Illustrator: Heinz Edelmann

1062
Art Director: David Hillman
Creative Director: David Hillman
Designer: David Hillman
Amanda Bennett
Client: Barrie & Jenkins

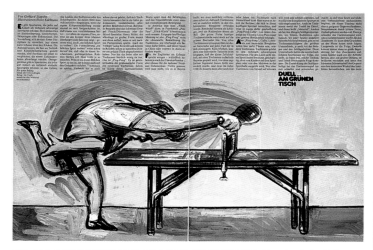

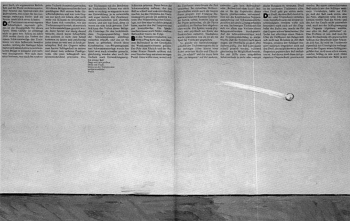

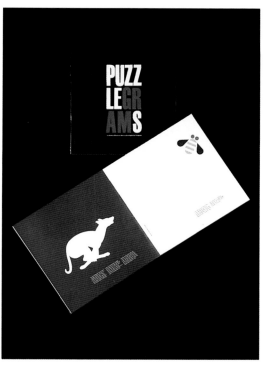

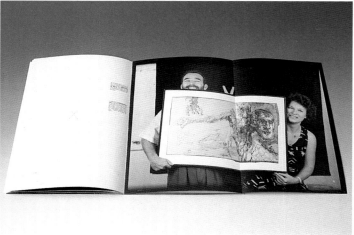

1063
Art Director: François Fabrizi
Studio: Studio Fabrizi

1064
Art Director: Shin Matsunaga
Designer: Shin Matsunaga
Publication: The Works of Shin Matsunaga
New York 1989

1065
Art Director: Brigette Sidjanski
Illustrator: Stasys Eidrigevicius
Client: Nord-Sud Verlag

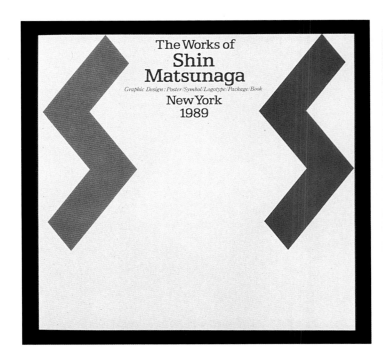

1066
Art Director: Ikko Tanaka
Designer: Ikko Tanaka
Photographer: Irving Penn
Client: Issey Miyake International Inc.

1067
Art Director: Pieter Brattinga
Designer: Pieter Brattinga
Producer: J. Vender Wolk C.S.
Publication: Joh. Enschedé

1084
Art Director: Pèter Pòcs
Designer: Pèter Pòcs
Photographer: Làszlò Haris
Copywriter: Pèter Pòcs
Client: SZDSZ

1085
Art Director: Kyösti Varis
Creative Director: Kyösti Varis
Designer: Kyösti Varis
Illustrator: Kyösti Varis
Agency: Varis & Ojala Oy
Client: Lahti Organ Festival

1086
Art Director: Bruno Monguzzi
Designer: Bruno Monguzzi
Studio: Bruno Monguzzi
Client: Kunsthaus Zurich

1087
Art Director: Takuya Ohnuki
Creative Director: Susumu Miyazaki
Shinsuke Kasahara
Designer: Soichi Akiyama
Yuji Masuda
Photographer: Herb Ritts
Copywriter: Masakazu Taniyama
Agency: Hakuhodo Inc.
Client: Sanraku Co., Ltd.

1088
Art Director: Noriko Amagai
Creative Director: Kōzō Koshimizu
Designer: Shigeharu Yamauchi
Photographer: Tamotsu Fujii
Copywriter: Kōzō Koshimizu

1089
Art Director: Niklaus Troxler
Creative Director: Niklaus Troxler
Designer: Niklaus Troxler
Illustrator: Niklaus Troxler
Copywriter: Niklaus Troxler
Studio: Grafik-Studio Niklaus Troxler
Client: Jazz in Willisau

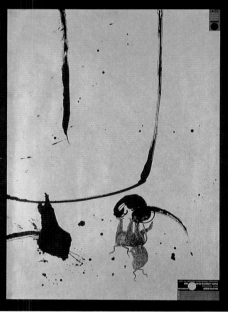

1090
Art Director: Takaharu Matsumoto
Creative Director: Takaharu Matsumoto
Designer: Takaharu Matsumoto

1091
Art Director: Fumihiko Enokido
Designer: Fumihiko Enokido
Illustrator: Fumihiko Enokido

1092
Art Director: Sandy Choi
Designer: Sandy Choi
Copywriter: Shona Brian-Boys

1093
Art Director: David Hillman
Creative Director: David Hillman
Designer: David Hillman
Karin Beck
Copywriter: David Gibbs
Client: Design Council

1094
Art Director: Seymour Chwast
Designer: Seymour Chwast
Agency: The Pushpin Group
Client: Zanders Feinpapiere AG

1095
Art Director: Noriyuki Tanaka
Yasuhiro Sawada
Creative Director: Noriyuki Tanaka
Designer: Noriyuki Tanaka
Yasuhiro Sawada
Illustrator: Noriyuki Tanaka
Photographer: Senji Urushibata
Client: Noriyuki Tanaka

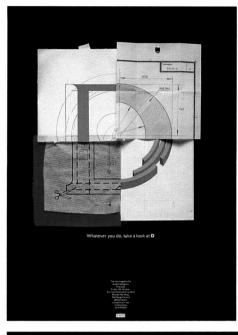

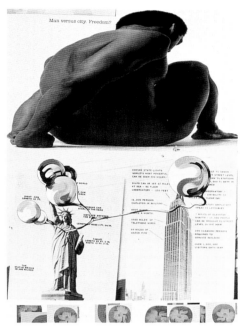

1096
Art Director: Makoto Saito
Designer: Makoto Saito
Photographer: Kazumi Kurigami
Agency: Cohwa International Co., Ltd.
Client: Shochiku Co., Ltd.

1097
Art Director: Daisuke Nakatsuka
Creative Director: Daisuke Nakatsuka
Designer: Wataru Hayakawa
Photographer: Eiichiro Sakata
Copywriter: Daisuke Nakatsuka
Client: Dai-ichi Mutual Life Insurance Co.

1098
Art Director: Ducki Krzysztof

1099
Art Director: Ikko Tanaka
Designer: Ikko Tanaka
Client: Takenaka Corp.

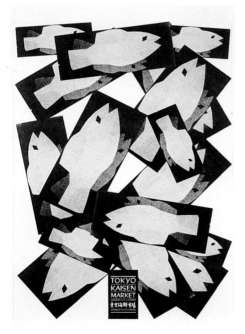

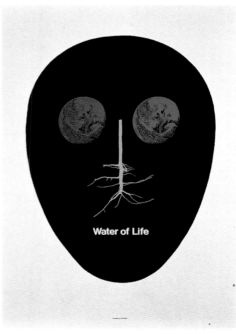

1100
Art Director: Kijuro Yahagi
Designer: Kijuro Yahagi
Client: Tokyo Kaisen Market

1101
Art Director: Ken Miki
Designer: Ken Miki

1102
Art Director: Masakazu Tanabe
Designer: Masakazu Tanabe
Illustrator: Masakazu Tanabe
Client: The Poster Execution Committee

1103

Art Director: Kenichi Samura
Creative Director: Kenichi Samura
Designer: Kenichi Samura
Client: Issey Miyake International Inc.

1104

Art Director: Niklaus Troxler
Creative Director: Niklaus Troxler
Designer: Niklaus Troxler
Illustrator: Niklaus Troxler
Copywriter: Niklaus Troxler
Agency: Grafik-Studio Niklaus Troxler
Client: Jazz in Willisau

1105

Art Director: K. Domenic Geissbuhler
Creative Director: K. Domenic Geissbuhler
Designer: K. Domenic Geissbuhler
Illustrator: K. Domenic Geissbuhler
Studio: K. Domenic Geissbuhler
Client: Zurich Opera House

1106

Art Director: Ducki Krzysztof

1107

Art Director: Kenichi Samura
Creative Director: Kenichi Samura
Designer: Kenichi Samura
Photographer: Chikao Todoroki
Publication: Bijutsu Shuppan-Sha Co., Ltd.

1108

Art Director: Shin Matsunaga
Designer: Shin Matsunaga
Client: JAGDA

1109
Art Director: Niklaus Troxler
Creative Director: Niklaus Troxler
Designer: Niklaus Troxler
Illustrator: Niklaus Troxler
Copywriter: Niklaus Troxler
Agency: Grafik-Studio Niklaus Troxler
Client: Jazz in Willisau

1110
Art Director: Tadanori Itakura
Designer: Tadanori Itakura
Photographer: Yasunori Saito
Client: Lexis Editorial Office

1111
Art Director: Holger Matthies
Creative Director: Holger Matthies
Designer: Holger Matthies
Illustrator: Holger Matthies
Client: Theater Oberhausen

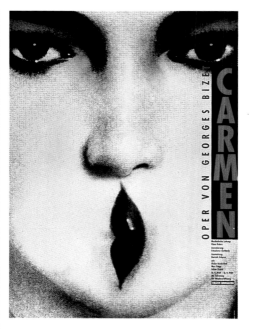

1112
Art Director: Osamu Furumura
Designer: Kenichi Yoshida
Illustrator: Osamu Furumura
Copywriter: Osamu Furumura
Client: Imayo Co. Ltd.

1113
Art Director: Takaharu Matsumoto
Creative Director: Takaharu Matsumoto
Designer: Takaharu Matsumoto

1114
Art Director: Cecile Rusterholtz
Laure Predine
Photographer: Claude Sauvagot
Studio: Tatoo
Client: Enfants du Monde

1115
Art Director: Atsushi Ebina
Creative Director: Atsushi Ebina
Mitsugu Hiroki
Designer: Atsushi Ebina
Illustrator: Atsushi Ebina
Copywriter: Hitoshi Yasui
Studio: Verve Inc.
Client: Herald Ace

1116
Art Director: K. Domenic Geissbuhler
Creative Director: K. Domenic Geissbuhler
Designer: K. Domenic Geissbuhler
Illustrator: K. Domenic Geissbuhler
Studio: K. Domenic Geissbuhler
Client: Zurich Opera House

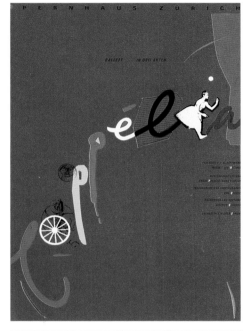

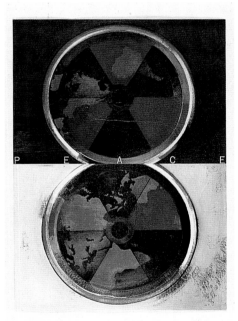

1117
Art Director: Shin Matsunaga
Designer: Shin Matsunaga
Client: JAGDA
ICOGRADA

1118
Art Director: Noriyuki Tanaka
Kentara Honzawa
Creative Director: Noriyuki Tanaka
Designer: Noriyuki Tanaka
Kentara Honzawa
Illustrator: Noriyuki Tanaka

1119
Art Director: Masaaki Izumiya
Creative Director: Masaaki Izumiya
Designer: Hiroshi Yonemura
Photographer: Yoshihiko Ueda
Copywriter: Mitsuhiro Koike
Agency: Hakuhodo Inc.
Client: Dai-ichi Mutual Life Insurance Co.

1120
Art Director: Toshiyasu Nanbu
Designer: Toshiyasu Nanbu
Client: Taste

1121
Art Director: Shin Matsunaga
Designer: Shin Matsunaga
Photographer: Noritoyo Nakamoto
Client: Takenaka Works Co., Ltd.

1122
Art Director: Kijuro Yahagi
Designer: Kijuro Yahagi
Client: Takeo Co., Ltd.

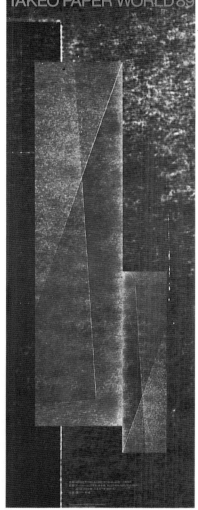

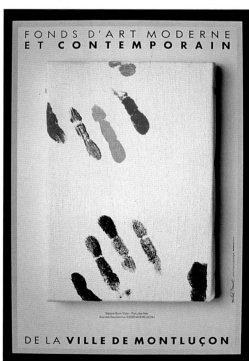

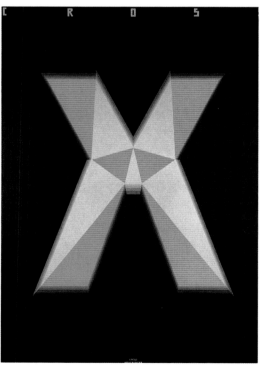

1123
Art Director: Michel Bouvet
Creative Director: Michel Bouvet
Designer: Michel Bouvet
Photographer: Françis Laharrague
Client: Ville de Montluçon

1124
Art Director: Shin Matsunaga
Designer: Shin Matsunaga
Client: Daiichishiko Co., Ltd.

1125
Art Director: Alan Fletcher
Creative Director: Alan Fletcher
Designer: Alan Fletcher
          Debbie Martindale
Illustrator: Alan Fletcher
Client: Geers Gross

1126
Art Director: Henry Steiner
Creative Director: Michael McLaughlin
Designer: Henry Steiner
Photographer: John Thomson
Client: Artspec Imaging Ltd., New Zealand

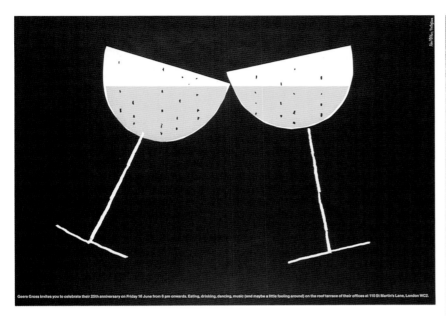

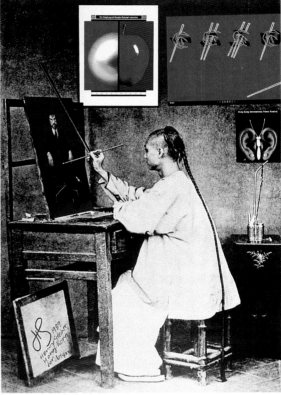

1127
Art Director: Andrew Lees
          Jackie Coates
Creative Director: Andrew Lees
Designer: Andrew Lees
Copywriter: Andrew Lees
          Chris Cudlipp
Agency: Chiat/Day/Mojo
Client: Club Mediterranee

1128
Art Director: Alain Le Quernec
Designer: Alain Le Quernec
Client: Artis

1129
Art Director: Andrew Lees
　　　　　　Jackie Coates
Creative Director: Andrew Lees
Copywriter: Chris Cudlipp
　　　　　　Andrew Lees
Agency: Chiat/Day/Mojo
Client: Club Mediterranee

1130
Art Director: Mervyn Kurlansky
Creative Director: Mervyn Kurlansky
Designer: Mervyn Kurlansky
Client: Polish Government

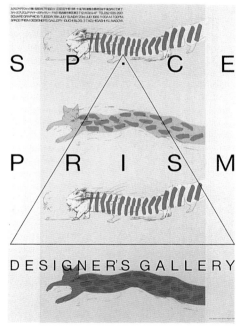

1131
Art Director: Heinz Handschick

1132
Art Director: Börje Stille
Copywriter: Ingemar Johannesson
Agency: Johannesson & Stille AB
Client: Folksam

1133
Art Director: Masakazu Tanabe
Designer: Masakazu Tanabe
Illustrator: Masakazu Tanabe
Client: Designer's Gallery Space Prism

1134
Art Director: Börje Stille
Copywriter: Ingemar Johannesson
Agency: Johannesson & Stille AB
Client: SIS

1135
Art Director: José Bulnes
Antoine Robaglia
Studio: Information et Enterprise
Client: Matra

1136
Art Director: Minoru Niijima
Designer: Minoru Niijima
Client: Kanazawa Sculpture Exhibition Committee

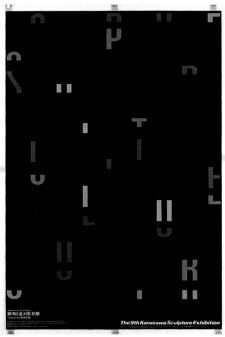

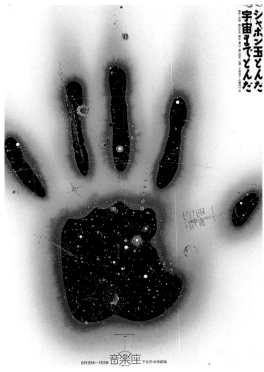

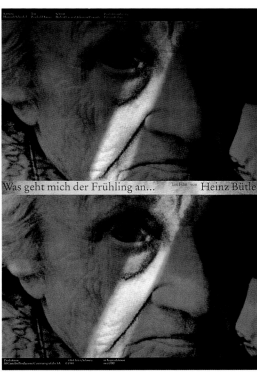

1137
Art Director: Koichi Sato
Designer: Koichi Sato
Client: Ongakuza

1138
Art Director: Bruno Monguzzi
Designer: Bruno Monguzzi
Photographer: Bruno Monguzzi
Client: Al Castello

1139
Art Director: Klaus Erwarth
Creative Director: Mariusz Jan Demner
Designer: Andreas Miedaner
Photographer: Stockfoto
Copywriter: Mariusz Jan Demner
Agency: Demner & Merlicek
Client: Wiener Festwochen

1140
Art Director: Bret Granato
Creative Director: Greg Starr
Designer: Eiki Hidaka
Photographer: Yukio Shimizu
Studio: Emphasis, Inc.
Client: Japan Airlines

1149
Art Director: Katsu Asano
Creative Director: Katsu Asano
Designer: Kinue Yonezawa
Photographer: Bungo Saito
Copywriter: Katsu Asano
Agency: ASA 100 Co.
Client: Japan Graphic Designers Association Inc.

1150
Art Director: Manfred Grupp
Creative Director: Erwin Fieger
Designer: Erwin Fieger
Photographer: Erwin Fieger
Copywriter: Erwin Fieger
Producer: AWS Ditzingen-Heimerd

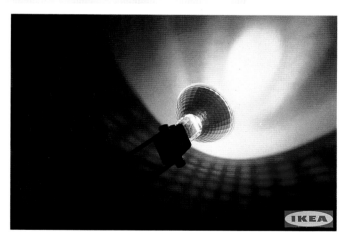

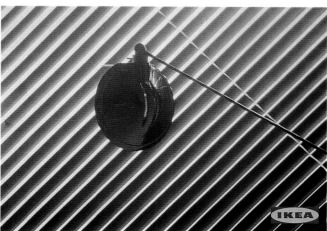

1151
Art Director: Helmut Klein
Creative Director: Edmund Petri
Designer: Gabi Wagner
Photographer: Helmut Klein
Agency: Young & Rubicam
Client: IKEA

1152
Art Director: Norbert Herold
Creative Director: Norbert Herold
Photographer: Monika Robl
Agency: Heye & Partner
Client: Optyl GmbH

1153
Art Director: Sigi Mayer
Creative Director: Sigi Mayer
Designer: Sigi Mayer
Photographer: Horst M. Stasny
Copywriter: Horst M. Stasny
Agency: Sigi Mayer
Publication: Modern Times Magazine

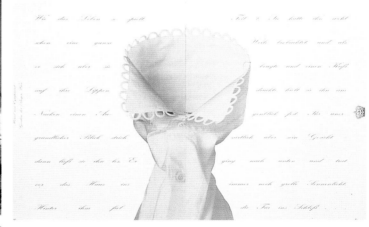

1154

Art Director: Darrel Shee
             Bill Martin
Creative Director: Gary Prouk
Copywriter: Bill Martin
Producer: Anne Phillips
Director: Richard Unruh
Studio: Partners Film Co. Ltd.
Agency: Scali, McCabe, Sloves (Canada) Ltd.
Client: Labatt Brewing Co. Ltd.

1155

Art Director: Noel Harris
Creative Director: Noel Harris
Copywriter: Harry Scott
Producer: Harry Scott
Director: Michael Ellis
Agency: Chiat/Day/Mojo
Client: Toyoto Motor Corp.

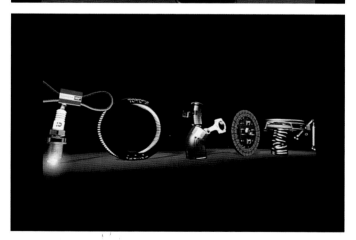

APE
30 seconds
LYRICS: Once I had a secret love,
    That lived within the heart of me.
    All too soon my secret love,
    Became impatient to be free.
VO: Carlsberg. Unbelievably good beer.

TOYOTA PARTS
30 Seconds
SFX: Latin American Music
VO: Toyota genuine parts and quality service…the only way to keep the feeling.

1156

Art Director: Randy Diplock
Creative Director: Gary Prouk
Photographer: Stanley Mestel
Copywriter: Randy Diplock
Producer: Sylvia Maguire
Director: Greg Sheppard
Agency: Scali, McCabe, Sloves (Canada) Ltd.
Client: Canadian Childrens Foundation

1157

Art Director: Neil French
Creative Director: Neil French
Copywriter: Neil French
Producer: Han Chew
Director: Neil French
Agency: The Ball WCRS Partnership
Client: Singapore Tourism Promotion Board

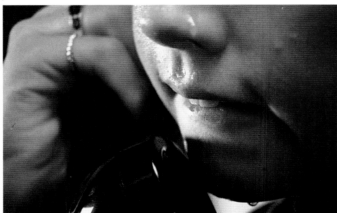

NOT IN SERVICE
30 seconds
SFX: Rain
VO: In Canada, like other countries, child abuse exists. The abuse can range from verbal to sexual. In fact, 1 in 8 Canadian kids are victims. And like other countries, we have a child helpline. But there is a difference.
BELL RECORDING: I'm sorry, the number you have dialed is not in service….I'm sorry, the number you have dialed is not in service.

SMILE
30 seconds
VO: Every year, tourism brings in 4 billion dollars to Singapore. And, it's up to everyone of us to keep it coming. But, of course, it isn't just a smile that matters, it's an attitude. And that's why we have The Singapore Tourism Awards. So, next time you meet a visitor, give him your billion dollar smile.

1158

Art Director: Kayleen Flanigan
Creative Director: Rob Freebody
　　　　　　　　Mark Busse
Photographer: Annie Westbrook
Copywriter: Melinda Kerr
Producer: Anne Hughes
　　　　　Catherine Hancock
Director: John Ware
Agency: Foote, Cone & Belding

1159

Art Director: Richard Dearing
Creative Director: Ray Ross
Designer: Richard Dearing
Illustrator: Justin Robson
Copywriter: Don Blackley
Producer: Di Kelly
Director: Peter Macintosh
Agency: Clemenger Sydney
Client: Ricegrowers Association

POWER

30 seconds
VO: The new Mazda T-Series not only…
SFX: Loud rumble of traffic; horns tooting
VO: …has a powerful four liter…
SFX: Gear change
VO: …direct injection engine and a split shift subtransmission…
SFX: Clunk
VO: …that gives you the control of ten gear ratios.
SFX: Gear change
VO: It also carries an unbeatable 12 month unlimited kilometer warranty. Making it a very powerful proposition indeed.
SFX: Traffic
VO: The new Mazda T-Series. You get more from Mazda.

HEALTH

30 seconds
VO: There is one food that's as natural as corn on the cob…with far less sugar. It's as cheap as chips…with a lot less fat. It's as convenient as a can of beans…with a lot less salt. And, it's as easy to cook as a boiled egg…with no cholesterol at all. It's rice. Yes, rice. Grown in Australia by Sunrice.

1160
Art Director: Darren Warner
Creative Director: Gary Prouk
Copywriter: David Martin
Producer: Leslie Collie
Director: Steve Chase
Studio: Champagne Pictures
Agency: Scali, McCabe, Sloves (Canada) Ltd.
Client: William Neilson Ltd.

TWO SPEEDS
30 seconds
SINGER: Live my life
    The two speed way.
    It may come easy.
    It may go the long way.
    Just don't tell me the way to go.
    I could take it fast or I could take it slow.
    I could take it fast.
    I could take it slow.
    I could make it last.
    I could make it go.
    Just do what you do.
    The two speed way.

1161
Art Director: Yuzuru Mizuhara
Creative Director: Wataru Tsuchiya
Copywriter: Atsushi Sugimoto
Producer: Tsuneo Usui
Director: Yuzuru Mizuhara
Agency: Hakuhodo Inc.
Client: Canon

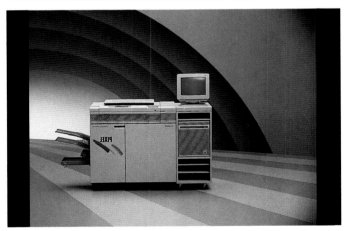

STRAWBERRY
30 seconds
VO: You may find it hard to believe, but everything around me is a copy. This high resolution is networked with a computer. It's here—the Canon Pixel Duo.

1162
Art Director: Mick DeVito
Copywriter: Derek Day
Producer: Sarah Shaw
Agency: Butterfield, Day, DeVito, Hockney

1163
Art Director: Anne Baxendale
Creative Director: Chris Whittaker
　　　　　　　　　　John O'Sullivan
Copywriter: Paul Wadey
Producer: Clare Hunter
Director: Ian McKenzie
Agency: KHBB
Client: Uniroyal Tires

LOOK AFTER YOUR HEART
50 seconds
SONG: "Stop in the Name of Love"
VO: Eat too much, smoke, do too little, and it may not just be *your* heart you hurt.
So make a new start. And look after your heart.

BRIBERY
30 seconds
SFX: Rain pounding; then the sound of a heavy crane
VO: In the wet, you can't choose a better tire than a Uniroyal.

1164
Art Director: Dave Baldwin
Creative Director: Chris Whittaker
John O'Sullivan
Copywriter: Pete Cass
Producer: Clare Hunter
Director: Ian Giles
Agency: KHBB
Client: Nouvelee

REVERSING LOGS

30 seconds

VO: Nouvelle announces a new kind of toilet tissue. It's very soft. It's very strong. It's even a little longer. The big difference is our toilet tissue is made from 100% recycled paper. So to make Nouvelle we don't have to cut down any more trees. Nouvelle Toilet Tissue. Soft on humans, not so hard on Mother Nature.

1165
Art Director: Rohan Caesar
Creative Director: Robin Archer
Designer: Sue Hitchcock
Copywriter: Joe Di Stefano
Producer: Film Graphics
Director: Phil Meatchem
Agency: SSB Advertising
Client: Colonial Mutual

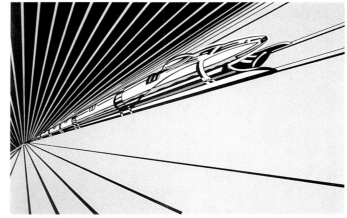

TRAIN

60 seconds

SFX: Station noises, crowds, whistles; then dramatic music
VO: In 1873, an Australian company started out with a vision. To forge a large insurance and financial services group built on security and strength.
SFX: Musical crescendo
VO: Today, it has evolved into a diverse financial force with $7.3 billion worth of assets worldwide. That company is the Colonial Mutual Group. A powerful, modern company that can look forward, because like few others it comes from a position of strength. The Colonial Mutual Group. Building on strength.

1166
Art Director: Richard Clewes
Creative Director: Richard Clewes
Copywriter: Richard Clewes
Producer: Charlene Kidder
Director: Greg Sheppard
Agency: 360 Degrees
Client: Credit Valley Hospital

1167
Art Director: Veronika Classen
Creative Director: Klaus Erich Küster
Copywriter: Veronika Classen
Producer: Käthe Pietz
Director: Lester Bookbinder
Agency: Michael Conrad & Leo Burnett
Client: Braun AG

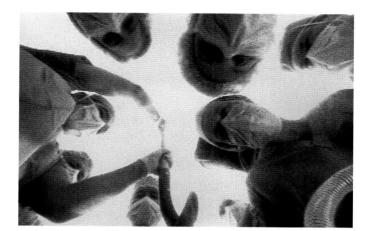

HEALTHY CONTRIBUTION
30 seconds
SFX: Operating Room sounds
VO: Recently, in Mississauga, The Credit Valley Hospital broke new ground in medicine. Of course, we can't finish Phase Two Expansion without your assistance. Please, make a healthy contribution to The Credit Valley Hospital.

BEO
30 seconds
SFX: Alarm clock beeping
BEO: Shut up!!!
VO: Braun voice control stops at a word.

1168

Art Director: Shigenori Arakawa
Creative Director: Wataru Tsuchiya
Designer: Toshikazu Ieda
Photographer: Satoshi Seno
Copywriter: Natsuko Kazami
Producer: Shinji Mita
Director: Jun Asakawa
Agency: Hakuhodo Inc.
Client: Meiji Mutual Life Insurance Co. Ltd.

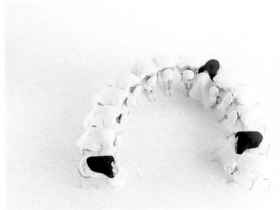

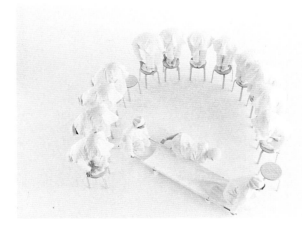

DENTAL INSURANCE

30 seconds
CHILDREN: Teeth!
VO: They are fine when they are healthy.
CHILDREN: Cavities! Teeth fell out! A denture!
VO: Dependable!
CHILDREN: Teeth!
VO: Dental Insurance by the Meiji Mutual Life.

1169

Art Director: Ryo Honda
Creative Director: Yasuhiro Ohnishi
Designer: Yasuhiko Yamamoto
Photographer: Toshio Yamaguchi
Copywriter: Ryo Honda
Producer: Ryoichi Manmi
Director: Yasuhiko Yamamoto
Agency: Dentsu Inc.
Client: Fuji Xerox Co., Ltd.

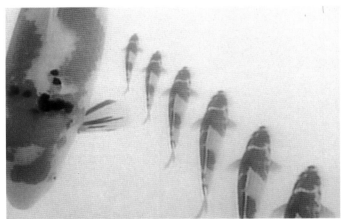

CARP SWIMMING ON PAPER

30 seconds
VO: Apply colors with an electronic palette. Increase the number.
Change the size. Documents can have new colors. Just a little fantastic.
XEROX's color copier Palette. Now on sale.

1170

Art Director: Richard Dearing
Creative Director: Ray Ross
Designer: Richard Dearing
Illustrator: Justin Robson
Copywriter: Gary Graf
Producer: Ron Spencer
Director: Peter Macintosh
Agency: Clemenger Sydney
Client: Ricegrowers Association

1171

Art Director: Jacob Cajaiba
Photographer: Klaus Meewes
Copywriter: Jacob Cajaiba
Producer: Ines Angiolillo
Director: Ernani Bessa
Agency: Salles/Inter-Americana
Client: ADVB

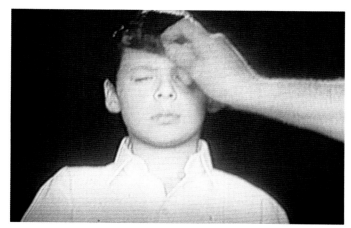

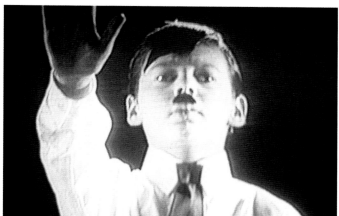

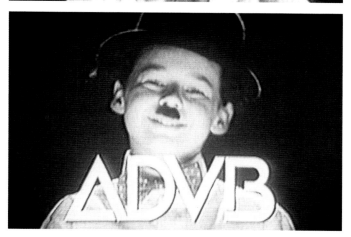

MADE IN AUSTRALIA

30 seconds

VO: There is something we export to the Orient that they really love…
and it's not a cuddly toy. Something they pay top dollar for…and it's
not liquid gold. Something they keep coming back for, again and again
…and it's not a boomerang. It's rice. Sunlong Rice…the only rice
Australia exports to the experts.

CHAPLIN

30 seconds

SFX: Drumroll

ANNCR: A child's future depends on you. Without affection…without
love…the only thing he is going to give back to the world…is hate and
violence.

SFX: Music reminiscent of Charlie Chaplin films

ANNCR: But if you give him love and affection…one day, he is going to
give it all back to you and the world in which you live.

1172
Art Director: Richard Dearing
Creative Director: Ray Ross
Designer: Richard Dearing
Illustrator: Justin Robson
Copywriter: Don Blackley
Producer: Di Kelly
Director: Peter Macintosh
Agency: Clemenger Sydney
Client: Ricegrowers Association

1173
Art Director: Jeff Layton
Creative Director: Boris Damast
Designer: Jeff Layton
Copywriter: Boris Damast
Producer: Gordon Stanway
Director: John Mastromonaco
Agency: Baker Lovick Advertising
Client: The Act Foundation

NUTRITION

30 seconds
VO: There's one food that provides protein to more people in the world than any other…and it's not fish. Fiber to more people in the world…and it's not bread. Energy to more people…and it's not red meat. And vitamins and minerals to more people in the world than any other…and it's not fresh fruit. It's rice. Yes rice. Grown in Australia by Sunrice.

JULIE

30 seconds
ANNCR: This is Julie. She's 12. Recently she saved a heart attack victim. Because she knew the simple skill of CPR. Learning CPR only took 4 hours out of Julie's life. In return she saved someone else's. Her father's. CPR. The reward of a lifetime. Anyone can learn it. Phone and find out how.

1174

Art Director: Peter van den Engel
Copywriter: Martijn Horvath
Producer: Frits Harkema
Director: Flip van Vliet
Agency: DMB&B Amsterdam
Client: Bavaria B.V.

1175

Art Director: Ikuo Amano
Creative Director: Serge Lutens
Designer: Yoshikatsu Okamoto
　　　　　　Yutaka Kobayashi
Photographer: Serge Lutens
Copywriter: Koichi Tsuchiya
Producer: Masaaki Sato
　　　　　　Tadashi Ichihashi
　　　　　　Takanobu Shiraishi

CONFERENCE

30 seconds
SFX: Various gurgling noises; the sounds of a bottle being opened and a glass being filled

PERSPECTIVE

60 seconds
VO: Brown, which has been stolen from the museum… Inoui

1176
Art Director: Terry Cheverton
Creative Director: Stuart Byfield
Copywriter: Paul Hand
Producer: Maureen Gibby
Director: Salik Silverston
Agency: Grey Advertising
Client: Salvation Army

1177
Art Director: Masatake Satomi
Creative Director: Toshiaki Nozue
Designer: Junichiro Akiyoshi
Photographer: Toshio Tateishi
Copywriter: Mamoru Kusakawa
　　　　　　Izuru Toi
Producer: Hiroshi Yoshida
Agency: Dentsu Inc.
Client: Matsushita Electric Industrial Co., Ltd.

BREAK THE SPELL

90 seconds
VO: He was 14, he was 16, he was somebody's son.
　　For a dollar he'd do anything for anyone.
　　He asked is this living or am I in hell,
　　God help me, God listen, please break the spell.
　　He didn't care about Gucci or a Merc in the drive,
　　His main interest was staying alive.
　　Come night he'd sleep wherever he fell.
　　God help me, God listen, please break the spell.
　　The pills looked inviting, they whispered their charms,
　　If only he could be held gently in somebody's arms.
　Thank God for the Salvos.

TAP DANCE

60 seconds
SFX: Tapping
VO: This floor is made of a newly developed, vibration-reducing steel plate that absorbs sound. No matter how hard he dances, he can hardly make himself heard. Using this material we've created a quieter washing machine with less vibration. The debut of the quiet, quiet National Washing Machine Day. Nowadays, you should choose washing machines by their sound.

1186

Art Director: Fumichika Kato
Creative Director: Tokihiko Okamoto
Designer: Tsuguya Inoue
Photographer: Minsei Tominaga
Copywriter: Hiroyuki Yoshimura
Producer: Yoji Watanabe
Director: You Sato
Agency: Dentsu Inc.
Client: Cosmo Securities Co., Ltd.

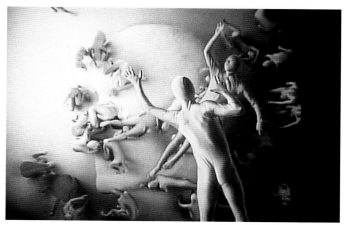

THE ANTENNA MAN

15 seconds
VO: Our antennae to the future react so sensitively that our brains tingle. Our heads are full of crinkles. Cosmos Securities.

1187

Art Director: Masahiko Satoh
　　　　　　　Miyako Maekita
Creative Director: Ryoji Nakagawa
Photographer: Hiroshi Machida
Copywriter: Masahiko Satoh
　　　　　　　Miyako Maekita
Producer: Yoshitada Kohchi
Director: Shinya Nakajima
Agency: Dentsu Inc.

MUSIC BOX

60 seconds
VO: If any one of these tines were missing, this music box would not play. With Toray, the strength of the 17 fields of enterprise represented by these tines are brought together to play one beautiful melody. Each one is crystal harmony, that's Toray.

1188
Art Director: Tony Beckly
Creative Director: Allan Crew
Copywriter: Julian Lloyd
Producer: Susie Cole
Director: Video Paint Brush
Agency: Lintas, Melbourne
Client: Schizophrenia Foundation

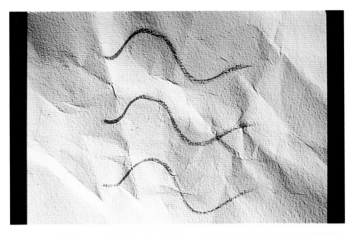

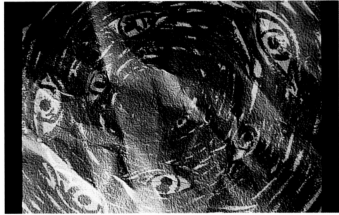

KIM

30 seconds

VO: For most of us the thought that our brains might malfunction is so frightening we don't like to think about it. But many thousand Australians will develop a disease which will make them think differently about the world. And the world think differently about them. Yet Schizophrenia is a disease like any other, except it affects your brain, not your body. There's much we can do. For a start, we can think differently about it.

PRESIDENT'S MESSAGE

It's hard to believe, but the Art Directors Club has been around for almost seventy years. I am fortunate to have a copy of an *Annual* from the early 20s. When you go through its pages, you get much the same feeling as when you leaf through this volume. They both have an air of authority, of final say about our profession. I think this special quality has never changed and is very much alive today. Sure, we have had competition from other organizations, but to me, at least, none have gained and maintained the importance of The Club.

To go back half way through our history, I remember the festive awards lunches held at the Waldorf-Astoria Ballroom over thirty years ago. There was an air of excitement around that room as the winners were called up that may not be duplicated in these more sober times, but it is still a landmark in an art director's career to be included in the yearly exhibition and in the *Annual,* which has remained the definitive chronicle of this profession.

All this tradition notwithstanding, we have gradually added many activities to make the club part of today's environment. The increasingly global aspects of advertising and design created the need for an international show judged by a jury from around the world. Their choices are also included in this book.

Activities to promote the participation of students and younger members are a priority on my list. We must provide for an enthusiastic and orderly succession. A new journal is being published and there are plans for a national conference.

The Board of Directors, the judges, the committee members, and especially the staff have given a lot of their time and knowledge to our club. If only for very selfish reasons, everyone in our profession must stay involved and keep the club a focus and a mainstay of our activity.

Henry Wolf

ART DIRECTORS CLUB

Staff

Executive Director
Diane Moore

Associate Director
Verice Weatherspoon

House and Project Manager
Leslie Buchan

Public Relations and Media Manager
Daniel M. Forté

Exhibition Manager
Jeri Zulli

Associate Exhibition Manager
Jonathan Gregory

House Assistant
Glenn Kubota

Exhibition Assistant
Denise Burns

Bookkeeper
Benny Carrasquillo

Administrative Assistant
Tracey Thomas

Chef
Chuck Lobl

Waitress
Margaret Busweiler

Advisory Board

Robert H. Blattner
William P. Brockmeier
Ed Brodsky
William H. Buckley
David Davidian
Lou Dorfsman
Walter Grotz
Jack Jamison
Walter Kaprielian
Andrew Kner
George Lois
John Peter
Eileen Hedy Schultz
Robert Smith
William Taubin

Executive Board 1989-90 Officers

President
Henry Wolf

First Vice President
Kurt Haiman

Second Vice President
Richard Wilde

Secretary
Ruth Lubell

Treasurer
Martin Solomon

Assistant Secretary/Treasurer
Peter Hirsch

Executive Committee

Robert Best
Seymour Chwast
Lee Epstein
Blanche Fiorenza
Sara Giovanitti

Committees and Chairpeople

69th Annual Judging
Lyle Metzdorf

Agency Relations
Kurt Haiman
Lee Epstein

Constitution
Jack Jamison

Call for Entries
McRay Magleby

Gallery
Richard Wilde

Hall of Fame Management
William Buckley

Hall of Fame Selection
Milton Glaser

Hall of Fame Patrons
Walter Kaprielian

4th International Judging
Karl Steinbrenner

Membership
Sal Lazzarotti
Carol Ceramicoli

Portfolio Review
Lee Epstein

Japanese Traveling Show
Shin Tora

Speaker Luncheons
Dorothy Wachtenheim

Newsletter
Sara Giovanitti
Seymour Chwast

ADC PUBLICATIONS PRESIDENT'S MESSAGE

The Art Directors Club's 69th *Annual*, which also includes the 4th Annual International Exhibition, marks the second year in our very successful relationship with Rotovision, who through their extensive international distribution network sold out every copy of last year's edition! I'm certain the book you now hold in your hands will be no exception.

McRay Magleby, the talented, award winning graphic designer from Brigham Young University Graphics did the striking cover and section dividers. Our panels of national and international judges were very selective this year, making for an even better publication.

My thanks go out to the ADC Publications Board, Pearl Lau, James Craig, Hugh O'Neill and Phil Thurman, and Executive Board liaison, Richard Wilde. A book of this magnitude could never have been published were it not for the invaluable assistance from the club's Diane Moore, Jeri Zulli and Dan Forté. We sincerely hope you enjoy this year's edition of the "Bible" of visual communication.

Dorothy Wachtenheim,
President, ADC Publications

JUDGES OF THE 69TH ANNUAL EXHIBITION

ADVERTISING
Carl Ally
Laurie Bleier
Dick Calderhead
David Davis
Lee Epstein
Elissa Querze
Michael Scheiner
Martin Solomon
John Steffy

EDITORIAL
Robert Barthelmes
Walter Bernard
Michael Brock
Bob Ciano
Carl Fischer
Claudia Lebanthal
D. J. Stout
David Walters
Fred Woodward

GRAPHICS
Charles Anderson
Peter Bradford
Lou Dorfsman
David Enock
Vance Jonson
Tana Kamine
Kiyoshi Kanai
Marie Christine Lawrence
Richard Moore
Minoru Morita
David November
Shin Tora

PROMOTION
Laura Bell
Carolyn Crimmins
Lynda Decker
Holly Jaffee
Andy Kner
Emil Micha
Jim Shefick

TELEVISION
Jerry Cotts
Ken Ferris
Harvey Gabor
Frank Ginsberg
Gary Goldsmith
David Jenkins
Jan Koblitz
Walter LeCat
Tom Monahan
Charlie Piccirillo
Robin Raj
Tina Raver
Phyllis Robinson
Nat Russo
Mort Sharfman
Michael Smith
Bob Smith
Karl Steinbrenner
Jerry Whitley

69th Annual Exhibition Chairpersons. Standing (left to right): Lou Dorfsman, Design; Carl Ally, Advertising; Andrew Kner, Promotion; Carl Fischer, Editorial. Seated (left to right): Lyle Metzdorf, Chairman; Phyllis Robinson, Television.

ART DIRECTORS CLUB 69TH NATIONAL JUDGING

In 1960, I saw my first *Art Directors Annual* and thought it was wonderful. Through the years, the ADC's *Annuals* have inspired me to do better creative work. So it is truly an honor and a privilege to have been this year's show chairman.

Hopefully, the work in this *Annual* will prove to be an inspiration to many future art directors. The *Art Directors Annuals* are also historically important because they are the only books that record the best in advertising, design, editorial, promotion and television in one volume.

This year's show, the 69th Annual Exhibition, received 14,075 entries including 24 hours of television from all over America. About 68% of the entries came from outside New York. It took 55 judges two weekends of soul-searching to select the 962 pieces that are in this *Annual*. They awarded 17 Gold, 45 Silver and 79 Distinctive Merit.

Not all categories received top awards. In fact, the club had no restrictions on how many pieces to select. This allowed the judges to pick only the best work. And picky they were! As a result, we ended up with a very good, quality show.

In order to select outstanding work, the judges used excellence in the following areas as a guide:

1. Concept
2. Art Direction
3. Design
4. Execution

I feel confident that few award shows have ever had better qualified section chairpersons for the judging than this year's exhibition. Thanks to Carl Ally, Advertising, Lou Dorfsman, Design, Carl Fischer, Editorial, Andrew Kner, Promotion and Phyllis Robinson, Television. Their leadership and expertise were invaluable. Thanks also to our judges. They were chosen by selecting top people with track records for producing award winning work. They came from within the club, outside the club and across the country.

And last, but not least, a special thanks to Ms. Diane Moore, the ADC's executive director, Ms. Jeri Zulli, exhibition manager, her staff and to Dan Forté for his help with the television judging. Through the combined efforts and talents of the ADC, you hold in your hands the best advertising, design, editorial, promotion and television done in 1989.

Lyle Metzdorf,
Chairman, 69th Annual Exhibition

JUDGES OF THE 4TH ANNUAL INTERNATIONAL EXHIBITION

Per Arnoldi
Ken Cato
Barry Day
Benoit Devarrieux
Gene Federico*
Kasumasa Nagai
Istvan Orosz
Francesc Petit
Gavino Sanna
Henry Steiner
Yarom Vardimon
Henry Wolf*
Maxim Zhukov

*Member of ADC Hall of Fame

ART DIRECTORS CLUB 4TH ANNUAL INTERNATIONAL EXHIBITION

This year marks the fourth exciting time the Art Directors Club of New York has been accepting, judging and exhibiting advertising, promotion, editorial and television communications from all over the world.

In 1984, when I was first given the go ahead from the Board of Directors to establish a long overdue international exhibition, it was the realization of a dream I'd had for several years. The idea came about while working overseas in Latin America, Japan and Southeast Asia with some temporary assignments in Europe. So much great work was being done in those areas that I felt it was imperative for the New York Art Directors Club to recognize that fact and honor the best.

What is particularly thrilling is to see the expertise and sophistication with which these communications are being accomplished. The recent geopolitical upheavals and dramatic changes we've witnessed in Europe, Asia, Latin America and Africa have such wide ranging effects that the next few years will be even more exciting. And it's more and more commonplace to see commercials and advertising production film crews popping up in once forbidden places.

We are seeing enormous changes in how the world perceives itself. And we—you and I, comrades—will aid and abet those changes for good or not so good.

The process will be fascinating, enlightening, informative and instructive. We'll continue to learn about each other and learn, underneath it all, that people the world over want to live better. Each year that we receive your entries from overseas, and a new international panel of judges makes its selections, we are seeing better and better work being done in more and more countries.

We'd like to see more representation from more countries. We'd like to see more of the best. We'd like you to enter your own work and we'd like to see you accept your Gold or Silver award at the next gala presentation here in New York.

We'd also like you to help us spread the word that every year during the month of December, we accept entries to the ADC International Exhibition of Advertising, Editorial, Graphic Design and Television.

Thank you for your enthusiastic response to our International Exhibition. And thank you for having helped make a dream come true.

Karl H. Steinbrenner,
Chairman,
4th Annual International Exhibition

A distinguished panel of experts review the submissions to the 4th Annual International Exhibition.

The ADC Traveling Show kicked-off its 1989 season at St. Louis's Loretto Hilton on the campus of Webster University. Over 500 people attended the opening night reception.

Photo: Bill Stover

TRAVELING SHOW

Last year's 68th Traveling Exhibition made successful stops in various cities in the United States and Japan. Among the places that played host to large opening night crowds in our country were:

The American Advertising Museum,
Portland, Oregon
Art Institute of Fort Lauderdale,
Fort Lauderdale, Florida
Art Institute of Houston, Houston, Texas
Art Institute of Pittsburgh,
Pittsburgh, Pennsylvania
San Antonio Advertising Federation,
San Antonio, Texas
Not Just an Art Directors Club,
St. Louis, Missouri

The club's 68th Annual Exhibition combined with the 3rd International Annual Exhibition toured extensively throughout Japan with the help of ADC members and goodwill ambassadors Minoru Morita and Shin Tora. Throngs of Japanese graphic designers and advertisers enjoyed shows in Nagoya's International Design Expo, Osaka's Design Center and at Tokyo's Gallery 7.

Anyone interested in sponsoring the club's national show may contact the exhibition department for further information.

GALLERY COMMITTEE

The Art Directors Club Gallery has emerged as one of the most important galleries exhibiting work from the visual communications industry. The exhibitions are varied, covering a wide range of shows from student work to international exhibits. The gallery openings have served as the meeting place for club members as well as enriched the advertising and graphic design community at large.

ADC Hall of Fame Show

ADC National & International Exhibitions

ADC/VCEF Benefit Art Exhibition & Auction

Association of Graphic Arts Show

Club of American Collectors Antique French Poster Exhibition & Sale

DESI Awards

Dimensional Illustrators Exhibition

Japanese Poster Show from Kyushu Graphic Design Association

Kazumasa Nagai & Nippon Design Center "Exhibition 90"

Package Design Council Exhibition

Society of Publication Designers Illustration & Photography Show

SVA Illustration & Photography Exhibition

SVA Photography Show

SVA Student Portfolio Exhibition

Richard Wilde,
Gallery Chairman

Photo: Dan Forté

Club of American Collectors gallery exhibit and sale, "One Century of Advertising Art," showcasing rare French posters.

Luncheon speaker Sam Antupit of Harry Abrams with Luncheon Committee member Pearl Lau.

Luncheon speaker Louise Fili   *Photo: Dan Forté*

LUNCHEON COMMITTEE

The creative industry is growing and expanding. New markets, new mediums, new people. I'm happy to report that the Art Directors Club is in step. During the year, we have introduced some new faces to show how computer animation is working for entertainment and research purposes (R. Greenberg and Associates). We've demonstrated how graphic designers can become experts in all levels of communication, as with the Access Guides (Richard Saul Wurman).

Lunchtime at the club has gone from the sublime (Peter Vitale, photographer for *Architectural Digest*) to the ridiculous (Michael Frith and the Muppets). There are two sides to every story, especially in design. The classic magazine designer represented by Walter Bernard and the off-beat represented by Fred Woodward of *Rolling Stone* are lunch speakers in point.

With presentation always being the key and the first thing taught in art school, it's a special pleasure to have people such as Nigel Holmes, who turned around the look of charts and graphs. Statistical information has never been the same! In opposition, we have the design of big, beautiful coffee table books by Sam Antupit of Harry Abrams. Of course, once you learn something, turn it upside down and throw it out the window with the Ad Brats, Richard Kirshenbaum and Julian Bond. Two prominent members of our club, Hall of Famer Lou Dorfsman and past president and BSB's senior promotion art director Andrew Kner, also took the time to enlighten our large luncheon gatherings.

Our lunchtime lectures at the club are by far the best on-going and consistent forum for learning, growing and meeting new people. It's the best deal in town for getting that blend of fun, education and delicious lunches! Thanks to our fellow committee members: Scott Menchin, Dale Moyer, Susan Newman, Robin Sweet, our chairperson Dorothy Wachtenheim and the club's staff for making our speaker lunches so special.

Pearl Lau,
Committee Member

Dorothy Wachtenheim,
Chairperson

PORTFOLIO REVIEW

Springtime is always a tough time for graduating seniors. A scary time when the womb of the school is displaced by the nakedness of job hunting. A disillusioning time when averages and grades don't matter--when all that really counts is the portfolio.

That's why the Art Directors Club sets aside a series of Mondays and Fridays in mid-spring to give seniors a chance to go one-on-one with professional art directors and designers. They hear critiques, argue back, get a feel for the real and then, hopefully, improve their portfolios based on what they've experienced.

Everybody involved gains. The participating schools, FIT, Kean College, Kutztown University, Moore College of Art & Design, New York City Technical College, CW Post College, Pratt Manhattan, University of Delaware, University of Massachusetts and Youngstown State University all get to see how well they're preparing their students and to detect possible lapses in their curriculum.

The volunteer professionals have a chance to gauge and screen the upcoming talent and to see how far the new generation of creatives will push the status quo. And, of course, the graduates will learn that the industry is a spectrum of creative tastes, temperaments and personalities. The sooner they learn to perfect and trust their own talents and instincts, the better.

Lee Epstein,
Chairman, Portfolio Review

Alan Zwiebel reviews a student's portfolio.   *Photo: Dan Forté*

1990 VCEF SCHOLARSHIP RECIPIENTS

THE COOPER UNION
Paul Carlos
Thomas Ferraro
Agnieszka Jane
Charles Robertson
Reva Weiss

FASHION INSTITUTE OF TECHNOLOGY
Sonia Biancalani
Shardona Hebblethwaite
Raffaella Isidori
Doreen Serpico

NEW YORK CITY TECHNICAL COLLEGE
Allene Edwards
(Roz Goldfarb Award)
Camilo Fajardo
Alicia Fernandez
Agnes Laygo
Xing Hong Lin
(Ruth Lubell Award)
Anamika Sharma
Paul Viola

PARSONS SCHOOL OF DESIGN
Glennys Anglada
Ron De La Pena
(Book of the Month Club Award)
Pauline Demanche
Christopher Follett
(Book of the Month Club Award)
Claudine Guerguerian
Bonnie Lau
(Richard Taubin Award)
Toshiya Masuda
(Book of the Month Club Award)
Ezra Petronio
(Richard Taubin Award)
Nobuyuki Suzuki
Cheung Tai
(Richard Taubin Award)
Siung Fat Tjia

PRATT INSTITUTE
Christopher Bean
Mateo Mulcare
Susie Shon

PRATT MANHATTAN
Mary Margaret Fraser
Anna M. Mondragon
Ann Y. Song
Esther D. Weitzman

SCHOOL OF VISUAL ARTS
Abigail Aron
Robert Carducci
Thomas Gianfagna
Robert Hawse
Mikko Meronen

VISUAL COMMUNICATORS EDUCATION FUND

Since its very inception 69 years ago, the Art Directors Club has worked towards the creation and execution of scholarships for promising art students in the various schools in the New York area.

The funding for these scholarships has never been an easy job, but one that has always succeeded in one way or another. The scholarships have provided great satisfaction to the members of our VCEF committees and given great help to those worthy students who have received them.

In recent years, while donations from corporations have become more difficult to attain, the committee has instituted several innovative ways of allowing us to continue this most important aspect of our club's being.

One dollar from every entry into the Art Directors Club Annual Exhibition goes directly to the VCEF for scholarships. An annual art auction to which members and friends contribute a piece of their talents in the form of a drawing, painting or photograph for auction has become another source of income.

The VCEF committee encourages the Art Directors Club membership, the corporations who so badly need good art directors for their own success and futures, and the related suppliers, friends and beneficiaries of good art direction to consider an annual donation to this worthy cause.

This year, upwards of $15,000 will have been given to deserving art students. These dollars are not easily gotten. The fund needs your help so it can help support and inspire the talents of tomorrow.

It is our goal to collect enough funding in the next five years to institute an endowment that will be self-perpetuating. One that will insure scholarships for years to come, no matter what economic factors come into play.

The VCEF wishes to extend its sincere gratitude to those who have helped us achieve the measure of success we already have and ask everyone who hasn't, to consider helping us obtain our goal of a permanent endowment.

The students listed here are the recipients of this year's scholarships. They are the latest of a long list that this VCEF Committee has full intentions of making longer and longer in the years to come.

Walter Kaprielian,
President,
Visual Communicators Education Fund

Photo: Dan Forté

VCEF President Walter Kaprielian with 1990 VCEF Scholarship winners.

Photo: Dan Forté

VCEF Scholarship recipient receives her certificate and Art Directors Annual *as Diane Moore, Walter Kaprielian and Martin Solomon look on.*